SPOKESMEN

S P O K E S M E N

Modern Writers and
American Life

BY

THOMAS K. WHIPPLE

Essay Index Reprint Series

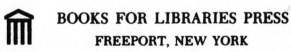

BOOKS FOR LIBRARIES PRESS
FREEPORT, NEW YORK

INTERNATIONAL STANDARD BOOK NUMBER:
0-8369-2179-8

LIBRARY OF CONGRESS CATALOG CARD NUMBER:
70-142711

PRINTED IN THE UNITED STATES OF AMERICA

ACKNOWLEDGMENT

Many of my obligations are indicated in the pages of this book, but there are others which could not well be acknowledged there, and which cannot now be specified. To two writers, however, my indebtedness is such as to require particular mention. How much I owe to Max Eastman, every reader of *The Enjoyment of Poetry* will be sure to see. My debt to Van Wyck Brooks is of the sort that cannot be defined; for me, as for many others, his acute analysis of American civilization first awakened the desire to try to understand the United States. I am glad to have this opportunity of avowing my belief that no one has done so much as he to make criticism a living force in this country.

For permission to reprint portions of some of these chapters I am indebted to the following: for "Henry Adams," to the *Nation;* for "Theodore Dreiser," "Sinclair Lewis," and "Eugene O'Neill," to the *New Republic;* for "Robert Frost," "Sherwood Anderson," and "Willa Cather," to the *Literary Review* of the *New York Evening Post.*

My thanks are due the following publishers for permission to make citations: Albert and Charles Boni, for the quotation from *Launcelot,* by E. A. Robinson; Boni and Liveright, for quotations from *Twelve Men, The Financier, Hey Rub-a-Dub-Dub* and *A Book About Myself,* by Theodore Dreiser, from Sherwood Anderson's

v

ACKNOWLEDGMENT

Notebook, and from *The Great God Brown, The Fountain* and *Marco Millions,* by Eugene O'Neill; Harcourt Brace, and Company, Inc., for the passages from Carl Sandburg's *Smoke and Steel* (copyright, 1920), and *Slabs of the Sunburnt West* (copyright, 1922), and from Sinclair Lewis's *Babbitt* (copyright, 1922); Henry Holt and Company, for the passages from the poems of Robert Frost, and from Carl Sandburg's *Chicago Poems* and *Cornhuskers;* Houghton Mifflin Company, for extracts from *The Education of Henry Adams, Charles Francis Adams, An Autobiography* and *A Cycle of Adams Letters,* and from Miss Cather's novels; the Macmillan Company, for quotations from E. A. Robinson's *Collected Poems, Dionysus in Doubt,* and *Tristram,* and from Vachel Lindsay's *Collected Poems* and *Adventures While Preaching the Gospel of Beauty;* Charles Scribner's Sons, for the passages cited from E. A. Robinson's, *The Children of the Night* and *The Town Down the River,* and from *Character and Opinion in the United States,* by George Santayana; the Viking Press, for excerpts from *Poor White,* by Sherwood Anderson (copyright, 1920, by B. W. Huebsch, Inc.), and from *A Story-Teller's Story,* by Sherwood Anderson (copyright, 1922, by B. W. Huebsch, Inc).

T. K. W.

CONTENTS

I

THE POETIC TEMPER

IS it possible for an artist to exist in the United States?" To many people that perennial question, now being debated more eagerly than ever, has grown exasperating. Obviously, they say, it is possible; are not the arts at present unusually prosperous? Whether the comparison is made with our own past or with the present condition of other countries, there is no reason for discouragement. Painting and music, for instance, are more flourishing than ever before on our soil. Probably never—certainly not for a hundred years—has our architecture been in so thriving a state; by general consent it is far more interesting than that of any foreign nation. Not for seventy-five years has our literature shown an equal vigor, and for the first time it measures well up to the contemporary literatures of Europe. Evidently, therefore, an artist can not only exist but do good work among us; and nowhere else would he be better off.

Such an answer, however, in spite of the truth it contains, implies a misunderstanding of the question; in fact, the question itself as stated above is misleading and needs to be rephrased. It should rather be: "Is the lot of the artist in the United States susceptible of improvement? Is he impelled by his environment to do the best of which he is capable?" For, after all, there is small cause for rational satisfaction in comparing the present situation

I

either with our own past or with conditions in Europe since 1914; such comparisons can show only that we might be worse off than we are. If there must be comparisons, let them rather be with lands and times in which the arts have most conspicuously thriven—but it is better to forget comparisons altogether and to be content with inquiring whether on the whole and in what ways American life and American civilization are favorable or unfavorable to the arts.

To some, however, the question even in this mild form is still irritating. They do not see why the topic should be discussed at all. A nation exists, they say, not to turn out statues and tragedies, but to make possible for all its citizens the pursuit of happiness. If the majority are less unhappy here than elsewhere, our national experiment has succeeded, and we are justified in regarding the production of art as comparatively unimportant. To claim for our country eminent figures in painting and literature might tickle our vanity, but not to have this pleasure is scarcely a cause for grave national concern. And, indeed, if art were no more vital than this, these objections would be valid. Only on one supposition can great stress be laid on art—the supposition, namely, that since artistic expression is a natural function of man and society, a nation's art affords an index to that nation's life, that a stunted art is a sure sign of unhealthiness in the body politic. If this assumption can be granted, the condition of the arts becomes a matter of real importance, because it is intimately related to the lives and to the welfare and happiness of the whole people.

It is with these questions in mind, then, that we approach contemporary American literature. What has it to tell concerning modern American life? Is it hampered or fostered by its environment? Above all, does it give any clues as to possibilities of improvement in our civilization or in the lives of the majority? On these subjects, our recent literature has much to say, both directly and indirectly: directly, because many of our present writers are realists and the imaginary world of their books presents and is intended to present a reflection of the world which they and we know, and also because many of them are avowed critics of the society in which they have lived. But these writers have even more to tell indirectly, for they have inevitably been influenced by their surroundings. In their view of life, in their art—in their temper, their philosophy, their purposes, even their style—they have been molded by American society. It ought to be possible, therefore, to derive from them, both from what they say explicitly and from what they unconsciously and unintentionally reveal, some notion of the American situation, of the merits, the flaws, and the peculiarities of American life. Before the individual writers can be considered, however, certain basic aspects of the artist's point of view and of his relation to society must be discussed. I refer to a view of life which I shall term the poetic view; to denote the artist's temper of mind I shall borrow a phrase from Max Eastman and call it the poetic temper.

Of the poetic temper, no description could be better than Max Eastman's at the beginning of *The Enjoyment of Poetry:*

A simple experiment will distinguish two types of human nature. Gather a throng of people and pour them into a ferry-boat. By the time the boat has swung into the river you will find that a certain proportion have taken the trouble to climb upstairs, in order to be out on deck to see what is to be seen as they cross over. The rest have settled indoors,

3

to think what they will do upon reaching the other side, or perhaps to lose themselves in apathy or tobacco-smoke. But leaving out those apathetic, or addicted to a single enjoyment, we may divide all the alert passengers on the boat into two classes—those who are interested in crossing the river, and those who are merely interested in getting across. And we may divide all the people on the earth, or all the moods of people, in the same way. Some of them are chiefly occupied with attaining ends, and some with receiving experiences. . . . We name the first kind practical, and the second poetic. . . .

Poetic people, and all people when they are in a poetic mood . . . are lovers of the qualities of things. . . . They are possessed by the impulse to realize . . . a wish to experience life and the world. That is the essence of the poetic temper.

Perhaps that admirable illustration is sufficient, but I should like to add another: Let us suppose that there is a grove of pine trees behind the house in which you live. Again and again you have hurried through the grove to catch a train or to get home in time for dinner. And you have gone there to rest after a day of hard work. Then some warm sunny afternoon, when you are neither hurried nor tired, you stroll idly into the grove. For the first time you really notice it—the smell of the needles and the pitch, the spring of the needles underfoot, the soft sounds and stirrings, and the grays and browns and greens of which the sunlight and the shadow make a thousand tints and shades. As you sit there, the whole place seems to come to life; all the colors and sounds and smells grow more vibrant; you forget yourself, you lose yourself in the experience. For, this time, you are experiencing the pine grove, you are realizing it. You have no ulterior purpose in mind; your consciousness is at flood, not at low ebb; for once, you are fully alive to your surroundings— which is to say that for the moment you are alive—living.

This is experience, this realization. It is not a passive thing; when complete, it demands that all one's faculties be keyed up to the highest pitch. To keep fully alive, to maintain a tension and an alertness, to be always on the *qui vive*—this is to have a large capacity for experience. It requires an extraordinary fund of energy, unusual vitality, and a rich emotional endowment, all of which are expended in the interest of a heightened awareness, an awareness that demands a steady outflow of feeling, a going forth of virtue. It is less a matter of observation or of sharp senses than of ability to let go, to give oneself, to surrender oneself, for one does not absorb experience—one is absorbed by it. Full realization involves a diminution of self-consciousness, a heightened consciousness of the object, a kind of vital and creative contact between subject and object, a merging, a fusion. At its utmost, it is in some sense akin to a mystic act of contemplation, even of communion. On its lower every-day levels it involves some sort of "passionate apprehension." It is known only to those who, in Eastman's terms, have the "poetic temper," or at least temporarily a "poetic mood." Other people, and people in other moods, do not experience; that is, they do not live. For experience is surely the stuff, the raw material, of life itself. We may disagree with John Drinkwater's saying, "With our human conception, we can see no good or desirable end beyond the perfect experience of life"; we may disagree with Pater's "Not the fruit of experience, but experience itself is the end"; but we cannot deny that experience,

5

though perhaps not the end, is assuredly the beginning, of life. Only when we experience do we live.

So far I have given illustrations of only one type of experience, sensuous realization, because that type is the simplest and the most familiar. But there are many others. For instance, there is intellectual experience, the "passionate apprehension" of ideas, of thought, a delight in the exercise of the mind as of the senses. So there is also the experience of action, as when the strong man rejoices to run his race, the joy of struggle and combat, familiar to all who care for athletic games—or for that matter to all who enjoy the conflicts of business or of politics. A closely allied kind of active experience is found in work when it is done *con amore*—the pleasure of doing things, of making things. Something of this sort Havelock Ellis had in mind when he wrote: "Life cannot be reached by the senses alone; there is always something that cannot be caught by the utmost tension of eyes and ears and nose; a well-balanced soul is built up, not alone on sensory memories, but also on the harmonious satisfaction of the motor and emotional energies." As the last phrase indicates, there is such a thing as the experience of a feeling or a mood, of anger, love, terror, loneliness—not that they are luxuriated in for their own sake, but that they are felt to the full. Or again, there is what may be called æsthetic experience, which is provided by art in its many forms. I do not understand those who set off literature and the other arts as a thing contrasted with or opposed to experience, of which surely the realization of a poem or a statue or a symphony is but one species. Yet another sort of experience is the religious— for whatever one may think of the mystic's explanations, one can scarcely deny him his experience.

Finally, there is the type which to literature is the most important of all: social experience, the realization of other people, of their peculiar traits and qualities, of their relations with oneself and with one another. It is by no means identical with what is called social life; on the contrary, during most of our intercourse with others, we and they are no better than so many mechanical dolls. We do not really get acquainted with one another, because we arm ourselves with impenetrable masks to prevent real acquaintance. We develop no personal relations; for one thing, it takes two to make a personal relation, which arises only when both parties to it give their consent. And only with the personal relation does social experience begin; it grows only in intimacy; it flourishes only in intimate groups all the members of which have some knack for it, for social intercourse is an art which not every one is competent to practice. It can be gauged by conversation: wherever conversation thrives, there is real social life and therefore social experience. There the barriers are let down, and people are both eager to know one another and willing themselves to be known. It must also be premised that, as human beings, they are sufficiently developed to be worth knowing. A rich social life is the final fruit of—and is possible only in—a society in which the poetic temper, the life of realization in its many phases, is properly valued.

But there is little point in attempting to classify and catalogue the varieties or the ingredients of experience, which after all is one and indivisible. The poetic temper is simply the disposition to live as fully as possible; the life of realization signifies, not any special activities or mode of life, but rather a point of view which may be carried into any human activity: it signifies a self-forgetful, disinterested point of view and includes all disinterested activities. The term is a more inclusive one than Aristotle's theoretic life or the medieval contemplative life, for it includes not only the artist's pursuit of beauty, the scientist's and the scholar's pursuit of knowledge, the philosopher's pursuit of truth, the mystic's pursuit of God, but also the several pursuits of such as the explorer, the craftsman, the huntsman, even the business man if he enjoys his activities for their own sake. Whenever, one might say, any one does anything "for love," the poetic temper is present. The life of realization is a more inclusive term than the "creative life" of which many modern authors write, for though it is followed by all creative workers, it does not necessarily imply creation: it may be followed by any one, in any situation whatever, whose primary concern is to live as fully as circumstances permit, to realize life as fully as possible.

But perhaps its essential nature can best be made plain by a description of some opposing points of view. Its chief enemy, as Max Eastman points out, is the practical habit of mind. The practical man, being wholly bent on his own personal aggrandizement, cannot afford to indulge in disinterested activities. His aim is not to become acquainted with his environment, to explore the world, to realize life, but to exploit all these for his own benefit. He shuns experience, for experience would divert his attention and his energy from the goal. To return to my earlier illustration, when you hurry through the pine grove to get home to dinner, you are being practical; it is in that spirit that the practical man goes through life. With his whole heart set on succeeding, making good, getting on and up in the world, he cannot let himself stop to look about him and take things in, to question and ponder, to ask himself "Why?" and "Whither?" He cannot, in short, afford to live. He sells his birthright for a mess of pottage.

Fortunately, the wholly practical man does not exist; the antithesis I have been setting up between the life of realization and the life of self-advancement is artificial and unreal, for it is obvious that every one must be practical part of the time, and that no one can be practical all the time. The question, therefore, resolves itself into this: which of the two is to be primary, which secondary, which the end and which the means, which the master and which the servant? For note that also when you go to the pine grove to rest, you are being practical. One cannot work continually; one must have refreshment and distraction. So the practical man goes off to the country or a play or a party or even to church, in order that he may return with renewed vigor to his practicality. Nature, art, social life, religion—all may be made handmaids of the practical life; indeed, it is the last triumph of the practical life to reduce the life of realization to this ancillary position. But it is worth observing that when experience is thus debased, it becomes wan and anemic.

Another foe to realization is timidity. There are people so constituted as not to be able to let themselves go, to surrender themselves. They instinctively shrink from experience, especially if it presents itself in a novel form. They contract and shrivel up like a sensitive plant at the touch of reality; they adopt a shy touch-me-not attitude, ready to withdraw into their shells at any moment. They are, therefore, incapable of much experience, especially social experience, since nowhere are they so hampered by their diffidence as in their relations with other men and women. Of course they commonly justify their fear by

9

finding good excuses for it: they hide it often behind a
mask of practicality; they must keep an eye, they say, on
the main chance—to cultivate experience would interfere
with their success. Or else they disguise their trepidation
in the form of scruples of morality or of gentility and refinement, as if it were somehow not right or not "nice"
to face life boldly—and indeed actuality is often not
"nice." The "genteel tradition," one form of the cult of
respectability, which springs from dread of reality and
which allies itself with practicality, is eminently hostile to
fullness of life.

One wonders how much of what passes as puritanism
has its root in this congenital timidity. The puritan is a
protean creature, and what I say of him is to be taken as
an account of only one of his manifestations. There is a
type of puritan who regards edification as the end of
existence. He cannot pay a visit to the mountains without
excusing himself on the ground that natural scenery is
elevating and ennobling; he cannot even go fishing without
a moral justification. His only interest in a novel or a
play is to ask how it makes people "better"—which in his
opinion means, not more complete or more fully developed, but more "proper" in behavior. For the morality
which governs his universe is negative; he is given, as
Van Wyck Brooks says, to thinking of what Galahad did
not do rather than of the object of Galahad's quest. The
whole mission of this puritan is to see to it that we have
life less abundantly. To his mind, any approach to life
in the spirit of curiosity or of love is wicked. He considers experience, of whatever sort, as valuable not for its
own sake, but only for such moral lessons as it may in-
culcate, as if life were a Sunday-school teacher. Like
the practical man, he puts the life of realization in sec-

ond place and regards it only as a means; for the life of material or social advancement he substitutes the life of moral advancement, as he understands morality. Since both are hostile to experience, the puritan and the practical man make excellent confederates; in fact, they are often one and the same person. For this sort of puritan, oddly enough, is apt to think of worldly prosperity as a duty, and to call it "social service."

Finally, among the enemies of realization there are the sentimentalists. They are easily detected. Bring one of them suddenly face to face with a fine view, and watch him take a deep breath and shut his eyes. You may be sure that a person who thinks a landscape can be best taken in with the eyes closed is a sentimentalist. His emotions, real enough in their way no doubt, are worked by conventional springs and are as it were detached from, unrelated to, the cause. A certain ecstasy, because it is conventionally associated with the sight of a large expanse of territory, is aroused in him instantaneously. As soon as the feeling has subsided, the sentimentalist is ready to go on; he feels no need of actually looking at this particular view. He has had and relished his "fine-view feeling"; why should he linger? That is, his conventional reaction has actually prevented him from seeing the scenery. The sentimentalist lives in an unreal world, usually prettier and sweeter, always much less difficult than the real world— in a world built up out of preconceived, established, traditional associations and conceptions, of cheerful and easy illusions. It is impossible to overstate the difference between the poetic temper, which insists on full realization of things as they are, however unpleasant, of the ugly and squalid and foul no less than of the fair and comely, and the sentimental temper, which is indifferent to reality—even hostile to it, inasmuch as the sentimentalist wishes to luxuriate in a warm emotional glow which the harsh external world is all too likely to dissipate. He has therefore an admirable defense against reality, and he makes great economies. To realize an experience takes energy, all of which he saves because he is protected against experience.

Practicality, timidity (or fear of life), puritanism, and sentimentality form a common and highly successful working combination. Being perfectly armored against life, the man who could unite them all would be likely to go far. Every jot of his force could be devoted to making good. However uninteresting, however complete a failure he might turn out as a human being, he ought to be sure of success as he understands success. To be sure, he would never live at all. He would experience nothing, and all his humane potentialities would remain undeveloped; his senses, his power of thought and of feeling, his æsthetic sensibility, his love of action, his social faculties, would all be in grave danger of atrophy. In any case, however, our concern is less with the individual fate of such a person than with the social consequences of the practical attitude, with what happens to a society when most of its members are indifferent or hostile to experience, and with the effect such a society is likely to have on an artist, especially a writer, who lives in it.

Inevitably, in such a society, the life of realization, in all its phases, becomes meager and debased. The physical manifestations of the practical attitude are most conspicuous. An indifference to the exercise of the senses shows itself in the ugliness of all the works of man, and most of all in the drab and sordid ugliness of his towns and cities, thrown together haphazard according to the exigencies of the moment. Nature, of course, will continue to provide her own beauty, but even Nature may be seriously marred if every human activity is opposed to her.

More serious, however, is the effect on the intellectual life. Any sort of speculation or reflection languishes in neglect and indifference, if it is not altogether taboo. Fundamental problems of philosophy, politics, ethics, economics, and the other subjects which have engaged human attention are seldom raised and never really debated. Such matters, such interests, would distract people's attention from the job in hand and thereby interfere with efficiency. That is why to all intents and purposes real thought cannot exist in a practical society. It is replaced by a kind of *Ersatzphilosophie,* a "cheerful optimism" which is valued because it makes for greater efficiency. "We care nothing for truth," the practical society says; "what we want is to succeed, and if illusions will make us more efficient, by all means let us have the illusions. If a rosy outlook aids the digestion, if a belief that life is good and that the world grows constantly better helps the circulation of the blood, by all means let us believe these things." There is no better illustration of how sentimentality plays into the hands of practicality, and of how both of them are opposed to a sense of fact. Thought, enslaved in the service of practicality, is debauched from the pursuit of truth and prostituted to the pursuit of a mean success.

To this same purpose, in a practical society, are prostituted art and religion. The latter—by rights the chief opponent of the practical life and the defender of the life of realization in its extremest form, the mystical—forgets its mission and descends to a series of "pep talks" which are calculated to send men and women back to their offices greatly refreshed on Monday morning, with renewed vigor for the week's work. The Infinite comes to be regarded as a source from which human energy can be drawn as electricity is drawn from a waterfall; workers are urged to practice prayer and contemplation in order that they may increase their output. Art in all its forms is similarly debased. It is used to create a factitious optimism which the victim of the fake as often as not knows to be false—but he does not care. He is after "inspiration" in the cant sense, not realization; he wants novels, stories, plays, pictures, which will encourage him to go thoughtlessly ahead, comfortably convinced that everything is going well and that he need not bother.

In short, every aspect of the life of realization becomes a drug to be taken in the interests of efficiency. Besides serving the purpose of promoting irrational cheeriness, the arts may be turned into mere distractions; if not used to build up a false optimism, they are used to divert the business man for a few hours from his work. Nature—the only form in this practical world in which loveliness is to be found—is thought of as a sort of refreshment booth, and the value of an outing Wednesday evening is measured in terms of selling-power Thursday morning. Sport is taken in doses like medicine, or else winning is so overemphasized that the sportsmen adopt a professional attitude. Even work, when all the interest is removed from the work itself and centered on the personal advancement of the worker, yields no satisfaction on its own account; the worker takes no honest pleasure in his work, but scamps it, and gets by: good work is nothing, quantity production of a passable grade is everything.

In a wholly practical society, social life is impossible.

It resolves itself into a mere search for distraction in groups, since these people have none of the social ingredients. At best they can talk shop, somewhat lackadaisically because their real interest is not in the "shop," whatever it may be, but in their own fortunes; or they can tell stories. They are more likely to flee for refuge to the card table or the radio, or to a movie or a cabaret, anything to avoid their mutual boredom. For, worst of all, they have no genuine interest in one another. Why should they have? The social level sometimes falls below the level of the individual members, but it can never rise above that level, and when one describes the practical man, one describes a type which, however efficient it may be, leaves much to be desired as a social being. Contemptuous of ideas and therefore destitute of them, without curiosity and therefore without interest either in or for others, uninteresting and uninterested—the type is most striking for its essential poverty. Since a society of such folk cannot help being an arid human desert, it must contain many provisions for distraction, few for pleasure or enjoyment, for enjoyment implies that one must supply something—at least appreciation—as is the case in any sort of experience or realization. And these people cannot supply even that. They are impoverished and undernourished because all their lives long they have systematically avoided realizing or experiencing anything—that is, they have deliberately avoided life itself—until their capacity for experience has withered. If it is a man's experience and his reaction to it that make a man interesting, plainly a man with neither experience nor reaction must be a deadly foe to life in any of its forms, but most of all in its social manifestations.

What of the writer, then, who is born into a society

adverse to the life of realization? Since all writers worth
considering, all artists indeed, by their very nature are
endowed with the poetic temper and predisposed to lead
the life of realization, such a society must also be adverse
to them. It affects them unfavorably in two ways: it
starves, and it warps, the writer's mind. It starves him
by denying him an adequate experience; the experience
with which it furnishes him can be at best but lean and
scanty. Above all, it is niggardly in that social experience
which, indispensable to a novelist or a dramatist, is vital
to every writer. He needs to establish manifold personal
relations with all sorts of people, and especially with people
who have lived largely and intensely and whose natures
have been fully developed. He needs to live in a close
network or web of society, to be part of a social organism.
In a practical world, however, where people are mutually
repellent particles, no social organism can be formed; and
the contacts which the writer may be able to make with
individuals must all be with a single type only, and that
a peculiarly undeveloped one. Moreover, he cannot really
manage even that; one cannot establish personal relations
with practical people because, being incapacitated for
human intercourse by their point of view, they will not
and cannot do their share. The experience they afford of
the human race and of human life cannot fail to be inadequate. To expect a writer to derive from them an
adequate realization of the rich profusion of human nature would be to expect an Esquimau of the tundras to
form in his own mind an adequate image of the Brazilian
jungle.

Nor is a practical society content with denying social
experience. It is deficient also in its appeal to the senses,
in the food it supplies the sensuous imagination. In such

a world, only nature offers sensuous gratification. Communion with nature, though no doubt better than none, is too limited and too one-sided to be a satisfactory substitute for communion with men and men's works. If a nation's literature abounds in fervid appreciation of nature and is correspondingly deficient in a sense of humanity and human achievement, the chances are that that nation has pursued the practical ideal. Its writers have turned to nature because it and it alone offered them the possibility of experience—that is, of life. Even more than in sensuous experience, furthermore, a practical society is wanting in intellectual and æsthetic experience. Ideas and disinterested speculation do not exist; the arts are reduced to a slavery of refreshment and distraction. For both, the writer must turn to other countries and other ages; and when so imported, when thus divorced from actuality, thought and art have the air of irrelevant bric-à-brac. What is needed is a living current circulating through the social medium.

Something too much has been said in the past as to the genius's superiority to circumstances. It is well to be reminded from time to time, as Rollo Brown has reminded us, that Mozart, born in the Samoan Islands, could no more have composed symphonies than Archimedes could invent the dynamo—or, we might add, than Shakespeare, in such a practical society as I have sketched, could have written his tragedies. However one may understand the term "creative imagination," no one is likely to deny that in composing a writer draws on his experience, that nothing appears in his writing which has not first been in his consciousness. Of course he transforms and transmutes his material—even the most abject realist does so; and often he transmutes it beyond recognition. Nevertheless, it is almost too obvious to say that literature is a record of experience, if that word is properly understood. Much of the best literature, to be sure, is the record of experiences which the poets have had in imagination only; but even these imaginary experiences are made from material accumulated in actual experience. It is less a question of finding "subjects" or material for writing, although one may doubt whether a practical society affords satisfactory material, than of the growth and development of the writer's mind, which, deprived of adequate experience, is bound to be undernourished, anemic, stunted. It needs sensuous, emotional, intellectual food and exercise, and as full and many-sided a life as possible. That is why a writer should have a full store of sensuous impressions, should have encountered many varied ideas and points of view and been touched with many moods and emotions, and above all should have an abundant direct first-hand acquaintance with human nature. It behooves a writer to have gathered as rich a harvest as possible because, if the harvest is poor, his work is sure to be meager and flimsy. Such will be the qualities of such genuine literature as may manage to be produced in a practical society.

In addition, a practical society, not content with starving a writer's mind and art, does all it can to corrupt and warp them. The writer is not only not impelled to do his best, but is positively discouraged from doing his best. He lacks, in the first place, all the incentives to good work which he might derive from an established literary tradition, from encouragement and sympathy, from discipline in taste and in critical standards. He is not made to feel that recognition will be commensurate with the merit of his work, that it is worth his while to make every effort to do the best of which he is capable, that only his best will be tolerated. On the contrary, he knows that the way to win applause is to prostitute his talents in the purveying of diversion, cheeriness, and sentimentality. But the lack of discriminating appreciation and the temptation to debauch his power are comparatively of little moment. More serious is the fact that, from birth, he is trained in false modes of thought and feeling. Throughout his childhood and youth he is educated in indifference to truth and in illusory sentiment, in the *ethos* of gentility and puritanism; so that on arriving at maturity he has to expend much energy in freeing himself from the cocoon in which he has been spun up. Then—at the age of twenty-five, say—he is where he ought to have been at birth: ready to begin. When one considers the enormous part played by the experience of youth in the work of those so fortunate as to have been born into a society which prizes the life of realization, in which a sense of fact and genuineness of feeling are prevalent, in which the writer begins from birth to accumulate experience and to reflect upon it, the wonder is that the less fortunate writer is able to accomplish anything at all.

Indeed, he is lucky if he ever succeeds in freeing himself entirely from the view of life in which he has been bred. He must be a person of extraordinary strength of character not to make some effort to conform to the local standards and to placate the tribal gods. And even if he does not make this attempt to deny his own nature, he may not escape unscarred. To wholly practical people, any impractical person is ridiculous, possibly dangerous; and by their hostility they evoke in him an answering hostility, they make him assume a defensive attitude toward his environment. Yet for him to be on his guard against experience and to repel it is suicidal; for if his mind is denied its proper nutriment so that it cannot grow and mature to its full strength, it will be wanting in inner substance. This central weakness may lead to self-distrust, to undue self-consciousness, to a lack of integrity which shows itself as an unstable, insecure point of view, and to the assumption of alien in lieu of authentic personal standards. Not improbably the writer may fly for escape from his predicament to the refuge of an easy romanticism, to foreign books and to day-dreaming and fantasy. At any rate, his rebellion is likely to drive him into some sort of isolation; the step from being regarded as a crank and a freak to becoming one is fatally easy.

We should expect, then, to find the literature of a practical country weak in sensuousness and thought, in sense of humanity and the human drama, strong in appreciation of nature, weak in literary critical sense and uncertain in style, marked by occasional flights into thin romanticism, sentimentality, jejune moralism, and commercial potboiling, and characterized in general by instability, immaturity, and a kind of emaciated gauntness. That, obviously, is not a description of contemporary American literature, a fact which alone suffices to show that the preceding sketch of a practical society is not a description of modern American life. Nor was it so intended: the society which I have outlined is as mythical as Plato's Republic. It is an "ideal" practical society such as could never exist on the globe. If asked for proof that the United States is not such a land, I should point to the extraordinary florescence of American literature, and indeed of the other arts also, which the last fifteen years have witnessed.

Much has been written, at one time and another, of the special hardships which the American writer must un-

dergo: our lack of tradition, our newness, our devotion
to money-making, our heritage of puritanism, our democratic uniformity or standardization. Without denying
the existence of these difficulties, I question whether they
are not all of secondary importance in comparison with
the practical attitude. For, while I cannot insist too
strongly that my picture of a practical society is not a
picture of the United States, it would be idle to deny that
I consider the one pertinent to the other. Since the days
of Benjamin Franklin, the practical has been the popular
American ideal. Even now, some of our most widely
read periodicals devote themselves to teaching success-
worship; our schools and colleges are full of it. It has
invaded our churches. Nor can we say that this pursuit
of practicality has been altogether in vain. At times large
portions of the nation have come perilously close to attaining the ideal, and among us still are communities which
are not far removed from it. The practical ideal, with its
attendant "genteel tradition," puritanism, and sentimentality, seems to me the central fact in our history, at least
in our literary history. My conviction that this view of
life is erroneous, that it does not make ultimately either
fo individual happiness or for national welfare, has led
me to try to see what light our current writers may shed
on the question.

For this purpose, I have chosen ten writers who treat
the American life they have known with special vigor and
directness. They have all also won for themselves established positions as leaders in contemporary writing. They
belong as a group to the time of the World War, in the
sense that in 1914 few of them had as yet achieved a widespread reputation: the present literary position of Henry
Adams, who might seem an exception, is based chiefly on

his autobiography, published in 1918; and although
Robinson and Dreiser had earned their places some time
earlier, they, like the others, were not accorded generally
acknowledged eminence until the period of the War.
Among our contemporaries these ten seem to afford the
best basis for an inquiry not only as to the lot of the
artist among us, but also as to the common lot in so far as
it has been revealed and discussed in current literature.
With their combined breadth of experience, with their ex-
ceptional insight and acumen, above all with their endeavor
to explore and interpret the American scene and to record
out of their findings some word of what we are as a
nation, they furnish valuable testimony as to the quality
of American civilization.

II

HENRY ADAMS

THOUGH it may seem strange to include in a discussion of contemporary writers a man who was seventy-six years old when the World War began, yet Henry Adams was so remarkable a herald or forerunner of the present and formulated a philosophy so typically modern that his story clarifies and helps explain the whole trend of American literature in the last fifteen years. Furthermore, he has himself told this story with such acumen in *The Education of Henry Adams* that his autobiography enables us as does no other book to watch the contemporary view of life actually in process of formation. Beginning, as he himself says, as a "child of the eighteenth century," and ending as an unexcelled exponent of the twentieth, he spans, and somewhat more than spans, an entire era. Intellectually, as well as physically, his life touches John Quincy Adams at one end and the World War at the other. That is why no other writer furnishes so good a basis and background for the interpretation of our contemporaries—one might say of ourselves—as he.

The conclusion to which his long lifetime led him was simply this: "In plain words, Chaos was the law of nature; Order was the dream of man." The universe, so far as he could discover, contained no trace of plan, much less of purpose; it seemed to lack even any sort of order or law, if law implies system. It was not, in fact, a universe at all, but a multiverse, for it was not under a single control, but was a congeries of warring forces. It was not a unity like a watch, but a multiplicity like a heap of fire-works set off by accident. "He found himself," he says, "in a land . . . where order was an accidental relation obnoxious to nature; artificial compulsion imposed on motion; against which every free energy of the universe revolted; and which, being merely occasional, resolved itself back into anarchy at last." This "multiverse" of his, that is, was sheer accident and catastrophe, unintelligible and meaningless, only a random manifestation of aimless senseless forces.

A senseless chaos—that is what life ultimately meant to Henry Adams. For he included in his view not only man's physical environment, but the whole of human existence: that too was an anarchic welter. He saw no reason to suppose that humankind stood in a peculiar position or enjoyed special privileges; man in his view was as much a subordinate part of nature as a rock or a chemical element. Even in early life, although he had not yet abandoned his conceptions of a cosmos, he had already given up all notion that man had a destiny different from that of other natural objects; in 1863 he wrote his brother:

My philosophy teaches me, and I firmly believe it, that the laws which govern animated beings will be ultimately found to be at bottom the same with those which rule inanimate nature, and, as I entertain a profound conviction of the little-ness of our kind, and of the curious enormity of creation, I am quite ready to receive with pleasure any basis for a systematic conception of it all.

But that "basis for a systematic conception" is precisely what in his old age he was forced to regard as impossible,

24

and as he came to see in nature only the play of meaningless forces, so he came to see in man only the unconscious sport of those forces. Nor did he hold this view in only its commonplace form; on the contrary, he denied that men learn how for their own purposes to control and govern natural forces. Men, in his eyes, were the victims, not the rulers, of their own discoveries and inventions. Gunpowder, steam, electricity—such things master us and do what they will with us; our dream of utilizing them for humane ends is an illusion.

Furthermore, man's conception of himself as a unit is as much illusion as is his conception of universal system. Personality, the self, whatever one calls it, is also chaos. Inspection at once reveals it as a multiplicity, not a unity, in which again order is obnoxious to nature. The single consciousness is a transitory and artificial exception, thrown off by nature at every opportunity in favor of dream and reverie; the lawless, inconsequent unconscious is the rule—"the simultaneous action of different thought-centers without central control." Man, in short, is a microchaos within, to match the macrochaos without. To this fact, not only psychology but also the whole course of human society bears witness. In spite of the innate human longing for unity and order, which Adams always admitted, men cannot succeed in imposing their wish even on their own actions and their mutual relations: hence "the persistently fiendish treatment of man by man; the perpetual effort of society to establish law, and the perpetual revolt of society against the law it had established; the perpetual building up of authority by force, and the perpetual appeal to force to overthrow it; the perpetual symbolism of a higher law, and the perpetual relapse to a lower one." His study of history convinced him merely that history was "in essence incoherent and immoral." He could detect in past events no rational sequence, no progress, no sign of cause and effect, nothing intelligible. Human beings, he therefore thought, could claim special consideration neither in their relations with external nature or with one another, nor in their own inner nature.

Henry Adams' creed, then, was one of pessimism and naturalism, of determinism as concerns human life, and of philosophic anarchism—a creed than which none, I suppose, is more repugnant to men in general. How was he impelled to a belief which was certainly as distasteful to himself as it could be? Undoubtedly he himself would have insisted that he was merely a passive learner, even an unwilling learner, of the lessons which science and history have to teach; nor can one prove his views false by pointing out (what is quite true) that he himself was neither metaphysician nor scientist. I have no intention of trying to criticize his philosophy or to "explain it away"; yet I think it not unfair to insist that in the formation of his opinions his own personal experience may be supposed to have played a part no less important than his studies. It is a fairly safe assumption that a philosophy is as much an expression of personal temperament as of logic and evidence. Indeed, Adams has recorded that certain particular incidents taught him anarchy. One such was his elder sister's death in 1870 under peculiarly atrocious circumstances, by which for the first time he was made to face nature's insensate waste and haphazard cruelty. Another such episode was his life in England, when his study of English politicians convinced him that they had been consistent only in their irrationality, so that the student simply lost himself "in the sheer chaos of human nature." But even more than by experiences like these his thought must have been affected by his own life as a whole, especially in relation to his environment, his time and place—namely, the United States in the second half of the nineteenth century.

In part, his philosophy was devised, perhaps unconsciously, to account for what he regarded as his own failure. *The Education of Henry Adams* is the apologia of a disappointed man. His brother Brooks warns us not to be deceived by Henry's pose, reminding us that Henry succeeded brilliantly in everything he undertook; nevertheless, though of course one must always allow for the irony which pervades the *Education,* and though every one knows that according to ordinary standards Henry Adams was far from a failure, one cannot, even at a brother's behest, make oneself believe that Henry Adams was content with the figure he had cut in the world. The vein of bitterness is too marked throughout his autobiography. His performance, no doubt, would have satisfied almost any one else; but he was an Adams, and also a man of unusual possibilities. By the exploits of his family in the past, by the inner powers which he was conscious of possessing, by the opportunities and advantages which he enjoyed, and by what he wished to accomplish—by these he judged himself, and was dissatisfied. And he had reason to be dissatisfied: he should have become one of the most conspicuous leaders of his generation, and such a position not his most zealous admirer can claim for him. To account for his comparative failure is to account in part for his philosophy; I suggest that the explanation is to be found in a three-cornered war waged between his natural endowment, his inheritance, and his environment.

It is plain for what sort of career he was fitted: for

27

the sort of which England in the nineteenth century affords many conspicuous instances—Ruskin, Arnold, Huxley, Mill, Sir Leslie Stephen, Lord Morley—well-rounded men who combined philosophic, literary, artistic, economic, and political interests, and who used their talents and acquirements for the criticism of life and civilization. For such a career Adams had a strong bias and every qualification. As he himself recognized, his whole bent was toward the life of *theoria,* not the life of action. By nature, his mind was of a speculative, questioning cast, reflective, sceptical, and critical. The inclination was inborn in him to think things over, to try to discover their significance and understand their causes and relations and effects. His disposition was, in the broadest sense, philosophical; he was born to be interpreter, commentator, critic—spectator, not actor—not to enter the arena himself, but to watch the combatants and to explain the meaning of the affair.

Moreover, his keenness of mind, his intellectual power, his alert and many-sided intelligence, his wide interests ranging from history, politics, and natural science to the arts, philosophy, and religion—all seemed to assure his success in his vocation. His preference for playing the spectator did not imply undue detachment; Adams was not by nature aloof from human affairs or indifferent to them, but rather the reverse: he wanted to take in the whole play, to see it as a whole—as only a spectator can. And, in the end, his achievements, far below his possibilities as they were, were those of the historian, critic, philosopher. Of all his works, *Mont St. Michel* and the *Education,* both written after he was sixty, are most indicative of his potentialities; in them, all the qualities I have been attributing to him are abundantly manifested.

These books are an earnest of what he might have accomplished.

Of all the forces which conspired against Henry Adams, the first was his New England heritage. The Adamses were the attar of New England, and therefore the distilled essence of puritanism. As Clarence King is said to have remarked, "Boston was 1,387,453 years under the ice; and then the Adamses came." The spirit or tone of the life which Henry knew as a child may be inferred from one typical incident. He and his brothers had been fishing all morning on a wharf at Quincy, and their father, contrary to custom, had kept them company. Here is the entry which their father made in his diary that evening:

The weather was charming. I idled away the morning on Mr. Daniel Greenleaf's wharf, with very little success. Perhaps this consumption of time is scarcely justifiable; but why not take some of life for simple enjoyments, provided that they interfere with no known duty?

The last sentence tells the whole story: the assumption that enjoyment, though simple, and though interfering with no "known" duty, is scarcely defensible. It was in this arctic atmosphere that Henry Adams grew up, in this world where no motive, no value, existed save duty. And this duty, in the phrase of C. F. Adams, Sr., was to become as soon as possible a "useful member of society." Only two passions were admissible—and the passion for self-improvement must be surpassed by the passion for improving others. One must go through life like a soldier marching at attention, head up, eyes straight to the front. Every hour, every moment of one's life must be tested by that touchstone: "How has it better enabled me to benefit others?" And even so, the answer was narrower in spirit than the question, for the improvement must be immediate and obvious. Delayed or indirect returns were not counted.

Henry's elder brother, Charles Francis, Jr., in his autobiography bewails the effect on himself of this upbringing; and the effect on Henry was even more unfortunate. It bred in him a morbid conscientiousness, with reference always to social utility. This doctrine of service, which clashed with the still older New England tendency to doubt and question, could not prevent him from using his mind; but it could and did make him unhappy and conscience-stricken over his incorrigible habit of thinking. And if it opposed intellectual experience, it opposed other sorts of experience ten times more. Henry Adams could never naïvely enjoy anything. Especially a taint of wrongness clung to vivid experiences; as he himself humorously confesses: "They must be hurtful, else they could not be so intense." He could not even take a walk in Thüringen with his friends in innocence of heart; in the midst of his pleasure in "the first fresh breath of leafless spring, and the beer," he had to torment himself with scruples of conscience. Yet what he needed above all was simply to loaf and invite his soul, to absorb experience and grow and mature. His puritan legacy did him incalculable harm, because it made him deny his nature the very food it most needed. He later became clearly aware that his mind was stunted on many sides, and he blamed his defects on the United States in general and Boston in particular; hence his remark in a letter to his niece, "I am too American myself, and lack juices." That is, he considered a certain meagerness or malnutrition or incompleteness of development a national and above all

Bostonian trait; witness the parallel he draws between himself and St. Gaudens:

St. Gaudens was a child of Benvenuto Cellini, smothered in an American cradle. Adams was a quintessence of Boston, devoured by curiosity to think like Benvenuto. St. Gaudens's art was starved from birth, and Adams's instinct was blighted from babyhood. Each had but half of a nature.

In *A Niece's Memories,* we are told that when in 1890 Adams went to the South Seas with La Farge, "a new world of perceptions opened out to him; . . . the education of the senses began." While it is probably true that on this momentous journey he became fully conscious for the first time of the tremendous importance of sensuous experience, the statement above cannot be altogether accepted. For in a striking passage of the *Education* he tells how in 1859 during his first visit to Germany he awoke to music; and of his "first plunge into Italy" he says: "Like music, it differed from other education in being, not a means of pursuing life, but one of the ends attained." Indeed, all his life long he felt a pull toward the life of realization, especially sensuous realization, and in that life, largely perhaps because of his association with artists, he came to see more and more value, until, at the close, his innate tendencies got the better of him, and he regretfully resigned himself to the life for which he was fitted. However, try as he might in later years, he could not make up for the lost experience of his first fifty years. And that he was so slow and so reluctant to confess this proclivity, this poetic temper, in himself—that his capabilities remained for the most part undeveloped and unused—he owed to his ancestral puritanism.

Nor was puritanism the only influence that went with

the Adams blood. To be an Adams was something like being one of the Atridae: the greatness carried a family curse. Or rather, greatness was the family curse. Not only did Henry grow up believing that duty was the whole of life and that it consisted in bettering society by leading an active, practical, useful life; but, since he was an Adams, he had the further duty imposed upon him of keeping up the family name, of not falling short of his ancestors. And this was not a duty merely; it appealed to a force more powerful than the moral sense—to pride, emulation, ambition. Nothing is more obvious, or more important for an understanding of the man, than the fact that Henry Adams was passionately ambitious. The irresistible union of ambition with sense of duty may be a salutary spur to some men, but to Henry Adams, who needed not to be goaded but to be relaxed, it was fatal. For his environment set this all-prevailing force to work against his natural bent and capacity, in the direction of a narrowly practical service to society. Succeed he must, at any cost—succeed conspicuously, with public acclaim, and in the Adams manner, by trying to improve large masses of humanity. Only this kind of success presented itself to his mind as conceivable; therefore, he regarded the bent of his own mind, not as opportunity, but as weakness. In 1862 he wrote to his elder brother:

The truth is, the experience of four years has done little towards giving me confidence in myself. The more I see, the more I am convinced that a man whose mind is balanced like mine, in such a way that what is evil never seems unmixed with good, and what is good always streaked with evil; an object seems never important enough to call out strong energies till they are exhausted, nor necessary enough not to allow of its failure being possible to retrieve; in short, a mind which is not strongly positive and absolute, cannot be steadily successful in action, which requires quietness and persever- ance. I have steadily lost faith in myself ever since I left college, and my aim is now so indefinite that all my time may prove to have been wasted, and then nothing left but a trun- cated life.

For him, there is only one alternative: to succeed in action, or to fail. To some, perhaps, the rôle of critic, the rôle played in various ways at various times by Swift, Voltaire, Rousseau, Carlyle, and others, might seem one of sufficient dignity and even of sufficient service, but not to Henry Adams. True, good critics are fully as rare and as valuable as good performers—in the United States, surely, much more so, for if ever a time and a nation cried out for criticism it was the United States in the lifetime of Henry Adams. But no: he had no taste for that kind of success. Criticism was not included in the New England scheme of service; the elder C. F. Adams would probably not have thought, for instance, that Voltaire was a useful member of society. Futhermore, prophets were peculiarly without honor in the United States after the Civil War; they passed unnoticed, and Henry Adams had no liking for obscurity. He was out to make good. The more clearly he realized his inclination to the speculative, the more sternly he girded himself for action. If his fierce resolve to be practical at all costs ran counter to all his instincts, so much the worse for his instincts. Instincts which opposed one's becoming a "use- ful member of society" must be, if not positively wicked, at any rate so debilitating as to amount to the same thing.

The mania for handling all the sides of every question, looking into every window, and opening every door, was, as

Bluebeard judiciously pointed out to his wives, fatal to their practical usefulness. . . . Mr. Adams, the father, looked on it as moral weakness; it annoyed him; but it did not annoy him nearly so much as it annoyed his son, who had no need to learn from Hamlet the fatal effect of the pale cast of thought on enterprises great or small. He had no notion of letting the currents of his action be turned awry by this form of conscience. To him, the current of his time was to be his current, lead where it might.

Even though it led to failure. He was determined to get rid of his birthright, pottage or no pottage. He called thinking ineffectuality, and ineffectuality was to him a haunting horror. For example, he disliked being in opposition in politics. After the Civil War, when he was a political writer at Washington, his whole idea was to support the Government. To be in opposition was to introduce friction and to waste energy, and he had no fancy, he says, for ineffectual politics. So it was as to all his age: he determined to belong to it, not to be a critic of it, but to be in it and of it, by an act of will. He speaks of his determination to be actual, daily, and practical. And again: "His single thought was to keep in front of the movement, and, if necessary, lead it to chaos, but never fall behind." Through the leaves of his autobiography one can still feel the virtuous glow with which he formed this resolution, as if it were somehow noble to abdicate one's judgment and to stultify oneself in unreflective action. In going counter to his natural gifts and capacities, in heaping self-contempt on himself for them, in trying to be contemporaneous and pushing, he felt that he was manifesting righteousness.

And what an age it was in which he resolved to sink himself!—the Age of Exploitation, of capitalism rampant,

and of industrialism triumphant. Every man of the slightest intellectual eminence, almost every respectable man, devoted himself to denouncing it: "Even among the most
powerful men of that generation," Adams writes, "he
knew none who had a good word to say for it." Aside
from its intoxicated exploitation of the sources of wealth,
the age was sterile; he calls it wearisome and stale, poor
in purpose and barren in results. All non-practical impulses languished.

The poet groped blindly for an emotion. The play of
thought for thought's sake had mostly ceased. The throb of
fifty or a hundred million steam horse power, doubling every
ten years, and already more despotic than all the horses that
ever lived, and the riders they ever carried, drowned rhyme
and reason.

Nothing is plainer than that Adams hated the modern
world, to which every one of his propensities was opposed;
from his first sight of the English Black Country in
1858 to the election of McKinley and the triumph of the
"banker's Olympus," he hated it all. Yet it is equally
plain that he despised himself for hating it, tried not to
hate it, tried to believe that he did not hate it, denied
again and again that he hated it, and admitted it as often.
He would not raise a lone American voice to echo the
great European chorus of protest; no, he had to regard his
dislike of it as mere weakness—as from the practical point
of view of course it was—rather than as good sense. He
could not content himself with the futility of criticism;
he must share in the mêlée.

If the age was bad elsewhere, it was at its worst in the
United States. The typical incident of American history
in the nineteenth century was the gold rush of '49; that

is what for nearly one hundred years life meant in the United States: a wild, savage scramble for nature's riches. "The moral law," as Adams observes, "had expired—like the Constitution." The control of society was no longer either ethical or political; if human at all, the ruling power was greed. But, when the era of pioneering had opened up and settled the country and discovered the sources of wealth, and had been succeeded by the era of capitalism and industrial development, Adams was led to the conclusion that the ruling power was not human, that men were helpless toys of inanimate force. As the whole occidental world more and more took on the likeness of a great empire governed by such potentates as Coal, Steam, Electricity, so also did the United States; but in addition the United States was commanded by a viceroy in the form of a railroad system: "The generation between 1865 and 1895 was already mortgaged to the railways, and no one knew it better than the generation itself." In this service, all society was remodeled, from the mines and the banks to the educational and political institutions. It was at the behest of such physical and economic forces, just as Gold had dragged thousands across and around the continent to the Sierras, that the Americans of the time with all their illusions of freedom devoted themselves body and soul to economic individualism and self-advancement. The superhuman powers had decreed a reign of social anarchy.

The American character was the product of these powers. The new American, though his progenitors came from all over the globe, was singularly uniform; "the child of steam and the brother of the dynamo," he showed no peculiarities save the mold and pressure of mechanical forces. The American mind was standardized, simple, positive, and conventional; strictly speaking, it was not a mind at all, but a "buzz saw," an economic thinking-machine, in Adams' words, which could work only on a fixed line, a mere cutting instrument, practical, sharp, and direct. The American could not have let himself care for other interests, had they existed for him.

The typical American man had his hand on a lever and his eye on a curve in his road; his living depended on keeping up an average speed of forty miles an hour, tending always to become sixty, eighty, or a hundred, and he could not admit emotions or anxieties or subconscious distractions, more than he could admit whiskey or drugs, without breaking his neck.

Perhaps the most signal triumph of the era was its victory over the two most powerful of human instincts, religion and sex. Religion had quietly disappeared, and sex counted for almost nothing. Such symbols as the antique Venus and the medieval Virgin were meaningless in the United States, because they were powerless. Instead of fear or awe, they inspired at best a mild sentiment. "An American Virgin would never dare command; an American Venus would never dare exist." Against a force strong enough to kill religion and sex, naturally such lesser interests as philosophy, art, and the other phases of the life of realization were helpless. In consequence, the American, for anything but work, was as useless as a machine. He was primarily a money-making machine, but he cared little for money after he had gathered it. He had no notion what to do with his wealth; his only pleasure was the pursuit of it. He was incapable of amusing himself or of imagining how other people enjoyed themselves. He could not even know that he was bored. All his desire, his intelligence, and his vitality were banked and confined in one narrow channel. His interest was as little discursive as a mill race; the world outside did not exist.

It was with these "buzz saws" that Henry Adams chose to compete in their own field—a contest for which he was unfitted not only by his temperament but also by his inheritance as an Adams. That, to be sure, was practical, but adapted to an earlier type of practicality than the nineteenth-century variety. His training, suitable for such a career as his great-grandfather's, was as disadvantageous in the Age of Exploitation as it would have been in the California gold fields of '49. The puritan standards of duty, dignity, and propriety, of public and private morality, and the puritan conception of the gentleman and the statesman proved to be impediments. He was fond of calling himself, and with justification, a child of the eighteenth century, meaning that all his ideas were inherited from that period; and he realized all too clearly that this legacy disabled him in the hurly-burly of 1865-1900. He was set to run a foot race in full plate armor, and he was left behind by those who brought only a moral loin cloth to the strife. The prizes went to the newcomers who traveled light, unhampered by heirlooms.

Not a Polish Jew fresh from Warsaw or Cracow—not a furtive Yacoob or Ysaac still reeking of the Ghetto, snarling a weird Yiddish to the officers of the customs—but had a keener instinct, an intenser energy, and a freer hand than he —American of Americans, with Heaven knew how many Puritans and Patriots behind him, and an education that had cost a civil war. He made no complaint and found no fault with his time; he was no worse off than the Indians or the buffalo who had been ejected from their heritage by his own people; but he vehemently insisted that he was not himself at fault.

That last sentence is a good specimen of the affected and insincere bitterness which springs from disappointment and failure. Yet he speaks only the truth when he says that he was not to blame: by birth he was destined for the life of realization; by inheritance he was taught that he must succeed in a practical career and was trained for early-republican statesmanship; and by bad luck he was thrown into the fray of nineteenth-century America. Certainly it was not his fault that he was born an Adams in 1838; nor was it his fault that in his lifetime his country had no place for such men as himself. He did, after all, make one effort to follow his proper vocation; after the Civil War, he went to Washington and set up as a writer on public affairs. But he soon abandoned this effort, partly because he found himself forced into opposition—not, surely, a very sound reason—but more because he saw that the nation could not support such a career. No one was interested in his or any one's ideas. In a letter of 1862 to his brother he states the case perfectly:

What we want is a *school*. We want a national set of young men like ourselves or better, to start new influences not only in politics, but in literature, in law, in society, and throughout the whole social organism of the country—a national school of our own generation. And that is what America has no power to create.

He was right: a school of one, existing in a vacuum, was impossible. And had it been possible, it was not the way for him, because it was not the way to generally recognized success. There was nothing for him but failure.

In the course of time, as we have seen, he had to abandon his practical ambition and resign himself to criticism and philosophy. But, though he gave up his own hopes of practical success, he never abandoned the practical point of view. Upon that, his whole scheme of thought was founded. His is preëminently the philosophy of practicality. Its center is a worship of power, of anything that "does work," that gets something done, irrespective of the merits or value of the result. He tells how he and his brothers, even as schoolboys, though vague about their purposes in life, "all were conscious that they would like to control power in some form." Until the very end, he had the viewpoint of the practical man, the man to whom nothing is an end, everything a means, valuable not on its own account, but because it leads to something else, because it produces results, with no question of the worth of the results—the man whose standard is quantitative, not qualitative, who asks always, "How much?" never "How good?" It is a very short step from indifference to qualitative standards to out and out denial of them. And that Adams was indifferent he discovered early in life.

To other Darwinians—except Darwin—Natural Selection seemed a dogma to be put in the place of the Athanasian creed; it was a form of religious hope; a promise of ultimate perfection. Adams wished no better; he warmly sympathized with the object; but when he came to ask himself what he truly thought, he felt that he had no Faith; that whenever the next new hobby should be brought out, he should surely drop off from Darwinism like a monkey from a perch; that the idea of one Form, Law, Order, or Sequence had no more value for him than the idea of none; that what he valued most was Motion, and that what attracted his mind was Change.

Like other people, the philosopher finds what he searches for; so Adams found Force, Motion, and Change—and nothing else. It was not mere whim that led him to address prayers to the dynamo.

Oddly enough, it was his devotion to force that took him to the study of the Middle Ages. In his own time, an age of multiplicity, the forces were innumerable and baffling; but the century from 1150 to 1250 seemed an age of unity, controlled by the one force of the Virgin— Woman and Mother—who united the impulses of religion and sex. She was greater than any of the twentieth century's mechanical forces, for "all the steam in the world could not, like the Virgin, build Chartres." He could not, as he confesses, himself feel the Virgin's power; he studied her as a problem in dynamics. She had for him, as he points out, precisely the same interest as a dynamo: she too "did work." With all his acumen and appreciation and imagination, he did not approach the twelfth century on its own terms, but rendered it into modern mechanical terms; and one cannot help feeling that his interpretation is somewhat vitiated by his point of view.

Henry Adams' ruling passion is also the clue to his use of the term "education." To him it means the pursuit of power, or, more accurately, that understanding of the world which leads to mastery of it. "Education," he says, "should try to lessen the obstacles, diminish the friction, invigorate the energy, and should train minds to react, not at haphazard, but by choice, on the lines of force that attract their world." A young man is a form of energy; he must be trained to "do work," to economize his force—nothing more. Here is practicality with a vengeance—not a syllable as to human values or as to comparative merit in achievement; the whole point is to achieve as much as possible, a sheer quantitative standard. Like any other machine, man is to be judged by two things only: by the amount of power he generates, and by his efficiency. The only criteria applicable to human beings are mechanical; there is no question whatever of ends, but only of means; no question as to doing what is worth while, but merely as to doing as much as possible. I doubt whether the philosophy inherent in the practical man's conduct has ever been more cynically and openly and brutally set forth. But in a world of disorder, Adams finally concluded, education, plan, or foresight was impossible. His own failure was less indicative than that of his friend Clarence King. King had everything in his favor, and if he, with all the advantages of nature and preparation and circumstance, did not succeed, how was any one to know by what path success could be reached? Adams was unable to answer. In the unintelligible jumble of raw forces which makes up the world and life, mankind is helpless.

Because all his own experience was a chaos, he was predisposed to accept the philosophy to which he was led by his studies. His own personality, frustrated because denied its proper nourishment and discipline, never had a chance to develop and grow strong. Within his own mind, all the fundamental compulsions of his being were at war with the puritanism and practical ambition which were instilled into him. Internally, he was an anarchy of antagonistic forces. And in his environment he found only still other forces opposed in turn to those within himself. Furthermore, this environment itself—the United States of the nineteenth century—showed no signs of order or control; it was the scene of a battle-royal among

insensate forces to which men were but unconscious slaves
and victims. It is no wonder that Henry Adams drew
the obvious moral: life is meaningless, a senseless tragedy
of futility and waste. To arrive at this conclusion, he
needed no knowledge of science or history; he needed
only to observe himself and his world. That is the importance of Henry Adams—that he has recorded the experience of a man endowed with the poetic temper and
forced to live in a practical society, that he first and
most fully formulated the philosophy implicit in American
behavior, and that therefore he affords the best of all
approaches to an understanding of modern American life
and literature.

BIBLIOGRAPHY

ADAMS, HENRY. *Democracy: an American Novel.* New
York, 1880, Henry Holt and Company.
———— *History of the United States of America during the
Administrations of Jefferson and Madison.* 9 vols.
New York, 1889-1891, Charles Scribner's Sons.
———— *Mont St. Michel and Chartres.* Boston, 1913,
Houghton Mifflin Company.
———— *The Education of Henry Adams.* Boston, 1918,
Houghton Mifflin Company.
———— *The Degradation of the Democratic Dogma.* (In-
troduction by Brooks Adams.) New York, 1920, The
Macmillan Company.
———— *Letters to a Niece and Prayer to the Virgin of
Chartres.* (A Niece's Memories, by Mabel La Farge.)
Boston, 1920, Houghton Mifflin Company.
ADAMS, CHARLES FRANCIS, JUNIOR. *Charles Francis
Adams, an Autobiography.* Boston, 1916, Houghton
Mifflin Company.

SPOKESMEN

FORD, WORTHINGTON CHAUNCEY, Editor. *A Cycle of Adams Letters.* 2 vols. Boston, 1920, Houghton Mifflin Company.

SHAFER, ROBERT. *Progress and Science.* New Haven, 1922, Yale University Press. (*See* Chapter IV for Henry Adams.)

THAYER, WILLIAM ROSCOE. *The Life and Letters of John Hay.* 2 vols. Boston, 1915, Houghton Mifflin Company.

III

EDWIN ARLINGTON ROBINSON

N the land of E. A. Robinson's poetry it is always late November, always

A dreary, cold, unwholesome day,
    Racked overhead,—
As if the world were turning the
        wrong way,
    And the sun dead.

Across the cold November moors blows the bleak sad wind, whirling a few withered leaves away from the barren boughs. On the blasted heath stands the skeleton of a tree, black against the wintry gray of twilight or the somber red of an autumnal sunset. It is a land of forlorn ruin and decay, of shivering desolation, where

        . . . there are dead men all around us—
Frozen men that mock us with a wild, hard laugh
That shrieks and sinks and whimpers in the shrill
        November rushes,
And the long fall wind on the lake.

In this chilly waste, living things are blighted and shriveled, for life is here an intrusive anomaly to which the elements are bitterly hostile. Struggle as they may to live, men pine away and die, and their bones are whitened by the frost and sleet. Human existence consists in suffering and ends in defeat.

Always defeat—always failure: surely the theme of human failure, with all its variations and nuances, has been treated so exhaustively by no other poet as by Robinson. One would not have believed there were so many ways to fail. Among his gallery of portraits, some are total failures, from every point of view and from the very beginning, like Miniver Cheevy, the feeble, futile romantic, or like Aaron Stark, the miser with "eyes like little dollars in the dark," who laughed when people pitied him. There are the failures who have belied an early promise. There are those who achieve a worldly success at the cost of a spiritual death, or others, such as Richard Cory, who seem to have everything man can ask for, yet who show how different things really are by putting an end to themselves. As a rule, Robinson regards his failures with pity rather than contempt; in our ignorance we should not judge them, for we do not know what aspiration or what will-o'-the-wisp misled them.

> *I say no more for Clavering*
>> *Than I should say of him who fails*
> *To bring his wounded vessel home*
>> *When reft of rudder and of sails;*
>
> *I say no more than I should say*
>> *Of any other one who sees*
> *Too far for guidance of today,*
>> *Too near for the eternities.*

Of all the failures the least complete are those whose manifest worldly success is atoned for by an inner victory,

46

like the pauper-vagabond Captain Craig; yet even these are failures, for Robinson sees how warping is worldly failure. In this world, however, where some sort of miscarriage is sure, the best one can hope for, he seems to imply, is to be true to one's self and die an outcast.

So far I have spoken only of his portraits or short biographies, mostly of the inhabitants of Tilbury Town, but through nearly all his work save the Arthurian romances runs the same theme. Few of the modern folk make a go of living; for some reason, they are denied a full normal growth; they are not only thwarted, but stunted, meager, undernourished. It is not only in their enterprises but rather as human beings that they fail; and it is in this sense that Robinson's persistent theme has been the tragedy of frustration; he has tended to see human life as an inescapable tragedy of frustration, which is only made the blacker because we cannot bring ourselves to admit it. The contrast between the dark actuality of defeat, ruin, and death, and the false brightness of human illusions and hopes is the source at once of his irony and of his tragic pity. Always on the one side are desire, dream, expectation; on the other, disappointment and wreckage. In "The Garden," an early poem, he wrote:

> He led me to the plot where I had thrown
> The fennel of my days on wasted ground,
> And in that riot of sad weeds I found
> The fruitage of a life that was my own.
>
> My life! Ah, yes, there was my life, indeed!
> And there were all the lives of humankind.

Life, he says again and again, is a curse. He cries:

God knows the gall we drink
Is not the mead we cry for;

and he has written the most terrible expression I know of
the horror of disillusion and unfulfilled desire:

Why pay we such a price, and one we give
So clamoringly, for each racked empty day
That leads one more last human hope away,
As quiet fiends would lead past our crazed eyes
Our children to an unseen sacrifice?

And the essential tragedy is heightened by the immiti-
gable loneliness and isolation of every man. We have no
real communion with our kind, and still less with the universe in which we find ourselves; each man is a friendless
stranger in a strange land, with which he has no kinship,
to which in no way he belongs, in which he is a kind of
enemy alien, living in solitary confinement in a dungeon.
Robinson's thought has been strongly affected by the current pessimistic naturalism; it looks to him, as it looked
to Henry Adams, as if the world were on a "blind atomic
pilgrimage" from nothing to nothing—in which case it is
all

. . . an idle and ephemeral
Florescence of the diabolical.

Why, he asks, if we believe in such a world, do we cling
to "the life we curse"? Why do we not all kill ourselves?

If after all that we have lived and thought,
All comes to Nought,—

48

If there be nothing after Now,
And we be nothing anyhow,
And we know that,—why live?
'Twere sure but weaklings' vain distress
To suffer dungeons where so many doors
Will open on the cold eternal shores
That look sheer down
To the dark tideless floods of Nothingness
Where all who know may drown.

Does not—here is the very kernel of his thought—the fact that we do go on living prove that we do not accept naturalism as the complete truth? Something, somehow, has given us, in spite of the appearances, ground for faith and hope; our not committing suicide shows our belief that life has some sort of meaning or purpose. Hence he asks:

What have we seen beyond our sunset fires
That lights again the way by which we came?

And therefore he concludes that

It is the faith within the fear
That holds us to the life we curse.

Perhaps our faith is illusory—as to that, Robinson cannot say; it suffices him that we all have it, that we have all caught glimpses of the Light, the Gleam, the Vision, the Word—

. . . an orient Word that will not be erased,
Or, save in incommunicable gleams
Too permanent for dreams
Be found or known.

49

His philosophy, in short, is a very much chastened and sobered transcendentalism. His inclination is to think that each of us has some sort of contact with the Infinite, which constitutes an inner illumination, an intuition of an absolute reality for which there is no explanation in the external, natural scheme of things. I daresay he would subscribe to the words he puts in Merlin's mouth:

> . . . *"I could see*
> *In each bewildered man who dots the earth*
> *A moment with his days a groping thought*
> *Of an eternal will, strangely endowed*
> *With merciful illusions whereby self*
> *Becomes the will itself."*

From this central tenet he develops the usual doctrines of transcendentalism: the need of self-reliance and self-development, of freedom and individualism. Since each has his own private revelation, the business of each is to make the most of it; and since all men share in the infinite mind, all men are important. The value of the individual is measured, if at all, only by his truth to himself.

But Robinson is too much the sceptic and questioner to be absolutely sure. It seems as if there were the Gleam —and yet there is also the horror of actuality, "the racked and shrieking hideousness of Truth." Robinson's Gleam is anything but a steady beacon. It is not a light that lightens the darkness, but, like that of Tennyson's Merlin, a Gleam that has "waned to a wintry glimmer," a glimmer so feeble that we merely suspect that it may be there. It is a surmise and a hope, rather than a faith—no more than enough to make us go on living. It is quite different from the mystic's illumination, which to him is the only reality, in the light of which all the rest of experience must be interpreted. The pragmatic value of Robinson's Gleam is slight; it does little work; it is not "good for much." Yet it saves him from total pessimism and supplies him with other standards and scales of value than the naturalistic. It makes him see mankind's failure as not quite hopeless.

Robinson's creed is most clearly and emphatically stated in "The Man Against the Sky," but his view of life is most elaborately, though I think not most characteristically, embodied in four long poems, of which two, *Merlin* and *Lancelot,* deal with legend, and two, *Roman Bartholow* and *The Man Who Died Twice,* with contemporary life. Though none of the four is altogether successful, yet they are important as his chief efforts before *Tristram* in direct presentment of life, in which criticism and analysis are secondary. It is noteworthy that in these poems, where he tells other people's stories, he is much more positive about the Light than in his more personal and private expressions. At the end of *Merlin,* since the sage finds that he cannot be happy with Vivian among the pleasures of Broceliande while his world is going to pieces, although he is unable to avert the ruin, he sets off to wander over the world after the Gleam. At the end of *Lancelot,* after a final interview with Guinevere at the nunnery, where she tells the knight that their life, their world, is ended, Lancelot rides away into the darkness.

> *Once even he turned his horse,*
> *And would have brought his army back with him*
> *To make her free. They should be free together.*
> *But the Voice within him said: "You are not free.*
> *You have come to the world's end, and it is best*

You are not free.   Where the Light falls, death falls;
And in the darkness comes the light." . . .
. . . Always in the darkness he rode on,
Alone; and in the darkness came the Light.

The parallelism is obvious: in both poems, since following the Light is the business of man, whatever holds
him from that purpose must be abolished; and since the
world and the life of the world hide the Light from men,
it is better that the world should break up so that men
may be set free from its insistence to seek the Vision.
Robinson, however, seems to hint that those who have
known the most of earthly love and love of the earth are
the ones to whom the Light is vouchsafed; or, to put it the
other way round, that those who have the most capacity
for following the Light are most likely to be too much
absorbed by the world.   In any case, these Arthurian
stories are characteristic in that they tell of human hopes
and passions doomed to frustration and destruction, and
in that out of the wreckage all that survives is the unearthly Vision.

There is less parallelism between his modern narratives,
but both deal with the relation of a religious experience
to ordinary life—and in both this relation is one of contrast or hostility.   In *Roman Bartholow,* the psychic Penn-
Raven, who cures the hero of some sort of collapse, becomes the lover of his patient's wife with the result that
she drowns herself; and Bartholow is left to reflect that
"strange bottles hold God's wine," and that

> *. . . the tangled roots of wrong*
> *Were drawing always out of hidden soil*
> *The weird existence of a tangled vine.*

The Man Who Died Twice, Fernando Nash, once a composer of music, after a fit of delirium tremens brought on by debauchery has an extraordinary religious or mystical experience which comes to him apparently in the form of musical inspiration, a last triumphant effort of his genius, and which leaves him burnt out and useless but happy. In both poems, the Vision is strangely mixed with evil, and from the human point of view does rather more harm than good; yet it of itself, and it alone, has supreme value, in comparison with which nothing else is of any moment whatsoever.

This view of Robinson's, which Lloyd Morris calls "a devotion to ideals so profoundly exclusive that it results in a supreme indifference to their material consequences," is, I think, unique. All who have held similar views, as far as I know, have tried to hitch wagons to their stars, to find in their intuitions some sort of practical guidance, and to establish a vital connection between their illuminations and their every-day lives. But Robinson is absolute, like a Manichee, in his opposition of light and darkness; the two realms, though strangely intermingled, are utterly hostile. Ordinary earthly life is valueless or worse; but we must try it and prove its worthlessness to ourselves in order to free ourselves of it. Robinson's concern has been with the twice-born, with men who have been delivered from "the body of this death." He implies, perhaps, that only those with a large capacity for life, with passion enough to live abundantly, are capable of seeing the Light; but between the beginning and the end there must be a complete shift or transmutation, a rebirth into another world. "Where the Light falls, death falls"; and one must arrive at the darkness before one can see the Light.

Such is the upshot of the two earlier Arthurian stories, and of most of Robinson's other work—but what of *Tristram?* In it there seems to be no such contrast of earthly blackness with a supernal Gleam. On the contrary, seldom has there been written such a glorification of love and joy as the heart of the book, the account of the lovers' summer together in Joyous Gard, a brief time of such happiness that the rest of their lives is negligible. But exactly there, I think, is where *Tristram* joins company with the rest of Robinson's poems: if, as is true, no one in *Tristram* forsakes the world to follow an unearthly glimmer through blackness and death, nevertheless the lovers attain their bliss only by some sort of escape from time, if not from space—an escape, that is, from this world, from this life.

> *"Was it enough?*
> *How shall we measure and weigh these lives of ours?*
> *You said once that whatever it is that fills*
> *Life up, and fills it full, it is not time.*
> *You told my story when you said that to me,*
> *But what of yours? Was it enough, Tristram?*
> *Was it enough to fly so far away*
> *From time that for a season time forgot us?*
> *You said so, once. Was it too much to say?"*

> *"Love, it was far from here*
> *And far from England and this inchmeal world*
> *That our wings lifted us to let us fly*
> *Where time forgot us."*

Robinson has scarcely been converted to this world. Yet there is a fundamental, though not a total, difference between *Tristram* and the other long narratives; and this difference consists in the fact that *Tristram,* though as tragic as a poem can well be, is not quite the same sort of tragedy as the others. The change is one rather of mood than of idea; Merlin, Lancelot, and Tristram all succeed in so far as they get free from the blackness of mundane existence, but whereas the others find only a wintry sort of consolation, Tristram attains to joy. Even so, "where the Light falls, death falls," though it is the light of love—and not for the lovers only, but for every one implicated in their story. One must not forget the forsaken figure, at beginning and end, of Isolt of Brittany, watching the sea waves and the white birds flying.

Such a world as Robinson's, whose only redeeming feature is a Light which, instead of illuminating, merely offers hope of escape—such a view of life and such a philosophy, we may be sure, are expressions of temperament, are emotional rather than logical conclusions. Robinson's point of view is a projection of a profound melancholy, a *Weltschmerz* of a peculiar sort. Often his poetry conveys an extraordinary sense of weariness, which bespeaks a deficiency in vital force or spiritual energy. This fatigue, which sometimes resembles the medieval *acedia,* indicates an inability to cope with circumstance; it is a sign, in short, of a kind of failure, of a defeat at the hands of life. To attribute this melancholy to Robinson's early struggles and lack of recognition would be too easy; it must spring from a basic trait in his constitution, from a revulsion against existence, against the ordinary process of living. This trait I think we must call morbid, a sign of spiritual sickness. Although it resembles somewhat hyperæsthesia, as if feelings and sensations were too keen to be borne, and somewhat the malady of the idealist who feels the imperfections of the world so acutely that he cannot forget or forgive them, yet it is not precisely either one, but rather a mere rebellion against being, as though the fundamental clinging to life had somehow been transformed into its contrary.

Some sort of sadness, it is true, has been common among poets, but not a melancholy like Robinson's. The most familiar form, from Mimnermus and Omar to Herrick and Keats, arises from a perception of the impermanence of, and from a strong attachment to, joy and beauty: "Alas, that Spring should vanish with the Rose!" Or there is such a view as Arnold's, that beauty is illusory, that

> . . . *the world, which seems . . .*
> *So various, so beautiful, so new,*
> *Hath really neither love, nor joy, nor light. . . .*

Or there is the ascetic view—not common, to be sure, among poets—that beauty is evil because it is seductive. All these kinds of melancholy have one trait in common: they all acknowledge not only the existence but the power of loveliness—and therein they all differ from the usual melancholy of Robinson. For his peculiarity is that he finds actuality, the "world of appearances," not too fair but too repulsive. I do not forget such passages in his work as those in which he describes Merlin's life at Broceliande or Tristram's at Joyous Gard; but I would point out that such passages almost never occur in his account of the actual world as he has himself known it, that he himself, as far as one can tell, has never felt the love of pleasure which he attributes to Merlin, or the fulfilled ecstasy which Tristram enjoys, that the whole episode with Vivian is a kind of unreal dream or spell which makes

Merlin for a time oblivious of harsh reality, and that the season with Isolt at Lancelot's castle was far away from "this inchmeal world"; and finally that whatever may be true of Merlin and Lancelot and Tristram and whatever may be Robinson's theory about the desirability of a complete experience, the commonest note in his work is a negation of life. But to have felt so little love of life, to have found so little joy in living, to have nearly lacked the vital impulse—surely, that is a sign of spiritual dearth.

I cannot call Robinson disillusioned; I cannot believe that he ever entertained an illusion about this world. One cannot imagine him as a child with a child's eager interest and trustfulness. One pictures him, judging from his poetry, as a gloomy little boy, on his guard against the world, hostile toward a hostile universe. Nothing is deeper in him than his sense of isolation and estrangement, nothing more marked than his congenital constraint. His aloofness and his reticence are results of his instinctive withdrawal from life, of his inability to make healthy, normal, fruitful contacts with his environment. This repudiation of the world, this movement of desire away from reality, is, it seems to me, the central fact about Robinson. It accounts for his chronic depression, for his philosophy, for his view of life, "the life we curse," so that for him to live is to "suffer dungeons"; perhaps it also accounts for his preoccupation with failure, with those who are unable to deal with the world.

This spirit of denial, this incapacity to live—which I think is not quite the same as "repression," a trait often attributed to Robinson—renders difficult that surrender or letting-go, that self-abandonment and self-forgetfulness, necessary for experience; and it has thereby tended to be niggardly with the food of experience and the exercise of living which are indispensable for fullness of vigorous growth. The passion which Robinson obviously has in plenty has been for the most part somehow dammed back and diverted from its proper end and use, the realization of experience. Clement Wood has pointed out his remarkable dependence on his early impressions and more than one critic has thought at times that he discerned in Robinson's writing an increasing dryness or atrophy of energy and emotion. While *Tristram* is ample disproof of those who believed that sterility had set in prematurely, it remains true that these critics had reason for their belief, and that too much of Robinson's writing records a rejection of life, an antagonism to reality.

Needless to say, this ingrowing habit of mind has determined Robinson's style. Since both are expressions of his personality, his style matches the world of his imagination; its dominant trait is its austerity or ascetic quality. In his poetry as in his landscape, he is always frugal and sometimes bare and bleak. His withholding of himself manifests itself, in his way of writing, as constraint and compression. His astringent irony also and especially his liking for prosaic understatement are weapons with which he combats the claims of the world and tries by depreciation to free himself from them. Throughout, his keynote is a spare economy—in sensuous imagery, in emotion, in diction. His general preference is for speech-rhythm rather than song-rhythm, and for the simplest of vocabularies. He is not without purple patches, but his restraint saves him from most faults of taste—at least from magniloquence and inflated rhetoric, from false sentiment or forced feeling. To the credit of his highly developed critical sense it must be said that no other contemporary poet more uniformly rings true. The pressure to which they are subjected guarantees that his crystals will be genuine at least, not paste.

Yet Robinson's work affords ample evidence, if evidence were needed, that genuineness, or sincerity, is not an all-sufficient safeguard. If in most ways he holds himself severely in check, in one respect he lets himself run amuck. Because his words are plain, one must not infer that his thought is plain or that his style is simple, direct, and natural. Quite the reverse is true. He atones for his emotional and sensuous chariness by running into intellectual riot. He reminds one of Henry Adams' dictum, "The mind resorts to reason for want of training"; and indeed there is much in Robinson of Adams' distrustful, questioning, sceptical quality, as also of Adams' melancholy, the reason being that in both men other phases of personality have been sacrificed to an intellectual forcing. Robinson is one of the most cerebral of poets; he belongs to that small "metaphysical" species, of which John Donne is an eminent member, among whom passion, instead of seeking a direct outlet, expresses itself indirectly by acting as a stimulant on cerebral activity.

Such men are distinguished at their best by an extraordinary subtlety of mind, at their worst by obscurity and by a trivial intricacy of thought. One may say that since Robinson sees everything as many-sided and difficult to understand, for him to state things bluntly and simply would be to falsify—but this is a half-truth. When his ideas are really acute and subtle, one admires the fineness of Robinson's mind; but too often the involution of expression corresponds to no involution of idea. The obvious bores him; therefore he often suppresses it, to the confusion of the normal reader. This horror of the obvious leads Robinson into unnecessary and irritating

mazes of circumlocution; at times he spins himself up in
a cocoon of sophistic gossamer, at times he tries to conceal
the commonplace by strained and artificial indirectness of
language. He shows signs of harboring the not uncommon fallacy that difficulty and obscurity are indications of
profundity and insight.

As to Robinson's repudiation of the world's loveliness,
I must insist that, while he is by no means indifferent to
beauty, various kinds of beauty must be distinguished.
Of his perceiving a sort of beauty in the pathos of human
life there can be no doubt; but this quality, beautiful only
for its poignancy, in no way reconciles him to the world.
As for the manifold appeals of the senses—certainly,
Robinson is neither blind nor deaf, and his writing is not
devoid of imagery; that most of this imagery, however, is
peculiarly gaunt, stark, and somber, though not on that
account unlovely, will not, I think, be disputed. The chill
winds, leafless trees, and barren heaths do not endear the
world to him. Of beauty in the commonest sense of the
word, the sort of sensuous beauty which we associate with
Keats, there is little in Robinson's work, outside the Arthurian poems, and what little there is appears not when
he is rendering the world as he himself has known it, but,
when he is most remote from his actual experience. It
appears, for instance, at the end of "The Gift of God," in
the mother's vision of her son's future:

> *His fame, though vague, will not be small,*
> *As upward through her dream he fares,*
> *Half clouded with a crimson fall*
> *Of roses thrown on marble stairs.*

And of course it appears conspicuously in the following
lines from *Merlin*:

> *He scanned again*
> *The immemorial meaning of her face*
> *And drew it nearer to his eyes. It seemed*
> *A flower of wonder with a crimson stem*
> *Came leaning slowly and regretfully*
> *To meet his will—a flower of change and peril*
> *That had a clinging blossom of warm olive*
> *Half stifled with a tyranny of black,*
> *And held the wayward fragrance of a rose*
> *Made woman by delirious alchemy.*

Concerning such lines two things, besides their loveliness, are noteworthy. The first is their extreme rarity in his writing; the second—I venture the suggestion with diffidence—is that they carry a sense of effort, if not of labor, as if all Robinson's skill as a poet were needed to hide the difficulty which he felt in their composition. They lack the gusto that is in the descriptions of desolation and destitution, where he is thoroughly at home. No such criticism can be made of the lovely passages which describe Tristram's life at Joyous Gard; of them, I should say only that it is a pity Robinson has not given us more of the sort. Because of their rarity in his work, such passages do not perhaps altogether invalidate the statement that Robinson himself and his poetry are somewhat deficient as concerns sensuous beauty.

On the other hand, although I spoke of Robinson's "emotional chariness," there is no question of his passion. On the contrary, he is primarily a man of feeling, and of feeling of remarkable depth and power—limited perhaps in range, confining itself largely to the pity of human defeat, not often as in *Tristram* sympathizing with the emotions, like love, allied to joy, more at home with Guinevere in the nunnery than with Merlin in Vivian's castle, but within its range unsurpassed. Who else has so felt the tragic irony of frustration? It is not that Robinson is weak in feeling—quite the reverse; but that he is frugal in his expression of it. On the rare occasions when he lets himself go, as in *The Man Against the Sky,* he rises to heights of magnificence, but usually he seeks other effects. Though governed and led by his feelings, he commonly translates his emotional conclusions into intellectual terms. Most often he gains his intensity, not by the lift or surge or rhythm of his language, but by implication, without raising his voice, by some sort of understatement, by the very contrast between the meaning of his words and their almost prosaic plainness. The end of "Richard Cory" is an extreme instance:

> *In fine, we thought that he was everything*
> *To make us wish that we were in his place.*
>
> *So on we worked, and waited for the light,*
> *And went without the meat, and cursed the bread;*
> *And Richard Cory, one calm summer night,*
> *Went home and put a bullet through his head.*

At first glance, Robinson seems primarily a poet of dramatic narrative; that is, he tells stories in which events are secondary and in which the interest is focused on character. Perhaps because of his constitutional reserve, he has less often expressed himself in personal lyrics, and excepting *The Man Against the Sky,* those he has written are not the work on which his reputation is based. Yet to call him simply a narrative or dramatic poet would be misleading. *Tristram,* to be sure, has great dramatic beauty; but in the other Arthurian legends in which he has essayed what Lloyd Morris calls a full "re-creation of reality," his success is doubtful. In his longer poems of modern life, he has composed psychological novels in verse; in these, he has paid less attention to circumstance and setting and has analyzed his people rather than presented them directly; but the result has proved cumbrous and obscure. Where his success is conspicuous and unquestioned is in the brief analytic sketch, the portrait-etching. Strictly speaking, that is to say then, his gift is really not so much either dramatic or narrative as descriptive. It is less for creation than for dissection; he does not embody or make men so much as take them apart. His is the imaginative insight or understanding that probes and anatomizes. Perhaps the most triumphant manifestation of his power is the portrait of Shakespeare in "Ben Jonson Entertains a Man from Stratford"; it likewise shows itself in almost all his most popular poems, the "Tilbury Portraits." These most fully illustrate his qualities as a poet, especially in that elimination which amounts sometimes to denudation. As an instance of poetry stripped to its bare bones, characteristic but too extreme to be quite typical even of Robinson, I cite "Exit":

> *For what we owe to other days,*
> *Before we poisoned him with praise,*
> *May we who shrank to find him weak*
> *Remember that he cannot speak.*
>
> *For envy that we may recall,*
> *And for our faith before the fall,*
> *May we who are alive be slow*
> *To tell what we shall never know.*

SPOKESMEN

For penance he would not confess,
And for the fateful emptiness
Of early triumph undermined,
May we now venture to be kind.

As Lloyd Morris says, "The mind only reluctantly and not for long accepts an incomplete record of what its own vitality demonstrates to be a complete experience." I quote this sentence from Robinson's eulogist because it seems to me to contain a judgment of Robinson's value. Robinson, like Donne, is a special rather than a general poet; his appeal must be to comparatively few, and to them only in certain moods. To draw a comparison from another art, Robinson's poems belong with the canvases of Blakelock and Ryder, or would, if they had elected to include portraits in their painting, belong with them not only in their somber darkness lighted by strange glimmers, but in their lack of the values prized by the multitude. The majority of readers demand of their favorites less parsimony than Robinson's; they demand a freer and fuller flow of emotion, a more abundant sensuousness in the form both of more lavish and opulent imagery and of ampler and richer music, and a greater variety and body. Above all, they demand a larger heartiness, refusing to be content with a poetry which, because it is an expression of the repudiation of life, denies satisfaction to all their instinctive hungers and cravings. On the other hand, a certain taste finds a special delight in a sharp, fine flavor, all the more exquisite because not grossly obvious and pleasurable; and a minority must always sympathize, at least now and then, with Robinson's attitude of condemnation and rejection. No one who has achieved perfection of expression need fear for some sort of audience; and

Robinson affords in its perfection an experience, not wide in range and sharp rather than full, but an experience which we should be far from willing to forego.

Has this poetry of Robinson's any relation to American life? It is not, surely, to any considerable extent a reflection of the United States: in so far as Robinson depicts his environment, he confines himself not only to New England but chiefly to Maine. Nor can one assume that Tilbury Town is an accurate picture of Gardiner or of Head Tide; at best, it can be but such a village as seen through Robinson's peculiar and strongly marked temperament. That is to say, not that he has falsified, but that he has rendered only such aspects of the life about him as were fitted to impress such a man as himself. The nature of these aspects we know: what Robinson tells us amounts to this, that in the country where he spent his youth many men and women managed in their several ways to turn out human failures, to be warped and twisted and stunted, that the luckiest were those who from worldly failure wrung some sort of spiritual benefit, though bent and distorted in the process, and that the least fortunate were those whom an early success betrayed to a spiritual death. By itself, this testimony would tell something about only one phase of life in a remote nook of the United States; only when combined with similar testimony from Robinson's contemporaries in other regions does it assume importance—I am speaking of it now of course not as poetry but as social comment. Only when other witnesses bring similar evidence from all over the country do Robinson's portraits take on a national significance as one version of that "tragedy of frustration" which is the favorite theme of modern American writers.

Whether Robinson himself was much affected by the

environment one phase of which he portrays, whether he should be called a product of New England, is a difficult question. No doubt most of his idiosyncrasies were innate; all one can hazard is a guess that there was an affinity between him and his surroundings which served not to correct his peculiar bias but to exaggerate it, to strengthen his natural antipathy to life rather than to broaden and open up his capacity for experience. There is a likeness between Robinson and the folk of his creation which accounts in part for his understanding of them; neither he nor they have been nourished on a rich diet of the food of life. Many men have said many things about Yankees, but no one has disputed their claim to be a peculiar people. Among them—among those, that is, who stayed in New England—there has always been a current opposed to success-worship; nor is the lust for making good the disease which ails Robinson's characters or against which he has had himself to fight. Nor are they and he afflicted with the neo-puritanism which is endemic in most of the United States, nor outwardly even with the old Calvinistic puritanism of the Fathers. If the latter survives at all, it is only as a virus in the blood. Although there have always been a number of New Englanders who have preferred moral and intellectual distinction to getting on and up in the world, even this saving remnant has seldom been distinguished for a frank and free love of experience or for regarding a full human life as desirable on its own account. The early Calvinists would certainly have thought completeness of realization a hellish doctrine; they were not friendly toward any allurements that might distract the attention from the main business of getting salvation (since they interpreted worldly prosperity as an outward sign of inner holiness); and it is a plausible theory that some of their descendants, however indifferent to seventeenth-century theology, may have inherited a hostility toward life and a blindness toward the charms of this world.

Not all Robinson's comment on American life is implicit in his portraits and semi-dramatic poems; some of it is explicit. This outspoken criticism is developed at greatest length in the poems "Dionysus in Doubt" and "Demos and Dionysus." Briefly, his complaint is the old one—essentially the same as Emerson's—against conformity, uniformity, standardization, mechanization, to which, as befits a latter-day transcendentalist, he opposes individualism, self-reliance, self-development. On the one hand, in Robinson's prophetic picture of the United States, there is the complacency of those who enjoy an anthill or beehive utopia; on the other, there is the dark shadow cast by this regimented millennium.

> *There are too many sleepers in your land,*
> *And in too many places*
> *Defeat, indifference, and forsworn command*
> *Are like a mask upon too many faces.*

Robinson, like his predecessors, seems to assume that the American's lack of individuality is due to sheer perverseness or to cowardice, that if they would take thought and "be themselves" all would be well. But surely, if the American scene is deficient in human variety and interest, if Americans are too much alike, too standardized, it is due to no mere weakness of compliance but to the fact that they really are uniform—that is, undeveloped. The cure is not to be found in exhorting them to be themselves, for the trouble is that they lack real selves, that they are "being

67

themselves" most when they conform. Until their selves grow beyond the embryonic stage, it is futile to preach self-reliance, as futile as to urge sleep not to be sheeplike. Until we can be persuaded to value living more than self-advancement, to care more for experience than for success, to make the practical subservient to the poetic temper, to prefer the life of realization to the life of exploitation, I think we must put up with conformity and standardization on the one hand and with "defeat, indifference, and forsworn command" on the other.

Robinson's repudiation of the world, that is, his distaste for experience—springing in his case not from subservience to practicality but from obscure constitutional causes and perhaps from his New England inheritance—has affected not only the literary value of his work by making him dwell on the theme, and that a peculiarly denuded one, of failure and frustration, but also his social significance. Robinson cannot communicate to the reader what he himself lacks, and since he himself has been unable to practice the life of realization, he cannot much increase the reader's capacity for experience. He himself, almost as much as the types which he likes best to portray, has something about him of "defeat, indifference, and forsworn command." On the other hand, one type of imaginative experience, one bleak mood, he affords as does no one else. And furthermore, in one way his work is of the very greatest avail: it sharpens one's sense of the situation, it gives one an eye, so to speak, for the tragedy of frustration; it gives one a more thorough comprehension of human defeat. If it contains within itself no remedy, it leads at least to a better understanding of the disease which is forcing itself more and more gravely upon the attention of Americans.

BIBLIOGRAPHY

ROBINSON, EDWIN ARLINGTON. *The Torrent and the Night Before.* Gardiner, Maine, 1896. Privately printed.

—— *The Children of the Night.* Boston, 1897, Charles Scribner's Sons.

—— *Captain Craig.* Boston, 1902. Revised edition, New York, 1915, The Macmillan Company.

—— *The Town Down the River.* New York, 1910, Charles Scribner's Sons.

—— *Van Zorn: a Comedy.* New York, 1914, The Macmillan Company.

—— *The Porcupine: a Drama.* New York, 1915, The Macmillan Company.

—— *The Man Against the Sky.* New York, 1916, The Macmillan Company.

—— *Merlin.* New York, 1917, The Macmillan Company.

—— *Lancelot.* New York, 1920, Thomas Seltzer.

—— *The Three Taverns.* New York, 1920, The Macmillan Company.

—— *Collected Poems.* New York, 1921, The Macmillan Company.

—— *Avon's Harvest.* New York, 1921, The Macmillan Company.

—— *Roman Bartholow.* New York, 1923. The Macmillan Company.

—— *The Man Who Died Twice.* New York, 1924, The Macmillan Company.

—— *Dionysus in Doubt.* New York, 1925, The Macmillan Company.

—— *Tristram.* New York, 1927, The Macmillan Company.

MORRIS, LLOYD. *The Poetry of Edwin Arlington Robinson.* New York, 1923, George H. Doran Company.

REDMAN, BEN RAY. *Edwin Arlington Robinson.* New York, 1925, Robert M. McBride & Company.

IV

THEODORE DREISER

HE importance of Theodore Dreiser as a writer is chiefly historical. That is to say, he belongs to that class of men, such as Edmund Waller, "Ossian," and Charles Brockden Brown, who for a time enjoy a considerable vogue, but whom later generations, after the novelty and the immediate applicability have worn off their work, find unreadable. Such men usually excel in some one particular: they introduce or perfect a trick of style; they exploit a new province of human life; they develop an odd, unknown mode of feeling. But shortly their specialty is mastered by other writers, by men perhaps of less originality, but of solider and better rounded talents; and, save by the historian of literature, the partial and incomplete work of the pioneer is forgotten.

So it must be, I think, with Dreiser. He is important because he was among the first to establish a point of view which has become more and more prevalent. As Sherwood Anderson says in the dedication to *Horses and Men,* Dreiser has made a path through the wilderness, and now the path is becoming a street—a street that show signs of growing overcrowded. But it is unlikely that future readers will care to acquaint themselves at first hand with the work of the trail-breaker. The labor of reading Dreiser is too arduous and not sufficiently profitable. Too often, while engaged with one of his novels, one has that sense of grinding despair which comes in nightmares when one is being pursued over endless wastes of soft sand. The experience, however instructive, is too painful to be sought out by normal humanity.

Even Dreiser's admirers admit his shortcomings as a writer of novels. His style is atrocious, his sentences are chaotic, his grammar and syntax faulty; he has no feeling for words, no sense of diction. His wordiness and his repetitions are unbearable, his cacophonies incredible. The following sentence is a specimen of what he can achieve:

He had vaulting ambitions and pretensions, literary and otherwise, having by now composed various rondeaus, triolets, quatrains, sonnets, in addition to a number of short stories over which he had literally slaved and which, being rejected by many editors, were kept lying idly and inconsequentially and seemingly inconspicuously about his place—the more to astonish the poor unsophisticated "outsider."

He violates English and even American idiom; he often shows himself ignorant of the meaning of words, as when he uses *satiation* for *satisfaction* or *fearsome* for *afraid*. He freely mingles the most colloquial expressions with poetic archaisms. Worst of all is his liking for the cheap, tawdry, and banal, for phrases that are trite and florid, for "below-stairs" writing in the manner of Bertha M. Clay and the Duchess or of the society column in a country newspaper.

Nor is his command of the art of fiction superior to his command of language. Of narrative form he seems to have no conception at all, of the clean, lucid telling of a story. He is constantly forgetting the plan or structure of his work, for he can resist no temptation to wander off into bypaths, sometimes of rambling general reflection and of philosophical disquisition, sometimes of social and economic history, even into explanations of biological laws and analogies. Perhaps because he takes for granted a total ignorance of everything on the part of his readers, he can let nothing pass without explanation. If he mentions Christian Science, he must devote pages to its theology and technique. But worse than his fancy for straying is his habit of amassing what is unimportant and insignificant. Because he cannot bring himself to leave out anything, he heaps up mountains of pointless detail. We must be told everything about every character, no matter how minor—where and when he was born, what sort of house he lives in, what articles of furniture he has in it and what is their material and design, what his business is and whether he is prospering, how often he goes to church, and so on. But there is no need to dwell on these aspects of Dreiser's work; they are commonplaces of criticism, and they have been abundantly and amusingly discussed and illustrated by Mencken, Dreiser's foremost champion.

Mencken, however, seems to regard these foibles as of little consequence, as petty irritations that the reader must try to put out of mind. I cannot agree: no author's style is unimportant, for it is always characteristic. Dreiser's style is a personal expression in which inevitably many of his qualities show themselves. Surely he could not write as he does if there were not in his mind something correspondingly muddled, commonplace, undiscerning, cheap, and shoddy. When he says in *The Financier* of an interior decorator:

His eyes brooded great, deep things concerning the illimitable realm of refinement in which he was working, the passage can be no mere slip of the pen, nor can that at the end of *The "Genius"*:

"What a sweet welter life is—how rich, how tender, how grim, how like a colorful symphony."
Great art dreams welled up into his soul as he viewed the sparkling deeps of space.

That sentence alone, if there were no other evidence, would suffice to show that the man who wrote it, however much he might talk about art and beauty, had no conception of either the one or the other. Indeed, that is what all his writing shows. Its lack of any sort of beauty —beauty of form, of imagery, of rhythm—indicates not only that Dreiser himself is devoid of æsthetic sense, but also—what is even more serious—that he has no natural knack for writing. If he had turned to sculpture, say— an art for which he had presumably as much aptitude as for writing—would he have received respectful attention from so intelligent a critic as Mencken? One doubts it, for statues must at least stand up; and it is easy to imagine the sort of figures Dreiser would have carved—like parodies by Goldberg of Rodin's "Thinker." Dreiser's defects are too grave to be dismissed as peccadilloes. After all, an author must in the nature of the case work in literary form, in words and nothing else; and we are forced to take his words for what they are worth, inasmuch as we have no other means of learning what he may have in his mind.

An excellent instance of this truism is Dreiser's characterization. For all we know, his people may live with the utmost distinctness in his mind, but if he lacks means of communication he cannot convey his conception to us with any sharpness. Perhaps he can really create them in his imagination—we cannot tell; all we can know is whether or not he gives us a well defined idea of them. I do not find that he does. On the whole, his minor characters stand out more clearly than his protagonists: Drouet, for example, the drummer in *Sister Carrie,* or old Butler, the Irish politician in *The Financier,* or Clyde's father and mother in *An American Tragedy.* Dreiser has done no better portraiture than some of the sketches in *Twelve Men.* His heroines, Carrie Meeber and Jennie Gerhardt, leave an impression of something soft and yielding, of a gently passive substance, and somewhat the same indeterminateness hangs about Clyde Griffiths. Perhaps their vagueness is part of the author's intention, but he can scarcely have meant them to be quite so blurry as they are, especially as the blur seems more in the drawing than in the subjects of the pictures.

His earlier heroes, on the other hand, Cowperwood of *The Financier* and *The Titan* and Eugene Witla of *The "Genius,"* are all but monstrosities, memorable but unreal. Cowperwood in particular is a bogey-man. The difficulty in both instances is that Dreiser has attempted to go beyond his own powers and is therefore reduced to the poor expedient of telling us about his heroes instead of presenting them, of asserting, that is, that these men possess qualities which the author is incapable of portraying directly. The result is a hopeless confusion, an odd effect as of a twice-exposed negative; or rather, we feel as if we were hearing things we cannot believe about a real person with whom we have some acquaintance. Cowperwood, so far as we are permitted to see him for ourselves unprejudiced by the author's comments, is dull, coarse, and mean, with the mentality but not the picturesqueness of a card-sharper or a tricky horse-trader, animated only by avarice and lust. There were such men no doubt who became wealthy and powerful during the Gilded Age of America; and Dreiser's novels would be admirably to the point if they were conceived and executed to illustrate the saying of Charles Francis Adams:

I am more than a little puzzled to account for the instances I have seen of business success—money-getting. It comes from a rather low instinct. Certainly, so far as my observation goes, it is rarely met with in combination with the finer or more interesting traits of character. I have known, and known tolerably well, a good many "successful" men—"big" financially—men famous during the last half-century; and a less interesting crowd I do not care to encounter. Not one that I have ever known would I care to meet again, either in this world or the next; nor is one of them associated in my mind with the idea of humor, thought, or refinement.

So to the reader's eyes looks Frank Cowperwood—but not to Dreiser's. Dreiser sees him as a radiant figure, of keen intellect and irresistible charm, witty and urbane, as dynamic as he is ruthless and unscrupulous, attracting and mastering men and women by his fascination and by an innate power which emanates from him in a sort of glow. He looks like a figure of wish-fulfillment, in whom the author has embodied and realized all the desires to which circumstances have denied satisfaction in his own life. Cowperwood is the sort of man Dreiser would like to have been; at any rate, he is endowed with all the gifts and graces of mind and body, and among them a dis-criminating passion for art. Precisely here Dreiser's failure is most disastrous, I think, because Cowperwood's creator has himself no comprehension of art. In short, Dreiser has attempted to depict a man rich in many of the traits in which Dreiser is himself most deficient—and the discordance between the sordid dullard he presents and the resplendent demigod he describes robs the figure of all reality.

The central character of The "Genius," Eugene Witla, is equally unconvincing, and even less interesting, as he is weak and vacillating and deficient in self-control. But he is supposed, at any rate, to be something of a "genius," to have the capabilities of a great painter, and to possess wit and social charm. He fascinates every one in the book—every one but the reader, who no more believes in Witla's virtues than he does in Cowperwood's, and for the same reason. Dreiser is again beyond his depth, or above his level. Drummers and shop girls, farmers, small storekeepers, bartenders, and clerks he does well with; but when he departs from that species he only emphasizes his own limitations. The lower middle class in the Midwest, in city and country and village, he knows and understands, but he succeeds with no other class and no other locality. His excursions to New York and Philadelphia are failures. And even in his own field his characterization, though I do not wish to deny it considerable merit, cannot be called first rate. Sherwood Anderson's portrayal of the same types, for instance, makes Dreiser's look slack, fumbling, and superficial.

I have dwelt at some length on Dreiser's characterization because his admirers, though they grant his other shortcomings as a writer, insist that he can depict people. Mencken is one; yet Mencken's admiration turns out on closer examination to be not for the people themselves so much as for the circumstances in which they are placed, for the whole complex rather than for the individuals. That is, it is Dreiser as social historian rather than Dreiser as creator of character that Mencken and the others praise. And therein they are right, for whatever one may deny to Dreiser one cannot deny him an amazing capacity for observation which goes far to conceal if not to atone for his defects as a creator. Even if indefatigability of observation cannot altogether make up for lack of discernment and imagination, or industry for bad taste and dullness of intelligence, those qualities give Dreiser's work an importance as social record which it lacks as fiction. *The Titan* and *The Financier* have the same merit as the official biographies of multimillionaires which are composed by hard-working but uninspired paid biographers. An epic sweep has often been attributed to Dreiser's novels, and correctly so, for they have the range and vastness which pertains to any minute record of an enormous area of human life. They are titanic undertakings, reminding one of huge natural phenomena; to traverse "these vast steppes and pampas of narration," to borrow Mencken's phrase, is like exploring the state of Nevada. And they have all been assembled, grain by grain, by never tiring, ant-like labor of observation.

These great talus-heaps of detail bear witness also to a voracious curiosity and an insatiable interest in everything, an interest so universal that to it nothing, nothing whatever, seems dull or tiresome. This unfailing zest is one sign of Dreiser's omnivorous love of life—of all of it, of all existence, good or bad, beautiful or ugly. To him it is all exciting, because it is all strange. His is a romantic love of reality, charged with wonder and awe. This sense of novelty is one of the clearest signs that Dreiser has freshness, originality, and independence of mind; this unflagging relish for what is and this feeling of its mystery is one token of the fundamental trait in

Dreiser's nature—his inexhaustible flow of emotion. From it spring his love of life, his energy, his observation; it is the moving and guiding force in all he does and says. He may like to consider himself a bold and penetrating thinker, but, as Mencken points out, "his ideas always seem to be deduced from his feelings." Everything he sees or touches he bathes in emotion. It is a source to him at once of strength and of weakness.

Many readers regard Dreiser's emotionality as mere sentimentality, but not, I think, justly. For his feeling is genuine, not spurious, and unlike the sentimentalist he does not gloat over it, revel in it, savor it with delight for its own sake. Nor is he blinded by it; it does not prevent him from seeing reality. If it sometimes gives an unpleasant effect, the reason is twofold: in the first place, the childish crudity of his expression lends an appearance of falsity. For example, when he cries out, once apropos of Chicago and once at the climax of *An American Tragedy*:

A very bard of a city this, singing of high deeds and high hopes, its heavy brogans buried deep in the mire of circumstance. Take Athens, O Greece! Italy, do you keep Rome!

But that look in the eyes of Roberta! That last appealing look! God! He could not keep from seeing it! Her mournful, terrible screams! Could he not cease from hearing them —until he got out of here anyhow?

it is difficult but also, I think, necessary to believe that words so inadequate could be called forth by true emotion. In the second place, Dreiser's feeling often looks false because it seems excessive, out of all normal proportion; and indeed it often is contrary to any normal scale

78

of values. It is like the feeling of an adolescent, which to an adult looks absurd because it overrates what an adult takes for granted, but which is none the less genuine.

Granting Dreiser's imperfect means of communication and his disproportion, one must still insist that in his power of feeling lies his chief claim to greatness. Whatever their delinquencies, his novels leave as their final effect an impression of tremendous passion which makes itself felt even through the slag and dross of his writing. Especially of course this passion shows itself in his tragic sense, in his profound consciousness of the tragedy inherent in all existence, in the very scheme of things—tragedy inescapable, essential, universal—a tragedy perceived by many but by few so strongly, so overwhelmingly felt as by Dreiser. This one quality the author of *Jennie Gerhardt* has in common with the authors of *Œdipus the King* and of *King Lear*.

> *If one should dream that such a world began*
> *In some slow devil's heart, that hated man,*
> *Who should deny him?*

Such is the feeling that actuates Dreiser's work. His brooding pity penetrates all life as he sees it, affecting every human being, from the most glittering superman to the forlornest prostitute. It is not only that most human hopes and desires are sure to be disappointed, and that those that are fulfilled bring no satisfaction—it is less that we do not get what we want than that misfortune hunts out even the most obscure and the most resigned, that even though we ask nothing we are still born to trouble as the sparks fly upward. Dreiser is especially acute in his perception of man's extraordinary capacity for suffering, a capacity for suffering which lends dignity, if not a touch of greatness, to even the weakest and most contemptible of Dreiser's creatures. Naturally, this aspect of his work cannot well be illustrated by quotation; yet, after all that has been said as to his shortcomings, I should like to cite a passage that shows Dreiser at his best, and that shows that at times when he contents himself with utter plainness he can be both effective and moving. The passage concerns a "small, homely, hard-worked woman, whose pinching labor of former years had removed nearly all traces of feminine charm," who has just been told by her husband that he is going to be sent to the penitentiary for embezzlement.

His wife went out of the room after a time; but it was only to go into another bedroom and stare out of a window onto the faded grass of the fall. What was to become of her and her husband? She always thought of him and herself and children as a collective unit. There were four children, all told, fortunately well grown now. They would be very poor again, and, worst of all, disgraced. That was what hurt her. She stared and twisted her bony little hands. Her eyes did not moisten, but an ineffable sadness filled them. Sometimes the mediocre and the inefficient attain to a classic stature when dignified by pain.

If only such writing were less rare in Dreiser's work, there would be no excuse for saying that his importance is chiefly historical. And it is true that not even the exacerbation roused by an enforced reading of his books can prevent one from feeling that one has been in the company of a man of unusual dimensions, a man of originality and of great depth and volume of feeling, a man filled with wonder, awe, and pity; yet when one turns again

from the author to the novels and surveys those misbe-
gotten Leviathans whose vital spirits are so ill-adjusted to
their bulk, one realizes again that it is the man, not his
work, that one chiefly admires. That no doubt is why his
defenders have paid so much more attention to Dreiser
as a man, as an innovator, as a sociologist, than they have
paid to him as a novelist. Furthermore, the period in
which he began writing made his virtues, even his negative virtues, shine brilliantly by contrast.

To understand the ardent championship which Dreiser
has received, one must mentally place him in the period
of his first work, remembering that *Sister Carrie* appeared
in 1900 and *Jennie Gerhardt* in 1911, and that among the
favorite and most typical novels of the time were *When
Knighthood Was in Flower, Graustark,* and *Rebecca of
Sunnybrook Farm.* No wonder Dreiser was welcomed
by the enlightened few. At least, he meant well. At
least, he was not facile, conventional, superficial, thoughtlessly optimistic. He did not content himself with the
pleasant telling of a pretty story, with the embroidering
of rosy decorations. At a time when refreshment and
distraction were all that was asked of literature, he man-
fully resisted the demand. Too much respect cannot be
paid to his unyielding steadfastness and integrity. Instead of dealing in confectionery, he set out to tell the
whole truth about American life as he saw it, even though
he saw it as unpleasant; and he brought to his task a
granitelike honesty and a strong sense of fact, seeing
for himself and seeing directly, seldom the dupe of general
illusions or preconceptions. Dreiser's project was so
fresh and strange, so boldly original, that it made all
the few who undertook it famous. The critics who ap-
proved of the attempt were not so ungrateful as to ques-

tion its literary success; indeed, they could not afford to, in the bitter war which was being waged by their party against the moralists and the censors. And ever since, they have been writing about Dreiser as if this were still the early Roosevelt period. They have busied themselves with defending his conception of the purpose and nature of fiction, not with weighing his actual achievement.

To insist upon the imperfection of that achievement is not to deny that in many non-literary ways Dreiser's work is of the very greatest moment. As portrayer, critic, and product of American society, no one is more important and, unintentionally, more illuminating. He has few rivals as social historian. The future student of our way of living will have little difficulty in reconstructing from Dreiser's books the Midwest of the late nineteenth and early twentieth centuries, in its finance, politics, business, and daily private life. There are phases of Midwestern life which Dreiser does not touch, but those he treats he treats with authority. American life as he renders it has two outstanding features: chaos and tragedy. It is a free-for-all of personal aggrandizement, a wild struggle to get what each can out of the general grab-bag. Without plan, purpose, or sense, it lacks even the rudimentary organization of the wolf pack. The strongest, the ablest and most unscrupulous win the prizes —a futile victory because it brings no lasting satisfaction. The others, the dull, the weak, the bewildered, who do not even know what they want, who are hampered by all sorts of meaningless moral prejudices, who mill helplessly about, kicked and trodden upon—they are doomed from the outset. In such a disorder there is no place for purpose; such a milieu offers—can in the nature of things offer—no rewards which would appeal to a rational being, no valid reasons for living. Its only prize is economic success; when that has been won, there is nothing for the victor but further and superfluous economic success. The best Dreiser's world has to give is primal elementary pleasure—the pleasure of fighting, of luxury, of sensual gratifications; it is no more humane than the aboriginal jungle of saber-toothed tiger and woolly elephant.

It is a tragic world because it is futile and wasteful, because all people have aspirations and possibilities which cannot be fulfilled in it. Those are happiest on the one hand whose instincts are most primitive and on the other whose aspirations are feeblest; the former get the most, the latter ask the least. It is a tragedy, like most modern American tragedy, of spiritual frustration, of degeneration and decay. How could it be otherwise? Where in such an environment is there chance for the proper growth and development of human personality? What food, what experience, does it offer for human nature to feed upon? It is indifferent to experience, to humaneness of living, because from start to finish it is dominated by the practical ideal: one could ask no better picture than Dreiser's of a practical society. Its material manifestations, its towns and cities and the like, are hideous, sordid, and squalid, because it is indifferent to beauty, to sensuous experience. It is an intellectual vacuum, because what thought it has is either concentrated in self-seeking or dissipated in a blind consolatory cheerfulness which is the negation of thought. Its only æsthetic pleasure is the millionaire collector's delight at having outbid his rivals at an auction. It is destitute of religion; a stale, insipid tribal moralism has replaced the love of God. Naturally in such a country the inhabitants, save for their grasping-muscles, remain undeveloped; and therefore they have no real social life. Existing as they do, not in a social cosmos but in a social chaos, social experience is impossible for them. They drift about, helpless, detached atoms, attracting and repelling one another, with no more cohesion than so many billiard balls. The social aspect of Dreiser's world is the saddest of all, and serves well to emphasize the obvious import of Dreiser's portrayal of American life: namely, that a world given over to practicality is inevitably a tragic world, because it denies full humanity to human beings.

Dreiser himself, however, does not make this deduction. On the contrary, since he can imagine no other mode of living, he accepts the world he has known, the Age of Exploitation at its worst, as typical of human life everywhere at all times, accepts the Chicago of the nineties as a true microcosm, or microchaos. Therefore his explicit social criticism is curiously one-sided. Since he cannot judge his world by any other standards than its own, he cannot criticize its practice; he can only point out the inconsistency between its practice and its professed beliefs and official creeds. As to the latter, his comment runs along familiar lines; he discusses thoughtless optimism and sentimentality, negative, puritanical, taboo morality, intolerance, conformity, and standardization—in short, all the defenses which a society bent on "making good" builds up in the interest of efficiency to protect itself from being diverted by the claims of life and experience.

Not that Dreiser so explains our inconsistencies. He sometimes attributes them to Anglo-Saxon hypocrisy, that handy bugaboo; at other times, fantastically but characteristically, he is inclined to lay the blame on the influence of the Federal Constitution, an "idealistic" document drawn up by "charming and gracious dreamers"—among whom he singles out particularly the author of *Poor Richard's Almanac!* Because he accepts the practical ideal as inevitable, yet objects to the camouflage with which it must always protect itself to avoid friction and maintain an oblivious illusion, he is led into all manner of self-contradiction. He complains at one moment that Americans are passionately religious and moral, fiercely determined to put the Ten Commandments and the Beatitudes into practice, and the next moment that they pay no attention to right and wrong, now that Americans care nothing for righteousness, and now that they care for nothing else. His social criticism is largely vitiated by this uncertainty, which is due to his inability to view the life about him from a detached position.

This same inability is the determining influence on his philosophy, which, needless to say, is one of naturalism. Henry Adams saw the universe as a chaos of warring forces and man as their victim; E. A. Robinson sees man as a waif, a stray, an alien in a world which is indifferent and even hostile to him. Dreiser would assent to both propositions. He is convinced that man is but one among many natural objects, not differing in his status or destiny from a stone or shrub or beast. Nor can he discover a plan or purpose in nature, with or without reference to humanity: it is a senseless jumbled mass of energies that fight it out among themselves—"accidental, indifferent, and bitterly cruel forces," "haphazard and casual," resulting in "the unsolvable disorder and brutality of life." He writes:

I admit a vast compulsion which has nothing to do with

the individual desires or tastes or impulses of individuals. That compulsion springs from the settling processes of forces which we do not in the least understand, over which we have no control, and in whose grip we are as grains of dust or sand, blown hither and thither for what purpose we cannot even suspect.

Dreiser, being a determinist, would deny that he has any ethics, but he has a view of life which comes to much the same thing: since life is senseless and nature immoral, it is best to be rich and powerful, able to buy love and luxury. He has only contemptuous pity for the weaklings who are bound by moral scruples, only admiration for the Titans who at any cost get what they want. Again he comes surprisingly close to Henry Adams, to whom education meant efficiency, or a mastery of the world; both men, that is, indulge in success-worship of the crassest sort, the ideal of the *American Magazine*. In Dreiser, to be sure, this spirit is somewhat chastened, partly by personal experience and partly by reading; in his autobiography he tells how he discovered Spencer and Huxley, and adds:

Up to this time there had been in me a blazing and unchecked desire to get on and the feeling that in doing so we did get somewhere; now in its place was the definite conviction that spiritually one got nowhere . . . that one lived and had his being because one had to, and that it was of no importance.

That is, he came to the conclusion that conspicuous worldly success was of little value, but could think of nothing else of any value at all; therefore, though he resigned himself to his own fate, he consistently in his novels depicts this

kind of success as the only thing worth striving for:
it may be worth little, but nothing else is worth more.

Though Henry Adams thought that he derived his
philosophy from his reading in the natural sciences, we
saw reason to suppose that he was really more influenced
by his personal experience and especially by his environment, the United States between 1870 and 1900. Dreiser
avows openly that his views are based on his own experience, particularly as a newspaper reporter in Chicago and
St. Louis, though they were precipitated by his discover-
ing the Victorian popularizers of scientific thought. In
other words, Dreiser has merely made explicit the view
of life which he found implicit in American society, merely
reduced American practice to a philosophical theory. He
grew up in the ultra-practical society which he depicts,
a society wholly given over to economic individualism,
and—once more like Henry Adams—though Dreiser has
himself abandoned hope of success in the American sense,
he has developed, with the aid of what he knows of science, the practical point of view into a view of life. No
other attitude occurs to him as conceivable. Through and
through he is a product of a thoroughly practical society.

Dreiser's peculiar state of mind is somewhat explained
by the circumstances of his life. He was brought up a
Catholic—but apparently in a very odd kind of Catholi-
cism. He describes the view of life which was imposed
upon him in his childhood, a view that was too simple and
too cheerful to stand the strain of reality, that was hard
and fast and exclusively moral. According to his account, he was taught to believe that good and bad were
as unmistakable as black and white, that mankind was
clearly divided into sheep and goats and that there were
few goats, that the virtuous throve and were rewarded

in this world and the vicious punished, that the universe was run in accordance with the Sermon on the Mount so as to favor the meek, the peaceful, and the pure in heart. Christianity is still to Dreiser synonymous with sentimental optimism; he has no notion how close he has come at times to writing an early-Christian treatise *De Contemptu Mundi*. Furthermore, he was early inducted into a negative morality: virtue consisted in not drinking or smoking, not dancing, not going to the theater. Sex was by its nature essentially sinful. "We were taught persistently to shun," he says, "most human experiences as either dangerous or degrading or destructive." From this atmosphere he plunged as a reporter into slums and police courts and all sorts of misery, filth, and graft. Later he read Huxley, Tyndall, and Spencer, and found his worst fears justified. He went through the experience, so common and so painful in the nineteenth century, of losing his faith. Like his contemporaries, he experienced a reaction—much the same sort of reaction that every one goes through on reaching adolescence and leaving the easy harmless world of childhood, but in Dreiser's case aggravated by many circumstances, among them his advanced age. His awakening came ten years too late, and was that much more severe.

No better illustration than Dreiser could be asked of the statement that in a practical society a writer is drilled throughout his youth in false modes of thought and feeling, usually a sham gentility and a spurious puritanism, so that not until he reaches maturity can he rid himself of these encumbrances and really begin to experience life. That is why in many ways it is as if Dreiser had got stuck mentally in the adolescent age. The pained amazement with which he views human imperfection and inconsistency, the confusion, the morbid emotionalism and excitement, the lack of scale in judging values, the intellectual naïveté, the enthusiasm with which he announces what all adults have always known—all are traits, I believe, of an adolescent state of mind. One is tempted to suggest that Dreiser's is a case of delayed or arrested development, that he has never quite grown up, developed, and matured. He is still capable of arguing with serious heat that an earthquake is not an instance of God's mercy. He has succeeded at best only in half-emancipating himself from his early surroundings. As Mencken vigorously puts it:

The truth about Dreiser is that he is still in the transition stage between Christian Endeavor and civilization, between being a good American and being a free man. . . . There is an almost moral frenzy to expose and riddle what passes for morality among the stupid. . . . The man is still evangelical.

But not only does Dreiser retain a preacher's fervor; as we have seen, though he has managed to give up the nostrums with which practical people quiet themselves and to forego his own self-advancement, he has not managed altogether to free himself from the practical temper. He is still half enslaved.

Dreiser's ignorance, already mentioned in connection with his notions of the Constitution and of Christianity, shows itself also in a more pernicious form. Because he is able to conceive only two views of life, the one in which he was brought up and the one to which he has attained— the two views, one followed and one professed, in the world in which he has lived—in all his thinking he sets up false alternatives and impales himself on a needless dilemma. On the one hand are chaos and jungle, "Nature"

89

undisguised, pessimism, determinism, naturalism; on the other, a fatuous cheeriness, a debased morality, and a religion prostituted to practicality. These two for Dreiser exhaust the realms of human thought. It is most unfortunate. Naturalism—the philosophy of Hardy and Conrad—is a view which lends itself well to powerful and profound literary interpretations of life. Furthermore, Dreiser has assembled superabundant material for a penetrating and radical criticism of American life. Yet as thinker, as social critic, and as artist, he has been rendered all but impotent by the influence of his environment.

More than most men, he has suffered from the absence of an established national literary tradition, with its attendant discipline in taste and critical standards. As a writer, like most American writers, he has "just growed." In consequence, all his art, even to his style, seems to have been molded by the pressure of his surroundings: at least, it is a perfect match for them in its crude and chaotic ugliness, its occasional lapses into a maudlin, barbaric showiness, its immaturity, and its lack of rational control.

In part, perhaps, these qualities in Dreiser's work may be due to an innate want of æsthetic sense, but also they are surely in large measure due to a deprivation of the proper experience. It is true that he shows little appreciation even of natural beauty, which must have been available to him; yet one can scarcely believe that if he had lived in an environment which prized sensuous experience and which was rich in sensuous loveliness, especially of human creation, he could have been so oblivious of the claims of beauty. At any rate, if he had known a society which eagerly busied itself with ideas and which cared much for the disinterested play of thought, he could hardly have remained at so raw a stage of intellectual development. And if he had been part of a social web or fabric, he must have had a more varied and affluent conception of humanity and human possibilities. The folk of his making are uncivilized and undeveloped, and so is he, because he has only an uncivilized and undeveloped experience to draw upon. That he should have been denied an adequate experience is the greater pity for the reason that no one ever had a larger appetite for experience than Dreiser. His zest and gusto for living are his most distinctive trait. He has certainly absorbed what his world had to offer, and, I think, as one contemplates the image of that world in his books, one's final wonder is not that he got so little but so much out of it. Who else, who has had the same world as his to deal with, has succeeded in extracting more?

Therein lies Dreiser's great contribution to American letters and to American life. Before either the literature or the life could attain to vitality, some one had to establish a fruitful, living contact with the American environment, to experience it and realize it to the full. Until such a contact could be made, American life must continue to be meager and anemic, providing little sustenance either for humanity or for art. To make that contact is the main work of contemporary literature, and in this achievement Dreiser has been the foremost figure. I do not forget the abortive movement of the nineties headed by Stephen Crane and Frank Norris; but for some reason it failed to impress permanently either the general public or the writers of the time. The present literary manifestation has far more vigor—and it has Dreiser largely to thank. No doubt he is but the channel through which various forces and tendencies effectuate themselves, and

no doubt they would have made themselves felt somehow
without him. Yet, because he was the first in time of our
contemporaries to express the new spirit, and because of
the power and massiveness of his work, he has assumed
the position of leader. To occupy such a position is in
itself a great feat, and one that could be performed only
by a man who possessed distinct elements of greatness.

BIBLIOGRAPHY

DREISER, THEODORE. *Sister Carrie.* New York, 1900,
Boni & Liveright.

——*Jennie Gerhardt.* New York, 1911, Boni & Liveright.

——*The Financier.* New York, 1912, revised edition,
New York, 1927, Boni & Liveright.

——*A Traveler at Forty.* New York, 1913, Boni &
Liveright.

——*The Titan.* New York, 1914, Boni & Liveright.

——*The "Genius."* New York, 1915, Boni & Liveright.

——*A Hoosier Holiday.* New York, 1916, Boni &
Liveright.

——*Free, and Other Stories.* New York, 1918, Boni &
Liveright.

——*The Hand of the Potter.* New York, 1918, Boni &
Liveright.

——*Twelve Men.* New York, 1919, Boni & Liveright.

——*Hey Rub-a-dub-dub.* New York, 1920, Boni &
Liveright.

——*A Book about Myself.* New York, 1922, Boni &
Liveright.

——*The Color of a Great City.* New York, 1923, Boni
& Liveright.

——*An American Tragedy.* 2 vols. New York, 1925,
Boni & Liveright.

THEODORE DREISER

DREISER, THEODORE. *Moods, Cadenced and Declaimed.*
New York, 1926 Boni & Liveright.
——— *Chains.* New York, 1927, Boni & Liveright.
RASCOE, BURTON. *Theodore Dreiser.* New York, 1925,
Robert M. McBride & Company.

V

ROBERT FROST

N September 6, 1620, the *Mayflower* sailed from Plymouth, England, with her cargo of unwitting Pilgrim Fathers. The intention was to land somewhere in northern "Virginia," perhaps not far from the site of Atlantic City. But stormy weather drove the ship from her course— and the consequences are matters of common knowledge. This storm should rank as one of the major phenomena of history. If the Pilgrims had settled the sand barrens and cranberry bogs of New Jersey, or if a northeaster had blown them to the vicinity of Charleston or Savannah, the United States would be a different land, conspicuous perhaps for light-hearted jollity and *dolce far niente*. As it was, the Pilgrims and their followers the Puritans were driven to the only part of the country where Nature is herself a puritan. From the moment that Bradford stepped from his boat to the granite bowlder among the sweet fern and juniper bushes beside Cape Cod Bay, the doom of future Americans was sealed. Transcendentalism, Harvard, abolition, Iowa, prohibition, and Los Angeles began to grow in the womb of Time.

In the title-poem of *New Hampshire*, Robert Frost demurs at being thought a local poet; he says that his books are "against the world in general," and that to apply them more narrowly is to restrict his meaning. This assertion Frost's readers outside New England are inclined to question. True, he is not local in the derogatory sense; he is not provincial. But to say that Frost is not a New England poet would be like saying that Burns is not Scottish or that Synge is not Irish. For good and for evil his work is the distilled essence of New England, and from this fact spring both his marked limitations and his unique value. Frost himself, with his belief that "all poetry is the reproduction of the tones of actual speech," must admit that his language is local, that his diction and his rhythms bear much the same relation to the talk of New Hampshire farmers that Synge's bear to the talk of West Irish fisherfolk. But Frost's localism does not stop there: his characters and their life as he pictures it, the natural setting in which they live, the poet himself in his point of view and habit of mind, are all peculiarly local, for better and for worse. Only in so far as New England is not entirely unlike other regions and Yankees are not entirely inhuman, and in so far as poetry of marked excellence appeals to every one, can Frost claim to write for "the world in general."

Frost's district does not cover all New England even; it is confined to the inland, to the hilly farm country. And needless to say, he concerns himself only with the present, not with the New England of witches, Jamaica rum, the slave trade, reform crusades, and elevated philosophizing. His is the New England which most of us know only from the verandas of summer hotels, a land of great natural loveliness, with a sprinkling of uncomfortably quaint natives, the Bretons or Basques of America, strange fragments of forgotten peoples, somehow more remote from us than the Poles and other immigrants who are settling the abandoned farms. Frost

maintains that it is the glory of his New England to produce nothing in commercial quantities, nothing to sell;
and as to commercial products it is true enough.   But
one must not infer that because corn and hogs will not
thrive in New England, nothing thrives there.   When I
said that Nature herself was there a puritan, I did not
mean that she was glum and niggardly.   On the contrary,
she is lavish enough with the things she approves of—
with jumbled hills and lichened granite and little cold
excitable streams.   Among these surroundings, in the
sharp, edged air, silver birches, fox grapes, blueberries,
wintergreen, and bayberry bushes grow freely enough.
All these things have distinctive traits in common; they
are useless, for commercial purposes, and they afford little
nourishment to man or beast, but they make up in peculiar
aromatic tang and flavor for what they lack as sustenance
for gross animal life.

Such is the background of Frost's poetry.   In their
little old gray houses, shingled or clapboarded, each shad-
owed with its great elms and surrounded with its gray
stone walls, his farmers live, and till their little reluctant
fields, much as their ancestors have always done.   Life is
difficult for them, but not impossible, and at least, as
things go nowadays, it is simple.   It is less specialized
than most modern life; because of their circumstances,
these people have to provide for themselves everything
they can, and most of them have to follow a trade or
craft besides.   In addition, they are in some respects fortunate in the tradition they have inherited.   Without meaning to imply that all the Puritans were unworldly, without forgetting the wooden-nutmeg side of New England,
one may point out that New England has always had its
strain of people who have valued knowledge and mental

independence and intellectual achievement, the strain which produced Emerson and his associates, and others who have rebelled against the dominant tendencies of American life. Perhaps because in the exodus of the mid-nineteenth century the more ambitious left home to spread like a swarm of locusts over the Mississippi Valley, and because their like nowadays go off to the cities, perhaps because the environment offers slight hope of outstanding economic success, Frost's farmers have succumbed less than other Americans to the mania for making good, and have continued, though in a rude and enfeebled form, the tradition just referred to. Their condition is such, as Gorham B. Munson points out, that "the acquisitive impulse gets no favoring headstart, and instead of haste we find reticence and deliberation characteristic." Theirs may not be the ideal human lot; yet, what with the variety of their toil and their heritage of self-reliance in opinion, it is a state better adapted to developing varied potentialities than the common American way of life.

But there is another side to the picture. The New England soil and climate seem to affect humanity as they do vegetation. Frost's Yankees are like wintergreen in the sharp pungency of their flavor and in their lack of sustaining body; they differ from other men as their fox grapes differ from muscat grapes. They are distinguished for individuality rather than for flourishing heartiness. In fact, it is a temptation to say that mankind is one of the crops which cannot thrive and grow vigorously in New England, that it, like corn, needs richer earth. It may be that the restraining influence of puritanism is responsible, for puritans, even to the ninth generation, though they go in for labor of body and mind, are prone to deny themselves other experiences of equal importance, such as loafing and sensuous pleasures. The puritan restraint and the puritan tension have cut these people off time out of mind from necessary sources of human nourishment. The result has apparently been recognized even by some New Englanders:

> Emerson said, "The God who made New Hampshire
> Taunted the lofty land with little men."
> Another Massachusetts poet said,
> "I go no more to summer in New Hampshire.
> I've given up my summer place in Dublin."
> But when I asked to know what ailed New Hampshire,
> She said she couldn't stand the people in it,
> The little men (it's Massachusetts speaking).
> And when I asked to know what ailed the people,
> She said, "Go read your own books and find out."

It was an apt reply. Frost himself, by saying that he writes "against the world in general," intimates that he considers his characters not essentially different from the normal, average run of humanity; but west of the Hudson he will find few to agree with him. To the rest of us, they look like very queer fish indeed. In brief, what ails them is their ingrowing dispositions. Not merely the famous New England reserve: it is a positive lack of frankness, an innate love of indirectness and concealment, which leads them not only to hide their own thoughts and feelings and motives, but to assume, naturally, that others do the same. Out of this tendency grows a suspiciousness, a tortuous habit of mind, which is a constant source of surprise to the more credulous and easy-going alien. To them, an act of kindness which other folk would think the sheerest matter of course seems so unnatural, so momentous, that it must be sedulously concealed. Even more striking is the meanness and the pettiness of these people. Not that they are unfeeling or frigid; on the contrary, they attach an excessive, often a morbid, intensity of feeling to the merest trifles. This makes them touchy, always with a chip on their shoulder, often close to hysterics. Most of them show an extraordinary capacity for dislike, hatred, and contempt—which may explain why New England has been the nursery of so many great reformers.

A good example of this exaggerated emotionalism is found in "The Code": a farmer tells his hired man, who is unloading hay, "Let her come," and the farmhand, injured in his dignity by the order, dumps the whole load on his employer. A more startling instance is "The Vanishing Red": a miller, because he does not like an Indian's tone of voice, proceeds to drown the Indian. Evidently, what at most would make a normal man swear, makes a Frost character commit murder. The most terrible and tragic illustration of this morbid excess, though here the cause is not trivial, is "Home Burial," the story of a woman so sunk in her grief for her child, so deliberately and purposely sunk in it, that she has contracted a violent hatred of her husband and is all but outright insane. In much of Frost's work, particularly in *North of Boston,* his harshest book, he emphasizes the dark background of life in rural New England, with its degeneration sinking too often into total madness.

Frost apparently regards the woman in "Home Burial" as abnormal, but he seems to approve the hired man's "independence" in "The Code" and to find nothing out of the way in the miller's murder of the Indian in "The Vanishing Red." The explanation is not far to seek.

These folk look normal to Frost because his own turn of mind is similar to theirs; his is the Yankee mind transmuted, raised to a higher level. Indirectness and suspiciousness are transformed in him into an extraordinary subtlety, which shows itself in his narratives as subtlety of analysis and portrayal of character, in his lyrics as subtlety of thought, feeling, and imagination. Similarly, he has all the Yankee intensity; but this keenness, instead of manifesting itself as meanness and pettiness, undergoes a metamorphosis and weights details with feeling and significance. Because he feels details so sharply, he is unexcelled for minute and exact observation. No less is Frost Yankee in his restraint. He surprises us, to alter Keats' saying, by a fine deficiency—perhaps omission or suppression would be the better word. He never whips up his emotion or strives for a spurious effect. His flashes of intensity, when they come, are the more effective because his manner is uniformly easy and unforced. Even at his climaxes the language and the rhythm remain colloquial; his method is to build up a dramatic situation and then, in the same even tone of voice, to condense the whole into one touch, as at the end of "The Fear":

> *"Joel!" She spoke as if she couldn't turn.*
> *The swinging lantern lengthened to the ground,*
> *It touched, it struck it, clattered and went out.*

In like manner the grotesque "independence" which is irritating in "The Code" is so altered in Frost as to become an astonishing sincerity. To many tastes his peculiar virtues may not appeal, but not his harshest critic would charge him with pretense. By the side of his genuineness most poetry of the day looks more than a little forced. He carries sincerity, indeed, to the point of absolute naturalness. It is a triumph of art to be so natural as Frost; only an expert artist could manage the feat. His is the *ars celare artem* with a difference: it is not merely that he attains the apparent ease which Horace had in mind, the classical simplicity, but that his poems seem spoken impromptu, not written at all, as if we overheard him speaking aloud. In part, of course, this is an amazing gift for mimicry, but it is more than that: to the mimetic skill is added a gift for condensation and selection and an exquisite sense of form, which give his work not only verisimilitude but also the typical and essential quality of high art.

Carl Van Doren has well said:

Poets understand that the love of reality is the root of most poetry. Diffuse love too much, and it loses meaning as well as power; fix it upon specific things, and they become first important and then representative. Always Mr. Frost reaches his magic through the door of actuality.

Indeed, Frost's love of reality is so pronounced as to constitute a danger, though so far eluded, the danger to which Thoreau succumbed, of coming to feel that any fact, however insignificant, was important. None of his lines is more characteristic than the early "The fact is the sweetest dream that labor knows," and it is evident that he regards poetry as not unlike an axe-helve.

He showed me that the lines of a good helve
Were native to the grain before the knife
Expressed them, and its curves were no false curves
Put on it from without.

Similarly he carves his poetry out of experience, merely educing what is already implicit. And yet—here we approach the inmost secret of his poetry—he values the fact because to him it is more than mere fact. He is reported to have said that "sight and insight" are the whole business of the poet, and the second term is even more important than the first. As Untermeyer has observed, Frost's writing possesses "the double force of observation and implication"; in it are sounded "spiritual overtones above the actual theme." Frost, in short, has not a little of the transcendentalist in his make-up. Sometimes his feeling as to the significance of the fact is worked out into overt and explicit symbolism and even allegory, as in "Mending Wall," "Birches," "Wild Grapes," "Two Look at Two," but in his most characteristic and appealing work the feeling of mystery is left merely as a mood of strangeness and not developed intellectually.

As an example of writing full at once of actuality and of the suggestion of wonder, I might cite "The Wood-Pile," in which the author tells how, when out walking in a swamp, far from home, he found a cord of maple wood piled years before and left to rot. Commonplace enough, and yet as he tells it conveying a sense of the eerie and uncanny, just the sense which the experience itself would give to any one at all impressionable. Perhaps it is a relic of the savage's primeval feeling on coming across human traces in a desert place. Still more strikingly, "After Apple-Picking" illustrates the same union of minute observation with the evocation of an enigmatic mood—here, the odd, indefinable state of mind which overtakes one in the fall of the year. But perhaps the clearest instance of the power which a detail may have so to elicit feeling is found in "The Death of the Hired Man." Mary sends her husband to speak to the hired man, and says:

> *"I'll sit and see if that small sailing cloud*
> *Will hit or miss the moon."*
> > *It hit the moon.*
> *Then there were three there, making a dim row,*
> *The moon, the little silver cloud, and she.*

The common-sense person, I suppose, will ask, "What of it?" but to any one sympathetic with Frost those lines contain the essence of his special magic. I say "magic" advisedly, for there is something primitive and archaic about it: those lines bring back the feeling with which men regarded a world they understood not at all, the feeling that in such coincidences there ought to be something important and significant, that there is certainly something mysterious. In fact, in all these cases the gist of the matter seems to be a suggestion of some elusive meaning; one feels that there must be some lurking import, if only one could guess what it is. And sometimes, as I said, Frost develops the meaning for us; but more often he probably has no more notion what it is than we have—if, as is doubtful, there is any at all.

Apparently, Frost is not so constituted that his reaction to a sense-impression is simple and direct, and in proportion to the force of the impression. His reaction bears no obvious and calculable relation to the stimulus; on the contrary, the relation of cause to effect is unpredictable, perhaps incomprehensible. It is a relation as incommensurate and arbitrary as that between pushing a button and turning on an electric light or ringing a bell.

With him it is not only—not, I think, chiefly—sensuous pleasure that counts, but a subtle train of emotion and thought which the perception rouses in his mind. He is devoted to the fact, true—but because the fact is necessary to light the fuses of suggestion in his mind. A birch tree is to him not primarily an arabesque in black and white: it is fraught with hidden import. Conversely, he may be greatly moved by something quite devoid of sensuous appeal—a grindstone or axe-helve or woodpile—because to him it is tinged with hints of meaning that impart a feeling of the mysterious and the wonderful. And this is especially true if the perception is such as to excite the buried savage who sleeps within the most sophisticated of us. Consequently, in such a man's account of what he sees and hears we get sounds and sights not simply as they are, but on the one hand almost denuded of their physical beauty, on the other so transfigured that we see and hear them as it were through the shimmering veil of the more or less vague ideas and feelings which they have served to liberate.

That this is Frost's habit of mind, that the subjective element is fully as strong as the external, I have perhaps cited evidence enough; yet I should like to add another bit, one of his slightest lyrics:

> *The way a crow*
> *Shook down on me*
> *The dust of snow*
> *From a hemlock tree*
>
> *Has given my heart*
> *A change of mood*
> *And saved some part*
> *Of a day I had rued.*

This aspect of Frost deserves emphasis because much has been made of his realism and his objectivity, qualities which I am sure have been overestimated. For one thing, in spite of his close observation and minute detail, he is not a markedly sensuous poet; in fact, he is markedly ascetic. Think, for example, what an imagist would have done, in the lyric just quoted, with the picture in green and white and black. Though Frost deals by preference in the concrete, though his writing abounds in images that are sharp and specific, he does not luxuriate in sensuous gratification, in a frank relish for savor and color and sound. A mere reference to Keats and Swinburne is enough to illustrate this point: there is no "purple-stained mouth," no "cloth of woven crimson, gold, and jet," no "lisp of leaves and ripple of rain" in Frost. Or perhaps the sensuous austerity is more in the expression than in the image itself. He all but eschews the appeal of musical sound, preferring the effect of talk to that of song; such lines as "The slow smokeless burning of decay" are conspicuous by their rarity. In his treatment of feeling also, as we saw, he is ascetic; his language seldom swells or rises; the emotion is conveyed by implication only, by economy and elimination. Consequently, a reader less abstemious by nature than Frost may make the mistake of thinking him severe and stark, even bleak and bare and cold.

One of the plainest signs of this ascetic temperament, this instinctive holding in, is the sense of loneliness and isolation which he often expresses, most emphatically in "The Road Not Taken":

> *I shall be telling this with a sigh*
> *Somewhere ages and ages hence:*

SPOKESMEN

Two roads diverged in a wood, and I—
I took the one less traveled by,
And that has made all the difference.

And the same sense of separation, of a temptation to
seclude himself from the world, appears in the first poem
of *A Boy's Will* and again in a "Grace Note" to *New
Hampshire:*

> *The woods are lovely, dark and deep.*
> *But I have promises to keep,*
> *And miles to go before I sleep,*
> *And miles to go before I sleep.*

Sometimes the fascination of solitude, sometimes the
terror of it—in either case he feels it strongly.   He carries
the matter a step further in "The Tuft of Flowers":

> *I must be, as he had been—alone.*

> *"As all must be," I said within my heart,*
> *"Whether they work together or apart." . . .*

> *"Men work together," I told him from the heart,*
> *"Whether they work together or apart."*

The sequel of this poem, "Mending Wall," by implication
sets forth the mystery of isolation and comradeship;
the one is somehow necessary to the other, the sense of
solitariness whets the longing for companionship.

> *Something there is that doesn't love a wall,*
> *That wants it down. . . .*

He says again: "Good fences make good neighbors."

In Frost there is a touch, but no more than a touch, of Robinson's feeling of estrangement from the world. For I take it that Frost refers not only to other men, but to all things. Frost, however, unlike Robinson, does not reject experience, or refer to "the life we curse"; on the contrary, the love of life is central in Frost's thinking.

He tells us little of his philosophy, for he is as chary with his reflection as he is with his feeling, preferring hints and implication to forthright statement. But he tells enough to show that his is a philosophy of attachment, of realization, of intuitive apprehension, of what Whitman unpleasantly called "adhesiveness."

> *Some say Love by being thrall*
> *And simply staying possesses all*
> *In several beauty that Thought fares far*
> *To find fused in another star.*

There can be no doubt of Frost's passion for experience; he calls himself "Slave to a springtime passion for the earth"; and he returns to the theme again and again— at the end of "Birches," of "Wild Grapes," and in his striking lines called "To Earthward," which conclude:

> *When stiff and sore and scarred*
> *I take away my hand*
> *From leaning on it hard*
> *In grass and sand,*
>
> *The hurt is not enough:*
> *I long for weight and strength*
> *To feel the earth as rough*
> *To all my length.*

He cannot take actuality for granted; he shows an almost bloodthirsty clinging to people and things. He never knows repletion; he is like a hungry man who never gets enough to eat.

How shall this paradox of Frost's asceticism and of his craving for experience be resolved? Would it be too fanciful to liken him to a newsboy gazing into a confectioner's window at Christmas time? Frost sees all the beauties of the world spread before him, but some mysterious agency prevents him from getting at them and absorbing them.

> *I cannot rub the strangeness from my sight*
> *I got from looking through a pane of glass*
> *I skimmed this morning from the drinking trough*
> *And held against the world of hoary grass.*

Perhaps it is the old transcendental streak which keeps him from a simple, naïve, unreflecting enjoyment of things, which suggests that a bird is not merely a song and a splash of color, but something mysteriously tinged with meaning, and which always sets up an inner experience to vie with, if not to outdo, the outer. The lines "For Once, Then, Something" seem to bear on the point.

> *Others taunt me with having knelt at well-curbs*
> *Always wrong to the light, so never seeing*
> *Deeper down in the well than where the water*
> *Gives me back in a shining surface picture*
> *Me myself in the summer heaven godlike*
> *Looking out of a wreath of fern and cloud puffs.*

Whoever it was told Frost he always saw himself was a discerning critic, though I think it is more accurate to say that he sees the world, not himself, but the world only as reflected in his own temperament, and that, if he could, he would turn from reflections altogether and deal direct with actuality. But in spite of his wishes, the New England reserve, the New England tensity, will no more permit him to abandon himself freely to the world than to pour out his heart in unpremeditated verse. Always in his attitude there is a check or rigor which he cannot let go or relax; he cannot lose himself and be absorbed wholly by experience.

Yet, in trying to account for the vein of austerity which is always in Frost, apparently in spite of himself, I do not wish to overstress it. There is nothing gaunt or famished about him. Rather the reverse: his work, as contemporary American poetry goes, is remarkable for its solidity and completeness. He has come to better terms than most of our poets with his environment, and has had a better environment to come to terms with, and has profited by both circumstances. That may explain why, as Munson says, "he spends no time dilating on the aloofness or indifference of nature to the fate of man," and why, though the tragedy of frustration is by no means absent from his writing, it is not set forth as the whole or even the norm of human life. Whatever may be Frost's limitations, he gives the impression of a wider and sounder and more many-sided development than that of any other living American poet.

The reason is to be found in the circumstances of his life—namely, that he has spent much of it in farming. His poetry is a standing argument in favor of such theorists as the Brook Farmers who held that poets and philosophers would profit from working with their hands, and is proof of Havelock Ellis's assertion that a well balanced mind requires not only sense-impressions, but also the exercise of the "motor and emotional energies." Frost has had the discipline and training which come from combining sensation and thought and feeling, and above all from applying them and putting them to use in doing things. To quote Munson once more:

Frost's imagination is the consciousness of a man who is using *more* of his equipment than most of the moderns do. I mean simply that Frost does not seem to work almost exclusively from one of three centers—from the intellect or the emotions or the body or sense-center—but from a sort of rude coöperation of all three. . . . In this development he . . gives a start to the speculation as to how far the conditions of modern mechanized life throw into disuse portions of the necessary equipment of a fully conscious being. Certainly Frost's lines give one more of an impression that a whole man is writing them than do the sharply intellectualized or thumpingly emotional lines of most of his contemporaries.

Robert Frost's is preëminently a farmer's poetry. His familiarity with nature and with objects is not, for all his deservedly famous observation, that of the observer or spectator, but that of the man who has worked with them and used them. His acquaintance with them is more intimate and more intuitive than that of the onlooker. A grindstone to him is not a quaint object with rustic associations, but something which has made him groan and sweat; a scythe does not remind him of Theocritus but of the feel of the implement as he has swung it. Blueberries and apples are less connected in his mind with their color or their taste than with the process of picking them. Frost's peculiar kind of knowledge is shown in his reference to the "highway where the slow wheel pours the sand"; in the lines:

My instep arch not only keeps the ache,
It keeps the pressure of a ladder-round.
I feel the ladder sway as the boughs bend;

and in this passage:

How Love burns through the Putting in the Seed
On through the watching for that early birth
When, just as the soil tarnishes with weed,
The sturdy seedling with arched body comes
Shouldering its way and shedding the earth crumbs.

Such knowledge pervades everything he writes; it even shapes his conception of poetry. As a poet, likewise, he is still the craftsman and the husbandman; he judges a poem by the same standards which he would apply to an axe or a hoe or a spade: it must be solid, strong, honest. And his own poetry meets the test, severe though it is.

It was characteristic of Frost that when he found himself obliged to earn a living, he went to farming, not to writing advertisements or selling bonds or real estate. Like the people of whom he writes, he is untouched by the rage for self-advancement. Indeed, judging from what has been made public, the integrity which distinguishes his poetry is only an outward sign of an equal personal integrity. That he believes in and practices the poetic temper and the life of realization has been made plain, I trust, already; what he thinks of the life of exploitation and the acquisitive temper is unmistakably stated in these lines at the end of "Wild Grapes":

I had not taken the first step in knowledge;
I had not learned to let go with the hands,
As still I have not learned to with the heart,
And have no wish to with the heart—nor need,

That I can see. The mind—is not the heart.
I may yet live, as I know others live,
To wish in vain to let go with the mind—
Of cares, at night, to sleep; but nothing tells me
That I need learn to let go with the heart.

Furthermore, though New Hampshire is not a poet's utopia, I doubt whether in the United States Frost could have found a better environment. For him, of course, there was no other: outside New England he is blind and deaf; from his poetry one would think that he had never been so far west as the Hudson nor so far east as the Atlantic. But, aside from this idiosyncrasy of his, no other region seems better fitted to be a poet's residence. In comparison, for instance, with Sandburg and the Mississippi Valley, Frost has the advantage; Frost's world may be simple and plain and rude, but Sandburg's is crude and chaotic, however teeming with raw vigor; and the work of the two bears the imprint of their respective surroundings. Inland New England, whatever its faults— and I have not tried to minimize them—is less hostile to the life of realization, in an elementary, primitive form, than the rest of the Union. Call the life which Frost portrays narrow, meager, monotonous, a backwater, a relic of a past age, say that his farmers are small, petty-minded, inhibited, as stony and thin as their soil—yet it is true that among these tillers of New Hampshire fields there is more of the stuff of life to be found than there is in many prosperous garden suburbs or among many gatherings of brisk young salesmen and of progressive and flourishing Babbitts. Among contemporary writers, Frost has been singularly fortunate in having found, for his incomplete but considerable capacity for experience, an environment which has yielded an experience not wholly inadequate.

His work, to be sure, is severely restricted by the bonds of his own nature and by the lacks of his subject-matter. His is a poetry of exclusions, of limitations not only in area and in localism, but equally in temperament. As he says of the oven-bird,

> *He knows in singing not to sing.*
> *The question that he frames in all but words*
> *Is what to make of a diminished thing.*

He has given us poetry with little music, little delight for the senses, little glow of warm feeling. He has introduced us to a world not rich in color, sound, taste, and smell, a world mainly black and white and gray, etched in with acid in deep shadow and fine lines and sharp edges, lighted with a fitful white radiance as of starlight. His predilection, among natural phenomena, for stars and snow is symptomatic. Even his people are etchings, or woodcuts—droll, bizarre, sometimes pathetic: when we see them crumple up, we know how they can suffer. But somewhere among their ancestors there was a snow man, and his essence runs in their veins, a sharper, keener fluid than common blood, burning and biting like snow water. Yet, like the etchings of the older masters and like the best of modern woodcuts, this poetic world of his has a good three-dimensional solidity. One cannot put one's finger through it.

And it has an even more valuable quality. Frost's poetry is among those useless, uncommercial products of New England which constitute her tenacious charm. It belongs with the silver birches and the bayberry, and it shares their uniqueness. It has the edged loveliness and the acrid relish and fragrance of every growth native to New England earth and air. It is the last flowering of the seeds blown to the Massachusetts coast by the storms of 1620. For it has about it the quality of the final and ultimate; it is an epitome. As perfect in its way as blueberries or wintergreen, what it lacks in nutriment and profusion it atones for like them in flavor. We may look elsewhere for our bread and meat; but nowhere else can we find in all its pungency that piquant aromatic raciness which is New England.

BIBLIOGRAPHY

Frost, Robert. *A Boy's Will.* New York, 1913, Henry Holt and Company.

———*North of Boston.* New York, 1914, Henry Holt and Company.

———*Mountain Interval.* New York, 1916, Henry Holt and Company.

———*Selected Poems.* New York, 1923, Henry Holt and Company.

———*New Hampshire.* New York, 1923, Henry Holt and Company.

Munson, Gorham B. *Robert Frost.* New York, 1927, George H. Doran Company.

VI

SHERWOOD ANDERSON

SHERWOOD ANDERSON combines an unusual number of activities: he is at once observer, interpreter, creator, and critic. To begin with, he presents a picture, as do most of our writers, of that portion of the United States which he has known intimately. Yet, since he has not contented himself with rendering the surface, his picture is not mere mimicry: he has tried to get beneath the appearances and to understand, by imaginative penetration, the vital processes of American life. He has digested the crude matter of experience and converted it into the substance of art, so that it has become a new thing, though still also a likeness of the old—a process as baffling to analysis as man's psycho-physical parallelism, yet familiar to every good portrait-painter. Furthermore, Anderson has pondered over his experience, both actual and imaginative, and has tried to draw tentative conclusions, not only concerning American civilization but concerning human existence in general. Not only has he, like the others, made a diagnosis, but also, unlike them, he has a remedy to suggest. Therefore, to one interested in the relation of current literature to modern life, he is the most instructive of our contemporaries.

Since his world is a representation of the Middle West, it has many familiar features. The country is rich and fertile, and highly cultivated; it is a succession of cornfields, cabbage fields, berry fields, and always cornfields again, with here and there a bit of woodland. Many of its details are pleasant—a pool in a brook near a bridge, a cluster of wild flowers in spring beside an old log, the sound of wind in the growing corn, the smell of freshly turned earth. But it is monotonous; it is so flat and so full of things that the eye cannot carry far in any direction. Since it is all the same, there is no use in going from one place to another. Walking along one of the roads, one passes field after field of the same crops, the same groves of the same trees, the same farmhouses. The road never turns, there is never a view. On and on one goes, hemmed in by an eternity of repetition. Even the towns do not help, for they are all alike and all as void of distinction as the country. They have all a paltry, mean ugliness, as one walks down Main Street past the livery stable, the drugstore, the hardware store, the frame hotel, to the red frame railroad station. Nor is even the big city much better, for the city is simply one of the towns enlarged, with endless blocks of identical buildings, grimy, featureless. It is a gigantic anthill, as they are little anthills.

The inhabitants match the country, not in luxuriant vigor and fecundity, but in absence of distinction. To be sure, they have features, but there is nothing memorable in their features: one has a red nose and two gold teeth; another is a large man with a drooping mouth covered by a yellow mustache; one of the women is tall and gaunt, her face marked with smallpox scars; another is a gray, silent woman with an ashy complexion. In a week spent in Winesburg, Ohio, one would not see one person who could be remembered for two days. And at first the habits of these folk look commonplace enough, as they go about their business, for the most part silently, stopping to speak for a moment with Shorty Crandall, the clerk in Sylvester West's drugstore, or with Sid Green, who works in Myerbaum's notion store. For a time, these people seem like the country, pointless, monotonous.

But their behavior is not always so quiet. As they walk along the street, they sometimes mutter to themselves, and their hands twitch; now and then one of them breaks out and begins shouting a stream of incoherent words. And in private they are much less restrained. On rainy nights they walk endless miles alone through the country, or they run wildly through fields and woods, sometimes groaning and sobbing and rolling on the ground. And other of their ways are still odder. Evidently, their usual composure is only a mask worn with difficulty, and occasionally thrown off willy-nilly. For beneath the uniform flat surface seethes a life of extraordinary intensity, a life which manifests itself in periodic explosions. These inarticulate and unrational people, always brooding and always uncomprehending, have immortal longings in them, and they burst for brief instants into electric activity. By their outbreaks they vindicate their humanity and become real and living. The conflict of the submerged life with the meaningless surface produces drama and significance.

Anderson affords a key to the understanding of this country in his sentence, "The living force within could not find expression." The people are baffled because their lives offer no channel through which their vitality can discharge itself. That is why they are all, as he himself has more than once pointed out, grotesque, misshapen, deformed by their own bottled-up energy. They are uncomprehending because their world offers them nothing to comprehend; their existence is an interminable reiteration of meaningless detail, and the innate incapacity of man to be a vegetable makes the tragedy. This is the land, not of repressed, but of unfulfilled, desires. Nor, although sex plays an enormous rôle in this country, is it true that these desires are exclusively sexual. The drama is not chiefly the struggle of sex with convention, nor even the struggle of desire in general with convention or with inhibition of any sort. It is something vastly wider: it is the rebellion of all desire against the inanity of life. Like all other men and women, Anderson's are fired with longings, dreams, ideals, aspirations—but these they cannot even formulate, much less effectuate. Desire, in this land, instead of being a creative force, is destructive, devastating, thwarted and made futile by the lack of any means of realization, by the pointlessness of life. Over the whole scene broods the tragic pathos of futility and waste. Here, life is unbearable commonplace tempered by lunacy.

Because, in this country, everything important happens below the surface, Anderson does not often develop the setting to any great extent. His writing is not conspicuous for the sensuous imagination it evinces. His landscapes, for example, are much less fully visualized than those, say, of Miss Cather. He makes little appeal to eye and ear and nose. Solidity and density are not characteristic of his world; his background is given as fully as his theme requires, but no more: it is not dwelt on for its own sake. And so it is likewise with his characters: there are no complete, rounded-out portraits; they do not possess an independent, tri-dimensional existence of their own—compare them in this respect, for example, with the grotesques of Dickens. There is no one in Anderson's stories who is remembered as an individual like Quilp or Micawber. For Anderson's great faculty is not the imagination that bodies forth the form of things unseen, but rather the insight which probes and penetrates. Yet the process by which he works is not analytical dissection; he is not in the usual sense a "psychological" writer. That is, he does not take the motives of his people apart and explain them. Perhaps he could not if he wished. A man in *The Triumph of the Egg* says: "I have entered into lives. I have gone beneath the surface of the lives of men and women." Anderson might say the same; he has "entered into the lives of men and women" by an intuitive and imaginative process. It is as if he had witnessed or heard of an incident, and had then brooded over it until he had come to feel sympathetically and participate in the emotions of the people concerned—not at all by any conscious intellectual process. He truly "enters in," as if the experience had been his own. And he enables the reader to do the same—not to watch an experiment in vivisection, but to explore the depths of living personality by himself getting inside the skins of other men and women.

No wonder then if in his pursuit of the secret essence he tends to neglect the surface. Life in his rendering is stripped to the stark essentials. In his world, we are ever watching the interplay of elemental forces, as elemental as heat, magnetism, or gravitation. His people are dismantled energies, almost as abstract as the diagrams of a treatise on physics, as simple as a corked bottle half full of boiling water. The austere bareness of this art may displease readers accustomed to the more comfortably upholstered worlds of other novelists; yet it is a prime cause of his chief appeal—his intensity.

Beneath the impersonality of his manner, a keen, a piercing sympathy makes itself felt. His pity is the prime motor of his work; the pressure of his compassion gives his world its potency and concentration. In some strange way—I suppose because his stories are conceived in passion—he has the power to convey feeling directly, as it is conveyed in lyric poetry. Drayton's sonnet, "Since there's no help, come, let us kiss and part," or Burns' song, "Ane fond kiss, and then we sever," is no bad parallel for some of Anderson's stories: there is the same absence of characterization, of explanation, of everything except the one sharp essential feeling. At his best, Anderson conveys precisely that sense of constriction about the heart and that difficulty of breathing which one gets from the finest lyrics.

How he does it is a mystery. His style is plain and bare, yet in the extremity of its simpleness lies this power, perhaps because it is so unforced and altogether natural. The author feels his people and his story so strongly and enters into them so fully that he is led instinctively to record the significant details, the significant speeches and actions; and when they are recorded in the most direct and honest of words, they convey what he wishes to convey. His writing has the quality of a well scrubbed plank floor—its clean freshness, its frank homeliness, and its slight roughness and unevenness. He uses no subterfuges and no tricks. In part, his art consists in a remarkable freedom from artifice. He is the opposite of an "artful dodger"; he knows no smartness. Such utter straightforwardness as his is a triumph.

And it is as characteristic of his structure and narrative as of his diction. His stories are as devoid of plot as they are of all the devices taught by correspondence schools for producing salable fiction. His best stories seem to have no technique at all: each deals with an episode, a crisis in one or two lives, and Anderson first gives what information is needed concerning the participants, and then proceeds with his anecdote. As a writer, his outstanding trait is his integrity; to maintain such integrity against all the lures and pressures of twentieth-century America is a notable feat which speaks highly for his instinct as a workman. To possess not only the story-telling knack but also the critical sense and the severity of taste necessary for strict self-discipline—for certainly he received no outside aid of consequence—that is singular good fortune. Anderson must have been endowed with the rigorous conscience of the true craftsman. He has repeatedly stated that that is his ideal of writing: to deal with words with the same honest skill and solid workmanship with which a good carpenter treats wood or a mason stone. He wishes to make a handicraft of literature, and his success has not been small.

Although I have been speaking primarily of his short stories, much of what has been said applies also to his novels. Yet as works of art the latter are inferior. The more complex chain of incidents he handles with less skill. Moreover, his novels all have a thesis to maintain or a theme to develop; they are not mere stories, mere presentations of human life, and what they may gain in significance they tend to lose in intensity and actuality. The faculty which works well in the lesser medium is apparently incapable of grappling with, shaping, and sustaining a long work. The beginnings of *Windy McPherson's Son* and of *Marching Men* have the excellences of the tales except their final poignancy; but both novels in later portions lose the narrative and dramatic interest and become treatises. Much the same is true of *Poor White,* although the hero, Hugh McVey, is the most fully embodied of all Anderson's characters, and the treatise, if I may call it that, takes the form of an extremely interesting sketch of the coming of industrialism to Ohio. *Many Marriages* is a short-story fantasy amplified into an essay in mystical philosophy. *Dark Laughter,* in form the best of the novels, is too preoccupied with exemplifying a theory to give much of any sense of character.

Some twelve years ago Anderson wrote:

For a long time I have believed that crudity is an inevitable quality in the production of a really significant present-day American literature. How indeed is one to escape the obvious fact that there is as yet no native subtlety of thought or living among us? And if we are a crude and childlike people how can our literature hope to escape the influence of that fact? Why indeed should we want it to escape?

If his own work is taken as commentary, to explain what he means by "crude and childlike," the statement holds good, and is especially salutary when "sophistication" is all the vogue. American writers who decide to be sophisticated produce the literary equivalent of those wooden châteaux modeled on Blois and Amboise which were popular half a century ago. On the other hand, the best of current fiction has the quality of a well built stone barn. The difficulty is that the artisan needs not only honesty and skill, but good material. He cannot do first-class work with rubble and shale, and Anderson's performance suffers from the sort of stuff he has had to deal with. Compared with the imaginative worlds of any of the major British or French novelists, of Fielding or

Balzac, say, the world of his making is a little poor, in the sense that it lacks variety, body, massiveness. He gets powerful effects with gray and drab and tan, but it is a pity that his palette is not fuller. As diet for the imagination, as æsthetic experience, his work is somewhat spare and lean—but the responsibility for this deficiency rests, not with Anderson, who has done the best he could, but with his environment.

When the verisimilitude rather than the creative qualities of Anderson's writing is considered, the first result is hesitancy. Can this scanty land, this penurious world, be the Middle West, notoriously dropping with fatness? Is not Anderson's country too different from Dreiser's or Sandburg's or Lewis's for them all to be true? On the contrary, these several accounts, so far from being contradictory, dovetail together into a complete picture. Sinclair Lewis provides the inert, thickly varnished surface; Sandburg the background of natural loveliness and of man's works, beautiful and ugly; both Sandburg and Dreiser the hurly-burly of city life, and Dreiser also something of the underlying economic processes and of the life lived by the victors in the struggle. Furthermore, *Main Street* and *Babbitt*, *Sister Carrie* and *Jennie Gerhardt* have many points of contact with Anderson's work, in the stress they lay on helpless, fumbling unfulfillment; and Sandburg shows that he is not oblivious of this aspect of his world when he writes in "Halstead Street Car" of

Faces
Tired of wishes,
Empty of dreams.

In his earlier novels Anderson deals with the bustle of the city and with prosperity and success and industrialism, but the reader tends to forget that side of Anderson's work because the author himself is comparatively little interested in it. He treats by preference not the enemies of life, but life itself, such as it is, going on below the surface, with random irruptions through the crust. Because he has penetrated more deeply than any one else into the submerged portion of mid-American life, one remembers chiefly that aspect and thinks of him as portraying only the type with which he is most successful.

No doubt Anderson's writing gives only one or two phases out of many, and gives those as seen through a highly individual temperament; yet that he has captured not only artistic but social truth any one may demonstrate to himself by standing on a favorable corner in any small town or industrial community and watching the faces that pass—faces commonplace, dull, apparently lifeless, yet touched with unspeakable pathos. That the reading of Anderson leads to a heightened realization and a new perception is the best proof that his transcript is faithful to its original. And what he leads one to perceive afresh is the old familiar tragedy which one encounters in almost all our contemporary writers—spiritual frustration. "The living force within could not find expression": could there be a better statement of that specific tragedy, of desire balked by the insignificance of life, of potentialities squandered in futility and waste? I do not know where a sharper feeling could be found than Anderson's of the senseless destructiveness, the inane wastefulness, the ugliness triumphant, of a life which wrecks and crushes the insubstantial wishes and aspirations of men, of a life in which the individual, in his struggle for spiritual existence, always goes down to defeat, overcome by an environment which is hostile to the very nature of life.

The difficulty is that the society which Anderson portrays was devised not for humane ends and is conducted without care for humane values. Historically, as he points out in *A Story-Teller's Story,* this society is the legacy of pioneering. Towns, cheap and ugly, were thrown together regardless, only to serve as way-stations or trading-posts where the newcomers might push their private fortunes. The pioneer's motive, in carrying out which he was willing to suffer any hardship or deprivation, was personal advancement; consequently, he created a world ill adapted to other motives—created, in brief, a practical society which his descendants have inherited, as they have inherited, at least in part, his point of view. If most of them lack his fierce practical ambition, yet they are the heirs and the victims of a tradition which they do not care to carry on and which they are unable to get rid of. They are at a standstill, for they would like to live, but, having no facilities for such an undertaking, do not know how to set about it. Except for the natural setting, their world is hideous, in material objects, in human appearances, and in human character. To borrow a phrase from Van Wyck Brooks, it "sends up to heaven the stench of atrophied personality." For that reason, these people are incapable of themselves remedying the defects of their surroundings; they have no source of beauty within themselves, nor even a conscious desire for it. Many interests—the secondary intellectual and æsthetic interests—are scarcely to be expected in a rural community, which can do well enough without them if it has the essentials—proper work and play, communal social life, religion. But, because it provides no outlets, this world is stagnant; it is devoid of amusement, of pleasure; it is joyless because its people have never known how to get joy out of working and playing together. Worse still, it is no social organism, and worst of all, it is destitute of religion. What passes as religion among a few is a debased fanaticism; the great majority have none of any sort, yet their lives are made bleak by the influence of a once lively faith which degenerated first into a timid constraint and then into a mere dead weight.

Though much of the foregoing is touched upon in Anderson's social criticism, most of his comment is devoted to another side of the situation, a side to which his novels are largely devoted. *Windy McPherson's Son, Many Marriages,* and *Dark Laughter* all deal with men who have made business successes and who have found themselves still dissatisfied with the futility of their lives. *Marching Men* and *Poor White* handle the question of industrialism. In Anderson's mind, industrialism and success-worship are intimately related, more intimately, I think, than the facts warrant, inasmuch as the practical ideal, as witness Benjamin Franklin, long antedated the Machine Age. However, there is no doubt that for half a century the two have been combined. Anderson's theory is that after the pioneer age a new civilization was beginning to develop, having as basis the work of craftsmen:

. . . A slow culture growing up—growing as culture must always grow—through the hands of workmen.

In the small towns artisans coming in—the harness-maker, the carriage-builder, the builder of wagons, the smith, the tailor, the maker of shoes, the builders of houses and barns, too.

As Slade and James were to be the fathers of the modern gunmen, so these the fathers of the artists of the generations to come. In their fingers the beginning of that love of surfaces, of the sensual love of materials, without which no true civilization can ever be born.

And then, like a great flood over it all the coming of the factories, the coming of modern industrialism.

In *Poor White* he says of this transition:

. . . A sense of quiet growth awoke in sleeping minds. It was the time for art and beauty to awake in the land.

Instead, the giant, Industry, awoke.

And he describes the Age of Exploitation in words reminiscent of Henry Adams:

It was a time of hideous architecture, a time when thought and learning paused. Without music, without poetry, without beauty in their lives or impulses, a whole people, full of the native energy and strength of lives lived in a new land, rushed pell-mell into a new age.

Anderson hates the standardized inhumanity of machines and machine-slavery, as he hates that practical ambition which turns a young American into "a mere smart-aleck, without humbleness before the possibilities of life, one sure of himself" . . . "blind, deaf, and dumb, feeling and seeing nothing." There is nothing to add to Anderson's own words. Of our ten writers, he is by all odds the profoundest and most searching critic of American life.

One reason is that he has himself lived through the whole process more completely than any of the others. Born in 1876 in Camden, Ohio, he watched the coming of the factories, of which he writes; and furthermore, as he says, "I was to take up the cry myself and become one of the most valiant of the hustlers." He uses his own experience not only in his social criticism but in the themes of his novels: he himself at one time owned a small factory, but he grew dissatisfied and one day walked off and left it, as do Sam McPherson and John Stockton. He became a writer of advertisements, in which occupation he saw still more of the ways of the boosters. But he has also taken part in other kinds of American life; like Sandburg, he has been a day-laborer and a soldier; he has been a factory-hand; and he has drifted about doing odd jobs, especially in racing stables. He has seen much of the picaresque side of American life which rarely gets into books. He therefore knows from the inside many types of life which his contemporaries know if at all only as spectators. Sandburg, for instance, seems never to have been touched by the go-getter's philosophy, and Dreiser, who has framed his notion of the universe on what he saw as a reporter in slums and police-courts, has had a less wide experience than Anderson. Moreover, he is more critically minded than Sandburg, less confused than Dreiser, and more reflective than Sinclair Lewis.

Yet he has many of the traits of his own most typical characters: he too broods over what he cannot understand, and gropes for he knows not what; he too is puzzled and uncomprehending, so that he often gives the effect of being inarticulate, because he cannot translate his feelings and his intuitions into logical terms. He was long in coming to know his own mind; he published his first volume at the age of forty, after he had tried all sorts of other activities. Evidently, for him it was long true that "the living force within could not find expression." As he appears in his books, especially *A Story-Teller's Story,* he has no self-assurance, but is wistful and shy, full of humility, and above all of reverence. Nothing is plainer than that he is endowed with a strongly religious nature; one hears throughout his writing that cry of the heart which is the source of all religion. That this need has found no satisfaction is the explanation of much of his insatiate random seeking. He has not found life a friendly and easy medium in which to effectuate his desires. His environment has been blankly impervious to his wishes. Hence comes that sense of the pathos of life, of *lachrymæ rerum,* which pervades his work.

Anderson, I suspect, is more strongly oriented to the inner than to the outer life—not, of course, that he is detached from or indifferent to his surroundings, but that he cares more for the subjective than for the objective element in experience. According to this conjecture, he is in this respect at the opposite pole from Sandburg; he absorbs rather than is absorbed by what goes on about him; with a kind of reticence, he draws it into himself, but does not surrender himself to it. In his autobiography, he describes the extraordinary vividness which has always characterized the life of his fancy; a snatch of conversation overheard by chance, a person glimpsed on a street car, any occurrence however trivial, is enough to start a train of suggestions in his mind— and it is with these suggestions rather than with the people who initiate them that he is preoccupied.

If there be any truth in this guess, many peculiarities of his work can be accounted for. While to deny him a large capacity for experience would be wrong, yet to maintain that he is much more open to certain types of experience than to others is possible. This theory would explain why he shows comparatively little regard for sensations or sensuous beauty, and thus—since his chief interest is turned away from the external world of solid physical appearances—why his writing makes little appeal to the senses and also why he is most sensuous when he is most fanciful, as in John Webster's vision of the southern river with the negroes and their boats drifting through a forest. It would also explain his neglect of people's outsides—looks, behavior, mannerisms—in contrast with his uncanny insight and singularly direct feeling for obscure emotions and hidden motives. And finally it would account for the fact that his creation is not full-bodied, if not indeed slightly bloodless, a quality which betrays a certain lack of gusto and at times even the weariness of a spirit which has not been able to establish fruitful, invigorating contacts with the surrounding world.

Since Anderson's stories are the product of such a temperament as his working upon such surroundings as he has had, into the result must enter not only the peculiarities of his personality but the peculiarities of his environment. The comparative poverty of his imaginative world is due to the fact that the environment has been ill adapted to meet the needs of his particular mental bias. It has been rich in those qualities with which he is little concerned: in the beauty of nature, in the obvious commotion of city streets, in the achievements of a mechanic civilization, in all that spectacular pageantry with its violent contrasts of which Dreiser is enamoured, in all those external or non-human aspects which fascinate Sandburg. But it has been poor in the things for which Anderson cares, for his interest is in the human soul, in dramatic or poetic human values, and in the relations and interactions of men and women with one another. Here his world has failed him, for it has been most deficient in the riches of human nature, in emotion, aspiration, endeavor, achievement, reverence, integrity—in the human quality which comes from work well and lovingly done, and in all those results for the human spirit of full lives well lived. Therefore his imagination has had to feed upon a somewhat scanty fare; his misfortune has been to live in a society which, being by its constitution practical and by its profession repressively moralistic and thus adverse to the life of realization, has deprived its members of satisfaction in work, of emotional and religious experience, and of well ordered social life, and has consequently failed in the development of full-grown personalities.

Except for the signs it shows of undernourishment, Anderson's work is singularly free from the qualities which are to be expected of the literature produced in such a society. In his pamphlet *The Modern Writer* he discusses the prostitution and standardization and sentimentality which are imposed upon popular literature among a people who do not value the poetic temper, but he himself has never yielded to the pressure, as he himself, so far as his writing is concerned, is remarkably immune from the dominant point of view. His imagination may have been somewhat starved, but it has not been warped. In spite of his critical attitude, he has not developed that hatred of his environment which prevents experience and leads to fleeing from reality into weak romantic reverie; at most, he betrays now and then a perhaps undue self-distrust and self-consciousness. In his work he has shown no instability or uncertainty of aim; from the first he has known what he was about. His sense of fact and truth of feeling have survived unharmed. Unlike many contemporaries, he is not deficient in critical sense and discipline. Yet in this respect he has not escaped altogether unscathed; not only did he find no aid or guidance outside himself, but it was only in spite of everything that he finally found his proper vocation. Not until comparatively late in life did he come in contact with a current of living thought, with men who debated vital questions of art, literature, and society. The strengthening he felt from this outside corroboration of his purposes he has amply acknowledged. But had he encountered something of the sort a decade or two earlier, his work might have profited, and surely his thought would have benefited in that it would have been less fumbling and drifting, would have had a somewhat more assured central point of rest.

Even so, of course, Anderson is too much the seeker ever to have arrived at a hard-and-fast philosophy. Among our present writers, he is one of the few real mystics. At first glance, he may look like much the same sort of naturalist as the others. The world as shown in his portrayal is naturalistic, like the world of Henry Adams, Sandburg, and Dreiser—chaotic, unintelligible, purposeless, with man the sport and victim of forces he cannot understand or control. It is a futile and a tragic world; yet Anderson, unlike certain others, does not make the assumption that it has always been and must always continue to be futile and disordered. He does not first reduce American behavior to a theory of life and then erect it into a scheme of the universe. His standard is never quantitative, and he is never an uncritical worshiper of mere force. The law of the jungle is not for him eternal and immutable. He obscurely apprehends that there may be a solution and a remedy, and this solution he finds in a mystical relation between the human unit and the universe. His quest has always been for the source of a more abundant life, and such a source he discovers in a union or identification of the individual with something outside himself, a merging of the single personality in something larger. Hence his preoccupation with the breaking down of the walls and barriers that hem in and isolate each man and separate him from the world about him and from the others of his kind.

In *A Story-Teller's Story* there are records of two unmistakable mystical experiences. One is the magnificent espisode of John Berners, than which Anderson has written nothing finer, which led him to ask himself whether one had "to come to the realization that oneself did not matter, that nothing mattered but a kind of consciousness of the wonder of life outside oneself," and which, in spite of his "having no God, the gods having been taken from me by the life about me, as a personal God has been taken from all modern men by a force within that man himself does not understand but that is called the intellect," ended thus:

I had suddenly an odd, and to my own seeming a ridiculous, desire to abase myself before something not human and so stepping into the moonlit road I knelt in the dust.

The other experience, which is plainly the foundation of *Marching Men,* Anderson had while in the army.

The constant marching and manœuvring was a kind of music in the legs and bodies of men. No man is a single thing, physical or mental. The marching went on and on. The physical ruled. There was a vast slow rhythm, out of the bodies of many thousands of men, always going on and on. It got into one's body. There was a kind of physical drunkenness produced. . . . One was afloat on a vast sea of men. There was a kind of music on the surface of the sea. The music was a part of oneself. One was oneself a part of the music. One's body, moving in rhythm with all these other bodies, made the music. . . . One's body was tired but happy with an odd new kind of happiness. The mind did not torture the body, asking questions. The body was moved by a power outside itself.

Since, as he says, he has no God, Anderson's is a nature-mysticism much like Whitman's. He advocates a return to a simpler and more primitive way of life, to the condition of savages and even of beasts and plants. In his first novel he wrote:

American men and women have not learned to be clean and noble and natural, like their forests and their wide, clean plains.

This point of view is at the root of his affection and admiration for horses and negroes; it recurs again and again in his stories, and explains his choice of title for his novel *Dark Laughter*. Hence comes his hatred of the intellect, as a dividing, separating force which will not let man "just be, like a horse or a dog or a bird." That is why he usually joins "dry" and "sterile" with "intellectual." As a character in *The Triumph of the Egg* exclaims:

What makes you want to read about life? What makes people want to think about life? Why don't they live? Why don't they leave books and thoughts and schools alone?

Even one who holds that the intellect need not be an impoverishing factor in experience and that to live like the animals is neither a feasible nor a desirable solution of the human problem may still concede that it would be better to live so than not to live at all, and be grateful to Anderson for the emphasis he lays on the importance of living.

The gist of all his philosophy is in these passages from *A Story-Teller's Story:*

Could it be that force, all power, was a disease, that man on his way up from savagery and having discovered the mind and its uses had gone a little off his head in using his new toy? I had always been drawn toward horses and dogs and other animals and among people had cared most for simple folk who had no pretense of having an intellect, workmen who in spite of the handicaps put in their way by modern life still loved the materials in which they worked, who loved the play of hands over materials, who followed instinctively a force outside themselves they felt to be greater and more worthy than themselves—women who gave themselves to physical experiences with grave and fine abandon, all people in fact who lived for something outside themselves, for materials in which they worked, for people other than themselves, things over which they made no claim of ownership. . . .

When you take from man the cunning of the hand, the opportunity to constantly create new forms in materials, you make him impotent. His maleness slips imperceptibly from him and he can no longer give himself in love, either to work or to women. "Standardization! Standardization!" was to be the cry of my age and all standardization is necessarily a standardization in impotence. It is God's law. Women who choose childlessness for themselves choose also impotence— perhaps to be the better companions for the men of a factory, a standardization age. To live is to create constantly new forms: with the body in living children; in new and more beautiful forms carved out of materials; in the creation of a

world of the fancy; in scholarship; in clear and lucid thought;
and those who do not live die and decay and from decay
always a stench arises.

These passages make clear Anderson's reason for laying
so great stress on craftsmanship and sex: he conceives
both as means by which man escapes from his prison cell
and joins himself to a larger life and a larger world, as
implements by which to destroy the partitions between
man and nature, between man and man, and between man
and woman. He recognizes the mystical element in love
of every sort, and he ranks love of creative work and
sexual love first. The theme of sex is thus treated in
Many Marriages, and in the most enigmatic and most unusual of his tales, and also the most avowedly mystical,
"The Man's Story" in *Horses and Men.* I do not understand this story, but so far as I can decipher a meaning
it is that through the love and possession of one woman
a man may attain to a similar kind of union with the
whole world. If sometimes one is tempted to demur at
what seems Anderson's obsession with sex, one must remember that sex is for him a key to a larger experience.

In his theory and thought, then, as well as in his practice, Anderson is a thorough-going champion of the
poetic temper and of the life of realization against all
their enemies. His work, for all its high merit within its
severe limitations, has quite as much social as literary
importance. No other poet, novelist, or dramatist is so
fully conscious of the American situation or drives it
home so forcibly as does Anderson, both in his imaginative creation and in his critical comment. His picture
of human starvation and frustration, his historical explanation of the condition he presents, his suggestions

concerning the way to a better and fuller life—all combine to lend him a unique significance in present American letters. In this achievement, he has brought into play all his faculties: he has used his insight into the natures of other people; to communicate his discoveries, he has availed himself to the best of his ability of his power as story-teller and worker in words; he has thought over what he has experienced and discerned in an effort to extract its import; in opposition to every outside influence, he has followed his bent and maintained his integrity. The appearance on the literary scene of such a man is a heartening portent.

BIBLIOGRAPHY

ANDERSON, SHERWOOD. *Windy McPherson's Son.* New York, 1916. Revised edition, New York, 1922, The Viking Press.

———*Marching Men.* New York, 1917, The Viking Press.

———*Mid-American Chants.* New York, 1918, The Viking Press.

———*Winesburg, Ohio.* New York, 1919, The Viking Press.

———*Poor White.* New York, 1920, The Viking Press.

———*The Triumph of the Egg.* New York, 1921, The Viking Press.

———*Many Marriages.* New York, 1923, The Viking Press.

———*Horses and Men.* New York, 1923, The Viking Press.

———*A Story-Teller's Story.* New York, 1924, The Viking Press.

———*Dark Laughter.* New York, 1925, Boni & Liveright.

SPOKESMEN

ANDERSON, SHERWOOD. *The Modern Writer.* San Francisco, 1925, Gelber, Lilienthal.

——— *Tar, a Midwest Childhood.* New York, 1926, Boni & Liveright.

——— *Sherwood Anderson's Notebook.* New York, 1926, Boni & Liveright.

——— *A New Testament.* New York, 1927, Boni & Liveright.

CHASE, CLEVELAND. *Sherwood Anderson.* New York, 1927, Robert M. McBride & Company.

VII

WILLA CATHER

T O the query whether it is possible for an artist to exist in the United States, the best answer would be: Go read Miss Cather. Her chief importance is neither historical nor social, but literary. True, she has done her part in the recording of American life; she has played, though not often, the rôle of critic of society; no doubt she and her work are products of the United States, in so far as any art and any artist must be affected by environment. Yet primarily it is as an artist that she is of interest. However one may estimate her achievement, no one, I think, will deny that fact. That her art has undergone development, that it was not born full grown, that it has been evolved in spite of difficulties both internal and external, all only serve to lend additional significance to her present position. Because, whatever may once have been the case, she is not now tied up in social influences, not "bogged and mired" in American conditions, because she has worked herself free from entanglements, she makes clearer what current literature has to reveal concerning the present United States: she shows that the American writer need have no peculiar or invidious relation to American life.

Miss Cather has been somewhat slow in bringing to fulfillment her talents and her purposes, and her progress has followed a zig-zag course. Her intention and her conception of her art have altered more than once. She began her career while still an undergraduate at the University of Nebraska; during her first three years, she wrote sketches of the immigrants whom she had known during her girlhood on the prairies, with the wish merely, it appears, to note down her observations and perhaps to defend people whom she thought misjudged. Not until her senior year, she has said, did she become interested in the art of writing for its own sake: "In those days, no one seemed so wonderful as Henry James; for me, he was the perfect writer." The reader of *Alexander's Bridge* is prepared to learn of this early enthusiasm, which indeed has left its traces in Miss Cather's later work as well; according to Miss Cather herself:

In *Alexander's Bridge* I was still more preoccupied with trying to write well than with anything else. It takes a great deal of experience to become natural. A painter or writer must learn to distinguish what is his own from that which he admires. . . . What I always want to do is to make the writing count for less and less and the people for more. I am trying to cut out all analysis, observation, description, even the picture-making quality, in order to make things and people tell their own story simply by juxtaposition, without any persuasion or explanation on my part. . . . Mere cleverness must go. I'd like the writing to be so lost in the object that it doesn't exist for the reader.

If her work is considered in connection with the preceding statement, which was made while Miss Cather was writing *One of Ours*, three stages are clearly perceptible in her development, in the first of which her object was to set down facts as accurately as possible, and in the second of which she busied herself with mastering her technique. The third stage may seem a return to the first, yet wrongly; for in it she is engaged primarily not in the faithful reproduction of an external reality but in telling a story—in creation, that is, not in imitation. And with *The Professor's House,* perhaps one may say, a fourth stage supervened, in which additional subtler motives of interpretation as well as presentation are at work. At any rate, since her student days her main interest has been not in mimicking actuality but in practicing one of the fine arts. In spite of all she may have said about being natural, it is obvious that so far from abandoning art in favor of a return to nature, she has simply altered her conception of art. Ever since her discovery of Henry James she has been the conscious artist, most of all in her efforts to conceal her art. And this shift in her views on writing has been accompanied by a corresponding change of emphasis in her choice of themes and in her treatment of her material.

The point that during the third stage of her progress, the stage to which belong all her novels from *O Pioneers!* to *A Lost Lady,* Miss Cather was first of all a creative artist, must be stressed, because many reviewers assumed that she was producing a sort of combined guide book and history of Nebraska. They insisted that *My Antonia* has "historical value for its minute and colorful depiction of life on the Nebraska prairies and in the Nebraska towns about 1885," that Miss Cather's volumes contain "a clear picture of the life of pioneers," that she "evidently studied this immigrant life close at hand," and that she has "reproduced it almost with the fidelity of a kodak picture or a graphonola record." No doubt her work has this anthropological interest; and no doubt, furthermore, those who thought of her chiefly as a recorder have this justification, that even after reaching maturity she has seemed at times so to regard herself. Her interest in the peculiarities of Nebraskan life has obviously been intense, and she has sometimes dwelt on them for their own sake. *O Pioneers!* is dedicated to the memory of Sarah Orne Jewett, "in whose beautiful and delicate work there is the perfection that endures," and Miss Cather has been much influenced by Miss Jewett, to whom she is indebted for friendly counsel as to the proper practice of her art. Possibly at one time she hoped to do for Nebraska what Miss Jewett had done for Maine; *O Pioneers!* is full of scenes which have no other end in view than verisimilitude, than local color, quaint and picturesque. Even *My Antonia,* though it shows marked advance, is still profuse in detail and minute in observation; it too contains many idyllic genre pictures which are their own excuse for being. But in *One of Ours* the background, though extensively developed, is kept in its place; and in *A Lost Lady* the setting is made altogether subservient to the theme, which is in nowise peculiar to a locality.

Yet Miss Cather was not an old-fashioned local colorist even when she wrote *O Pioneers!;* its appeal is not mainly to the curiosity which likes to see how people live in strange places, but to universal emotions. It draws from wells of feeling at which Miss Jewett never dipped, though it lacks Miss Jewett's "perfection that endures." Alexandra's struggle with the soil, though it could occur only in a new country, is epic, not quaint, in quality; and Emil's tragic love, which holds the center throughout the second part, is a subject unrestricted as to time and place. *O Pioneers!* is distinguished chiefly for a sense of essential human nature and above all of tragic passion. Alexandra might have been—is, almost—a classic heroine. The weakness of the novel is not that it is limited in range, but that it is not focused. The author's aim is scattering, her interest divided among two themes and a desire to tell the world about immigrant life in Nebraska.

In *My Antonia* the irrelevancies have been enormously reduced; the background is almost all required for the presentation of the subject, the portrait of Antonia, upon which all attention is concentrated. And Antonia herself, so far from being peculiar to an age or a region, has the quality of the immemorial. *A Lost Lady* has attained classic severity; the development away from snap-shot photography and from uncertainty of aim is complete. Mrs. Forrester's career would have been different in details only, not in essentials, in another setting, under the Ancien Régime or in Ancient Rome; no one even thought of dismissing her as a painstaking study of a Nebraskan type. Although in choosing the indirect method of narration Miss Cather returned to the example of Henry James, she has achieved, in her subordination of all detail, in her clarity and unity and order, in the apparent ease which shows her mastery, in her restraint and finish, a rigorous perfection of form for which there is no word but classic.

With *A Lost Lady*, Miss Cather arrived at what can only be called perfection in her art. Since then, her gain, which has been marked, has been not in her mastery of form—in which further gain was hardly possible—so much as in the substance of her novels. The change, to put it briefly, has been that she has penetrated farther into the mysterious depths of personality. *A Lost Lady,* I think, shows more of this penetration than its predecessors, but is surpassed in this respect by *The Professor's House, My Mortal Enemy,* and *Death Comes for the*

Archbishop. These books have all a complexity and an inscrutability of which there is none in the earlier novels, and only a trace in *A Lost Lady.* The theme, or at least the chief theme, of Godfrey St. Peter's story, is a strange sinking or regression of desire and of energy, of the love of life, which almost causes his death before he sees the necessity of learning to "live without delight"; and this state of mind is linked on the one hand with the difficulties that attend a newly acquired prosperity and on the other with a psychological return to his youth, partly to his own childhood, to the primitive that he had been as a boy, but still more to his youth in imaginatively sharing the experience, primitive like his own, of Tom Outland. Again, Myra Henshawe, who asks: "Why must I die like this, alone with my mortal enemy?" raises questions as difficult as does St. Peter: Miss Cather entered into those intricate secrets of the heart which are insoluble. And in *Death Comes for the Archbishop,* if these mysteries are more lightly touched upon, they are none the less present.

To speak thus of these books, however, is no doubt to give one who has not read them a false impression. They are not in the usual sense of the term "psychological novels," or novels dealing with psychological problems: Miss Cather does not dissect and explain her people; she presents them, but more, so to speak, from the inside— presents not only their surfaces but their most hidden recesses. This presentation is perhaps less simple and direct, and is accomplished somewhat more by use of implication and symbol, and is more colored or shot through with interpretation—but she is still making "things and people tell their own story." Furthermore, the aspect of the stories upon which I have been dwelling

is only one among many: these are novels which are
conspicuous for their many-sided richness and fullness,
for their commingling of many interests. In particular,
Death Comes for the Archbishop is a portrait of a whole
country and of a whole era and a whole society, as well
as of individuals and their interrelations. Finally, one
thing certain about these recent books is that they mark
Miss Cather's total emancipation from Nebraska.

As her conception of her art has deepened, then, her
artistic power has correspondingly grown, and not in her
management of form alone: especially she has strength-
ened that particular power which is all-important to the
novelist, power in the delineation of character, power by
virtue of her words to make people live in her pages.
The change, in a word, is that she has become increasingly
objective. Perhaps it is because our knowledge of
actual people is derived solely from the outside, from
seeing and hearing them, that the objective treatment
is so superior to the analytical, that in novels the characters are dissipated, vaporized, by explanation and dissection; however that may be, it is certain that as Miss
Cather has restricted herself to showing us her people,
they have taken on a firmer reality. In *O Pioneers!* there
is much description and elucidation of character; in *My
Antonia* comparatively little, the people being so solidly
set before us that little is needed; and in the later novels
there is practically none. If in these it is true that we
know the characters from within as well as from without,
and if these stories are psychological in the sense that the
main events take place in the mind only, yet these events
are exhibited rather than explained.

Her insistence on objectivity no doubt explains Miss
Cather's success in the biography and portrait-painting to

which she is inclined in preference to drama. The reader can fully visualize the appearance of her people; he knows what they look like, as well as what they think and feel. They are independent and three-dimensional, made of substantial flesh and blood, entirely projected. Their pictures and their natures are depicted by a multitude of minute touches, none of which in itself seems of much moment. Of this the early chapters of *One of Ours* afford excellent illustrations—work to which justice has not been done because the second half of the book is disappointing. Miss Cather brings Claude himself, his family, and his associates visibly before us and gives us an intimate knowledge of their personalities by infinitesimal but graphic detail. This cannot be illustrated by quotation; without the context, the fact that "Claude muttered something to himself, twisting his chin about over his collar as if he had a bridle-bit in his mouth" looks insignificant; yet in its place that sentence contains all of Claude Wheeler. It is subtle, strong, and penetrating. Such portraiture is the result of insight and imagination, as well as of observation.

Being primarily a biographer concerned with transmitting a sense of the personalities of her people, Miss Cather is comparatively indifferent to action, whether narrative or dramatic. She eschews exciting incident, and she is sparing of those scenes and deeds in which character is elicited and crystallized and made permanently memorable. True, as Stevenson says, "this is the highest and hardest thing to do in words; the thing which, once accomplished, equally delights the schoolboy and the sage"; yet the novelist who foregoes the appeal of the big scene, in which character and emotion at their utmost come to a crisis in physical action, is foregoing the strongest appeal which literature commands. It is the height of fiction, and I doubt whether any story-teller who lacks it can attain greatness. It is not altogether absent even from Miss Cather's earlier books—witness the snowstorm in *One of Ours* and the scene with the long-distance telephone in *A Lost Lady*—but for the most part until lately her scenes have tended rather to idyllic picture than to dramatic crisis or stirring action.

Not that excitement is absent from her earlier novels, but that it is commonly obtained in them by other means than the dramatic, by means similar to those she employs in her characterization, by the use, that is, of details and minutiæ. Sidney Howard has well said of her: "To treat the small facts and the microscopic phenomena of every-day as significant of the dominant energies and emotions of living, this pretty generally is the woman's method of novel-writing." So Miss Cather has imparted her thrills, by means of the subtly significant. In *A Lost Lady*, Neil overhears the murmur of two voices, a man's and a woman's, or Captain Forrester picks up a letter written by his wife and comments on the handwriting— such are the exciting crises of the story. It is such incidents, commonly two or three to a novel, that give intensity to Miss Cather's work. Her most recent writing, to be sure, may indicate some development on Miss Cather's part, for in Tom Outland's story and still more in some of the episodes of *Death Comes for the Archbishop* there is more narrative interest, and in *My Mortal Enemy*, there is tenser drama—there is more in all three of these of what Stevenson called "the highest and hardest thing to do in words"—than in any of the preceding volumes. Yet even if she is learning to sustain a longer lift and sweep, I should say that she still stirs the reader chiefly by means of the detail charged with meaning, the implication which creates a brief flash and a sharp, poignant instant.

If in her method of characterization and in her handling of intense crises Miss Cather is feminine, she is not pecularily so in all her qualities. Nothing is more striking than the vein of hardness, as of iron or flint, that runs through her world. Sometimes it is harsh, even brutal. No other trait of hers is more impressive than her sense of fact, her clearness of eyesight and honesty of mind. Yet her hardness is not incompatible with sensitiveness; those who confound strength with crudity will get no comfort from her. Her work is refined and fastidious; these qualities, however, come not from squeamishness, not from shrinking, timorous *noli me tangere* which vitiates much American writing, but from disciplined taste and controlled force. In *A Lost Lady* she has achieved an exquisite delicacy without fragility, and in *The Professor's House* she has carved a set of Chinese filigree boxes, one within another, out of a substance as firm as ivory; it would be difficult to find two stories at once more subtle and more powerful than *My Mortal Enemy* and *Death Comes for the Archbishop*. Hers is the delicacy and the refinement of mastery, not of weakness; her uncommon union of fineness and strength more than anything else distinguishes her among her contemporaries.

Oddly enough, it looks as if Miss Cather's truth of feeling were at least in part an acquired trait, self-imposed and self-cultivated. That she has avoided a dangerous pitfall there is evidence in her earlier work, particularly in *O Pioneers!* The chapters leading up to Frank Shabata's murder of his wife and Emil are admirable in their austerity, the most moving in the book; and then, at the very climax, is found this passage:

But the stained, slippery grass, the darkened mulberries, told only half the story. Above Marie and Emil, two white butterflies from Frank's alfalfa-field were fluttering in and out among the interlacing shadows; diving and soaring, now close together, now far apart; and in the long grass by the fence the last wild roses of the year opened their pink hearts to die

The butterflies are bad enough, but the roses surely are unforgivable. All one can say is that such roses open their pink hearts with less and less frequency in her later books and have long since become extinct; they are only a sign of a tendency which Miss Cather has conquered, but of one, nevertheless, which she has had to conquer. Downright sentimentality, it is true, is rare even in her first writing, but a tender sensibility and a wistful mood of reverie are not uncommon in her prose, and are dominant in her verse, *April Twilights,* of which the title is itself symptomatic, and in which prettiness of sentiment is general. These poems show how easily Miss Cather might have gone off on the sentimental track, had she not known better; they show to what extent the unsentimental tone of her novels is due to conscious elimination and restraint. Miss Cather's taste has not always been faultless.

Many signs—her not infrequent sentiment and rare sentimentality, her original difficulty in focusing her subject, her early inclination to irrelevancies, her initial preoccupation with local color, avoidance of big scenes, dramatic crises, and stirring action, and infrequent communication of emotion, and then by implication—all point to a central limitation in Miss Cather. Hers is an extraordinarily conscious art, and in the beginning one chiefly of conscious exclusion. Her original deficiency, I hazard, was in the high pressure and the intense heat of imagination which fuse material and burn out impurities. Surely a writer who is sufficiently possessed by his theme does not have to lop off irrelevancies, to be always on his guard. He finds appropriate expression, with difficulty perhaps, but instinctively; his expression may sometimes be inadequate, but it cannot be false. Such intensity of conception I suggest that Miss Cather has had to acquire. The completed work was not at first the crystallization of the conception; if it had been, she would not have been tempted to digress or to strike false notes. Her unity she attained, not under compulsion of an inner force, but by careful pruning off of excrescences. Her earlier novels seem not to have grown from a germ but to have been put together. They look as if she were afraid of letting herself go, as if reticence were her only defense, and she had need to be watchful. This defect was hinted by Francis Hackett:

It is her admirable gift to discern certain excellent themes and to treat them with fastidiousness and sympathy. It is apparently the paucity of her gift that she does so deliberately, with her inspiration perfectly in hand. . . . She burns illuminatingly and steadily, but mainly because she is sane and capable.

Her signal skill in her self-management is a token of her extraordinary tact and taste. She has developed a remarkably keen critical sense, and has subjected herself to the strictest sort of discipline. The result is even better than one would have thought possible: all adages to the contrary notwithstanding, she has added several cubits to her stature. One no sooner thinks that he detects her limitations than she triumphantly outgrows them, until at last one learns to look forward expectantly to unpredictable improvement, believing that Miss Cather is capable of anything—or everything.

Her style is a case in point. Until her later writing seldom was there emotional tension or lift in her language, seldom did it rise to a dramatic pitch and communicate strong feeling directly. Within its range, however, it was marked by a quiet, unobtrusive competence and on occasion by what Randolph Bourne called a "golden charm." As another critic remarked: "Her style has distinction, not manner"; simple, easy, lucid, and smooth, it has always had finish and beauty of texture— the texture of broadcloth, rather than of silk or of homespun. Yet when a reviewer wrote, in the London *Athenæum:* "Her real shortcoming is that she is at present quite without a 'style': placed beside any European model of imaginative prose she is dowdy and rough, wanting in rhythm and distinction," he was not indulging merely in the absurd blundering common to English discussion of American books; he was justified to the extent only that Miss Cather's way of writing is inconspicuous, as she wishes it to be, and in a sense impersonal. It stands outside the English tradition; its polish is not that shiny gloss imparted by the *eloquentia* which Englishmen have learned from French and Latin. Her style is her own natural mode of expression painstakingly cultivated, and it constitutes a perfectly modulated instrument which can attain to surprising range of compass and volume.

Nowhere does Miss Cather manifest her power over

words more successfully than in her description, especially of nature. I trust she will never manage, if she still desires, to eliminate "the picture-making quality," and suppress such passages as this:

There were no clouds, the sun was going down in a limpid, gold-washed sky. Just as the lower edge of the red disc rested on the high fields against the horizon, a great black figure suddenly appeared on the face of the sun. We sprang to our feet, straining our eyes toward it. In a moment we realized what it was. On some upland farm, a plough had been left standing in the field. The sun was sinking just behind it. Magnified across the distance by the horizontal light, it stood out against the sun, was exactly contained within the circle of the disc; the handles, the tongue, the share—black against the molten red. There it was, heroic in size, a picture-writing on the sun.

For sheer sustained beauty of description I know nothing that surpasses the account of the Blue Mesa in *The Professor's House*—far too lovely and too cumulative to injure by quotation. Here, unless it is the pictorial element in *Death Comes for the Archbishop,* is the final triumph of a gift in which Miss Cather has always been eminent, of evoking concrete sensuous imagery, an ability which lends full-bodied solidity as well as beauty to her work. Not only is she thoroughly alive herself to the appeals of the senses, but she is able to impart her impressions with added glamour. As in Hardy's novels, though less obviously, the setting which she so creates plays an integral part in her stories, as in *The Professor's House* always behind the figure of St. Peter, as well as of Tom Outland, stands the huge purplish mass of the Blue Mesa, and as in *Death Comes for the Archbishop* the land is independently and for its own sake as interesting and as important as any of the persons. The way in which the farm traps Claude in *One of Ours* is plain enough; and in *O Pioneers!* and *My Antonia* the rôle is yet more evident: the land becomes a great antagonist in the dramatic conflict. The plains and prairies, friendly or hostile, are always present—often terrible but always beautiful, most terrible and most beautiful in winter. The sense of space which they add is all important in lending an effect of greatness to the novels, an epic scope which would have been denied by a more restricted background.

In all the novels from *O Pioneers!* to *One of Ours,* the human life which is set in this country is closely related to it either by sympathy or by contrast. Among Miss Cather's protagonists, the women have a peculiar kinship with the land: they are simple, primeval, robust with a strain of hardness, heroic. Alexandra is a heroine of the Sagas, Thea Kronborg in *The Song of the Lark* has the integrity of a single driving force, Antonia is elemental motherhood. Much of the quality of these figures is in this picture of Antonia:

She lent herself to immemorial human attitudes which we recognize by instinct as universal and true. . . . She was a battered woman now, not a lovely girl; but she still had that something which fires the imagination, could still stop one's breath for a moment by a look or gesture that somehow revealed the meaning in common things. She had only to stand in the orchard, to put her hand on a little crab tree and look up at the apples, to make you feel the goodness of planting and tending and harvesting at last. . . . It was no wonder that her sons stood tall and straight. She was a rich mine of life, like the founders of early races.

The only adequate comment on this is Carl Van Doren's:

It is not easy even to say things so illuminating about a human being; it is all but impossible to create one with such sympathetic art that words like these at the end confirm and interpret an impression already made.

On the other hand, the young men in the early books, including Claude Wheeler of *One of Ours* and Neil Herbert of *A Lost Lady,* are antipathetic to the environment; they are sensitive, artistic, idealistic, deficient in force if not weaklings, fitted to thrive in favorable conditions but unable to conquer difficulties. A more complicated social picture is presented by *One of Ours, A Lost Lady,* and their successors, a wider range and greater diversity of character, and less typical, more sharply individualized portraits. The Wheeler household and Claude's friends, Mrs. Forrester and her husband, the old railroad pioneer, Professor St. Peter and all his family and in-laws, Tom Outland and Rodney Blake, even the seamstress Augusta; above all, Myra and Oswald Henshawe, and not only the Bishop and his friend, but the minor characters such as Señora Olivares—they have the variety and the separate uniqueness of life itself. Humanly speaking, Miss Cather's world is not made to fit a plan or theory and it is growing constantly richer in its multiplicity.

Yet her favorite theme persists throughout: the conflict of the superior individual with an unworthy society. And since this society is her version of the world in which she has lived—of the West primarily, and incidentally of the United States—it may be taken to embody implicitly her conception of American life. Her view is that the pioneers in general were folk largely endowed with creative power and imagination, but that the second generation, except for a few artists who have inherited the spirit of the fathers, has degenerated and succumbed to the tyranny of ease and money and things. Usually she sets off society against the background of natural grandeur. I cannot agree with Van Doren that she has few revenges to take on her environment. On the contrary, her scarification of it, repeated again and again, is as vitriolic as that of any contemporary. The American community, whether family or town or neighborhood, is always the villain of the piece. It is the foe of life; it is worse than sterile—deadly, poisonous, adverse to human growth, hostile to every humane quality. She shows us communities of people who are little and petty but withal complacent and self-satisfied, who are intolerant and contemptuous of what differs from themselves, who are tightly bound by conventionality—not the sort that springs from free, deliberate approval of conventions, but the sort that has its source in cowardice, stupidity, or indolence—of people who hate whatever does not jibe with their twopenny ha'penny aims, who hate everything genuine and human—genuine thought, or religion, or righteousness, or beauty—everything that means being genuinely alive, everything that shows true mind or feeling or imagination. In consequence, the living individual is not only of necessity isolated and cut off from sustaining human relationships, but thwarted and frustrated so far as possible. There is no social life save among peripheral settlements of foreigners. No wonder Miss Cather's characters find more sustenance in the companionship of the prairies than of their neighbors; the prairies are better company.

For such folk as her Nebraskan protagonists, placed in

such a natural and human world as theirs, life is bound to have a tragic aspect, for it is bound to involve a needless waste of human possibilities. Whether their undertakings end in success or in failure, the waste, and therefore the tragic element, is there: if they fail, as Antonia and Mrs. Forrester do in part, and as Claude does wholly so far as his struggle with his surroundings is concerned, they are thrown away because their world is not worthy of them; if, like Alexandra and Thea, they succeed, it is at a great cost in suffering and in a sort of hardening of the spiritual arteries.

Yet the upshot of Miss Cather's tragedy is not a meaningless futility, for there is compensation in the very fineness which separates her characters from their neighbors. Theirs is not a tragedy of frustration, for even at the worst they have been true to themselves and maintained their own integrity. Besides, one infers from Miss Cather's work, the only real failure is indifference, tepidity, timidity, the fear which shrinks from encountering experience and possible unhappiness, for the reason that to have lived so, without passion and without valor, is not to have lived at all. To have cared intensely about anything, even if one has not gained it, is to have lived not altogether in vain; mere living, living as ardently, as wholeheartedly as possible, is an end that justifies itself. Miss Cather always tacitly champions the poetic temper and the life of realization against practicality. The quarrel between the two furnishes the theme of *The Song of the Lark* and of *One of Ours,* and is prominent in *O Pioneers!* and *My Antonia,* as well as in most of her short stories. All her chief characters have the poetic point of view, and are forced by their viewpoint into conflict with their families and neighbors.

Miss Cather sees the faults of American life clearly enough; that, unlike some contemporaries, she does not take refuge in sheer denunciation, nor accept it as the only possible life, nor inveigh against the useless sense-lessness of all life, is an indication of her poise. If she is not ready with remedies, beyond illustrating what she holds to be the proper point of view, it is because she is too much occupied with making the most of her world to fret over causes and cures. She writes without the rancor of disillusionment because she has perfect balance. She has a sanity and a wholeness which prevent her from being one-sided. For example, she does not exalt the body with contempt for the mind, nor does she go to the other extreme: though she knows that passion is rooted in physical vigor, she sees the man or woman as one piece, alive in both body and spirit, with therefore a strong vein of sensuality which may find its proper outlet, as Antonia's does in motherhood, but which may prove calamitous as it does to Mrs. Forrester. This sense of personal completeness may account for her preference for robust if simple types, and for her liking for the primitive, evident in *The Professor's House* and elsewhere, on the ground that modern civilization has entailed the loss of elements essential to an entire human development.

The shrewdest criticism yet made of Miss Cather is that she represents "the triumph of mind over Nebraska." Not only has she found matter for literature—which in itself speaks highly for her keen scent and her avidity for experience—but she has converted that matter into the universal forms of art. If the victory was not bloodless, if it left its scars, if some of her books suffer in comparison with those of writers who have grown in a more fertile society, yet they are richer and more varied than those of any other living American novelist—they are opulence itself compared with those, say, of Sherwood Anderson. The marvel is that she has been able to achieve so much, to discern so much humanity in the flat and vacant land she pictures, with its teeming soil and human dearth. She has worked this wonder by having the strength to give herself to her native environment and to extract what juices and sustenance it afforded. By not dwelling on the aspects of her world which had nothing to offer, by leaving what she disliked in the background, she has managed to find a surprising amount of nutriment for her imagination—sensuous and emotional experience, and a considerable acquaintance with human nature, among isolated individuals, which goes far in the stories of Nebraska to atone for the absence of any healthily functioning social complex. And even the latter makes its appearance in the later novels which signalize her graduation from Nebraska.

Her triumph over Nebraska implies that Miss Cather has also conquered the Nebraska in herself. At this self-conquest we can only guess; but that poise, that disciplined taste and unfailing tact, that clear integrity of thought and feeling of hers are not products of any western farm or village, nor of any state university. From the first no doubt they were latent possibilities; but since a child can scarcely help assuming the point of view that surrounds it, the development of these possibilities must have cost a struggle. Perhaps the ten years after college during which she wrote little were her period in the chrysalis when the transformation took place. At any rate, she has finally emerged showing no marks of undernourishment or of that warping to which a practical and puritanical society subjects its members. She has been able to go ahead and do the best of which she was capable —an achievement so rare in American literature as to verge on the miraculous. Had she been born into any happier clime or age, I doubt whether, save for rendering more abundant social relationships, she would have done notably better. Though she began by largely subordinating herself to her subject-matter, she has ended complete mistress of the situation and produced books which enlist interest not as social documents but as fine art. She proves that the rule that American writers must be partially incapacitated by their environment has conspicuous exceptions—and she also proves the rule that they succeed in spite of their environment.

BIBLIOGRAPHY

CATHER, WILLA. *April Twilights.* Boston, 1903. Revised edition, New York, 1923, Alfred A. Knopf.
—— *The Troll Garden.* New York, 1905, Doubleday, Page and Company.
—— *Alexander's Bridge.* Boston, 1912, Houghton Mifflin Company.
—— *O Pioneers!* Boston, 1913, Houghton Mifflin Company.
—— *The Song of the Lark.* Boston, 1915, Houghton Mifflin Company.
—— *My Antonia.* Boston, 1918, Houghton Mifflin Company.
—— *Youth and the Bright Medusa.* New York, 1920, Alfred A. Knopf.
—— *One of Ours.* New York, 1922, Alfred A. Knopf.
—— *A Lost Lady.* New York, 1923, Alfred A. Knopf.
—— *The Professor's House.* New York, 1925, Alfred A. Knopf.

SPOKESMEN

CATHER, WILLA. *My Mortal Enemy.* New York, 1926,
Alfred A. Knopf.
——— *Death Comes for the Archbishop.* New York, 1927,
Alfred A. Knopf.

VIII

CARL SANDBURG

HE final impression left by Sandburg's four volumes of poetry is one of much power ill controlled. Not only has his work variety, ranging from a harsh strident realism through a romantic, tender feeling for natural beauty to a dim evocation of hinted mystery; it is not only varied, but variable—that is, uneven and uncertain. It is a medley of high poetry, flat prose, and showy counterfeit. Such unsureness is a sign that Sandburg is quite uncritical, that his taste is lax and undisciplined. His is an extraordinary aptitude for poetic utterance, ruled by little judgment. That is why his poetry is seldom a finished product, a thing absolutely done; in that sense, it is generally crude and raw. It constitutes a first-rate collection of matrixes, with a cut stone only here and there. It is, in short, chiefly ore—singularly rich ore, with perfect though usually tiny crystals embedded in it, but still ore that has not been passed through the crucible, that remains untransmuted, full of dross and slag.

To such imperfection Sandburg is peculiarly liable because he conceives of poetry as a running commentary on the poet's daily life, outer and inner. There is of course no reason why poetry should not serve this purpose, as it did with Wordsworth; but the very mention of Wordsworth indicates to what perils a poet exposes himself when he depends mainly and directly upon observation and memory—the peril above all of substituting annotation for creation, of falling into the trivial and the banal, into a welter of unorganized, undigested impressions. Much of Sandburg's work is not fully projected; it is unable to stand alone because it is insufficiently detached from the flux which gave it birth. The imaginative world which we enter through the door of Sandburg's poetry is scarcely more poetic than the actual world—I mean that it is scarcely more select or exclusive, scarcely less scrappy and jumbled. It is not merely that his poetic world, like reality, is kaleidoscopic, but that his kaleidoscope is too full of dull and muddy colors, that he has carried over into his poetic expression the unshaped confusion of his environment, which he has mirrored not only in his imagination but also in his style.

But if Sandburg's world is mischievous in its effects upon the art of poetry, it is none the less in itself a fascinating spectacle, strange, bizarre, chaotic—its unmistakable resemblance to the world in which we wake and sleep must not blind us to that fact. Its unintelligible disorder is full of inconsistency and contrast, of manifold beauty jostled by ugliness. It contains much natural loveliness of the traditional sort, of landscape, of tilled fields, of trees and birds, of sea and river, upland and valley, and much loveliness of the newest human make, of skyscrapers and steel mills and overland trains. But it also contains the Chicago River, and slums and stockyards and endless miles of monotonous grimy houses. It is exquisite, delicate, squalid, sordid, gorgeous, and at times sublime. It is as far from pretty fragility and decorous neatness as it is from pettiness and insipid languor; it has tremendous sweep, approaching grandeur, immeasurable spaces in which gigantic forces are at work, forces natural and human.

Not that the two should be thought of as opposed: in this world human life is thoroughly assimilated to the physical background, or has not emerged from it. All men are enslaved to some machine or engine or force—to steam or electricity, to coal or iron, or, like the farmer, to the soil and the force of reproduction, or to money, the symbol of all forces. Therefore, since the setting is dominant and mankind subservient and the two are all of a piece, human existence in Sandburg has all the traits of the world at large: it is anarchic, brutal, pathetic, powerful, drab, and gay. The inhabitants of this land are as varied and contradictory as the other material objects, and even more interesting: farmers, pig-stickers, harlots, dynamiters, milkmen, gunmen, shop girls, cabaret dancers, undertakers, pawnbrokers, pioneers, hoboes, soldiers, prospectors, aviators, laborers, policemen, railroad presidents—Poles, Jews, Hungarians, Bohemians, Greeks, Indians, negroes, gypsies, a few Americans. And they are all up to something, all after something or other for all they are worth—a vast menagerie let loose, trampling pushing, gouging, biting, in the freest of free-for-all: Never a sign of order or common purpose or intelligent direction or law, except the law of might; never a trace of organized effort to attain the greatest possible well-being in a *politeia,* to arrange some sort of decent communal life.

With this world Sandburg's life has been in as close accord as his poetry—not, needless to say, that it has been one of unleashed animalism, but that it has been variegated and full of contrasts. His story is like a romantic legend, mythical, epic. Born in Galesburg,

Illinois, he is the son of a Swedish immigrant; at thirteen he left school and took to driving a milk wagon; he worked in barber shops, potteries, and brickyards; he was a harvest hand in Kansas, a dishwasher in Denver, a coal-heaver in Omaha, and a soldier in Porto Rico during the Spanish War. He worked his way through Lombard College; he became a socialist, a politician, a newspaper man, and finally a poet. Such scope of experience is rare even in the United States, especially among poets. A biography of this sort leads one to expect a kind of Jack London in verse, glorifying abysmal brutes and glorying in being something of one himself. And indeed those who did not distinguish the man himself from his ideal portrait of Chicago thought of him as a roughneck, a slugger, at best a brawny, untamed Illinois viking; but no one who had really read him could hold such a picture of him. For he himself, as well as his life, is in his work.

No trait is more prominent in Sandburg's writing than his unusual sensitiveness, compounded of alertness of senses and quickness of feeling. He reacts keenly to impressions because he is highly susceptible. His work is full of the utmost precision and subtlety of perception and emotion. In "Nocturne in a Deserted Brickyard" delicacy of observation is united with an exquisite evocation of a mood in a peculiarly characteristic manner:

Under the curving willows,
And round the creep of the wave line,
Fluxions of yellow and dusk on the waters
Make a wide dreaming pansy of an old pond in the night.

No less symptomatic of his extreme sensitiveness is his occasional raucousness. It is difficult to understand how he could ever have been mistaken for a calloused rough. His noisiest passages indicate only how violently an almost supersensitive man reacts to the violence and racket and turmoil about him; the fierce ugliness and horror on which he sometimes dwells show only how strongly he feels filth and wretchedness and injustice. All these things would be taken calmly enough as matters of course by the hardened, thick-skinned ruffian whom many have erred in thinking Sandburg; but they make Sandburg's voice grow feverish and strident.

It might be expected that one so excitable and irritable (in the biological sense) as Sandburg would have shrunk from the harsh contacts of reality and taken refuge in a withdrawing, touch-me-not attitude. But this is pre-eminently what he has not done. So far from fleeing rough actuality, he is conspicuous among American poets for his immense gusto, for his avidity for experience. His zest for living is evident on every page of his books. And, fortunately, his capacity is equal to his appetite. His great distinction is his power of realization. He has that rare ability to yield himself to the moment, the action, the scene, to let himself be absorbed by the object, to throw or project himself into it, which is the basis of all experience, of all fullness of life. This capacity, which in Sandburg is so plentiful, bespeaks a large fund or reservoir of feeling, for, as has been pointed out already, complete realization makes great demands on emotional energy. That he has been able to meet these draughts is evinced by the wealth of experience to which his poems bear indisputable witness.

For his poems are the product of his peculiar faculties brought to bear on his particular environment in the special fashion and circumstances of his life; they are the embodiment of his experience. Sandburg, like Frost, has known things not only by seeing them but also by working with them and handling them, and therefore his acquaintance with them, like Frost's, is immediate, inward, and familiar. I doubt whether a mere spectator of the harvest fields would have written the following:

> *After the sunburn of the day*
> *handling a pitchfork at a hayrack,*
> *after the eggs and biscuit and coffee,*
> *the pearl-gray haystacks*
> *in the gloaming*
> *are cool prayers*
> *to the harvest hands.*

And surely more than observation and imagination went to the making of the "Psalm of Those Who Go Forth before Daylight":

> *The policeman buys shoes slow and careful; the teamster buys gloves slow and careful; they take care of their feet and hands; they live on their feet and hands.*

Labor and sweat and weariness, with their attendant satisfactions, have contributed to Sandburg's poetry and given it sinews. One kind of experience that he has known well is the muscular experience of action and work, and his writing has profited in proportion. Of all types of experience this is the scarcest among modern writers, and as soon as one discerns its effect, one realizes its vital importance to the development of the individual and so to his achievement.

As might be surmised of one whose senses are so acute as Sandburg's, his writing abounds particularly in the fruit of sensuous experience. His world has not been meager or monotonous in its appeal to eye and ear and nose, and he has responded to the appeal, delighting in sounds, textures, scents, and above all colors. Anything but ascetic, his surroundings have supplied him with a lawless, untrammeled riot of the senses, and he has taken it all in, from the flavor of the pawpaw and the red of ripe tomatoes to the stench of the Chicago River and the crash of steel-casting, from the silver of the new moon over the prairie to the silence of fog at sea. Therefore his poetry teems with concrete images of an unusual vividness. It is no pallid or denuded realm to which his verses introduce us, but a solid, noisy, bright-hued, smelly place. Above all else, Sandburg gives us things, the poetry of things.

He has the knack of getting at and conveying the essence of an object because he first apprehends it intensely, and because he selects the significant aspect of it and hits upon the precise phrase to carry this aspect. His felicitous selection is illustrated in two lines of "Buffalo Bill":

> *Buffalo Bill is a slanting look of the eyes,*
> *A slanting look under a hat on a horse.*

Both selection and phrasing are in "Sketch," especially the third stanza:

> *The lucid and endless wrinkles*
> *Draw in, lapse and withdraw.*
> *Wavelets crumble and white spent bubbles*
> *Wash on the floor of the beach.*

167

There can be no doubt that Sandburg possesses the specific poetic gift, the gift for conveying to words and through words the heightened intensity which makes poetry. When this function is not in abeyance, as it too often is, his phrases are fresh and crisp, as if stamped in a mint under high pressure. Such writing is by no means mere recording; it is creative, for by kindling our imagination it enhances our realization. It vivifies reality for us; it does, as I believe Coleridge pointed out, what water does to a pebble—intensifies the markings and colors and makes them more brilliant. It is found throughout "In Tall Grass":

Let there be wings and yellow dust and the drone of dreams of honey—who loses and remembers?— who keeps and forgets?

In a blue sheen of moon over the bones and under the hanging honeycomb the bees come home and the bees sleep.

This world of Sandburg's is richer in things than in people. Not that the latter are not numerous, but that they are somehow treated as if they were objects. Somehow the "Jew fish crier down on Maxwell Street" whose face "is that of a man terribly glad to be selling fish, terribly glad that God made fish, and customers to whom he may call his wares from a pushcart," and Mrs. Gabrielle Giovanitti, who

. . . comes along Peoria Street every morning at nine o'clock
With kindling wood piled on the top of her head,

168

and the rest seem exactly on a par with the crows which
"march their black feathers past a blue pool" and "cele-
brate an old festival," or with the cornstalks that "come
on with a high and conquering laughter." It may be, of
course, that there is no essential difference; yet, without
debating that question, we may still insist that some poets
have got farther into the insides of men and women than
anybody can get into a crow or a cornstalk. Whatever
the status of mankind in the universe, it is surely possible
for persons to have a more inward knowledge of other
persons than of birds and vegetables. This more inward
knowledge I do not see that Sandburg has. Perhaps it is
because his interest in humanity is generic or social rather
than individual; whatever the reason, he seems to feel
little of that hunger to go below the surface of the minds
of men and women, to paraphrase Sherwood Anderson, of
which one expects to find something even in a lyric poet.
There is singularly little of the dramatic or the analytical
or psychological in Sandburg.

Furthermore, there is singularly little in his writing of
a social web or nexus—for the reason, no doubt, that
there is nothing of the sort in his chaotic world. Does
not this fact account in part for his lack of curiosity as to
the interior of individual minds? Only in a social order
or organism can those close contacts and personal relations be set up which are the raw material of all social
experience, and it is difficult to see how such contacts and
relations could be established among the unattached re-
bounding atoms of such a disorder as Sandburg's society.
With all his absorption in his environment, scarcely a
single one of his poems grows out of the interaction
between another person and himself. Copious as his
poetry is in depicting the connections of human beings

with fields and factories and tools and work, it is poor in depicting their connections with one another. Even Robinson's world is opulent in its portrayal of human interplay and mental processes, as compared with Sandburg's. One might assume that the latter was defective in sense of personality, were it not that his version of a social anarchy is corroborated by others like Dreiser and Anderson; but with this corroboration one must conclude that Sandburg's poetry is shallow in its treatment of men and of the human drama because his environment had no deep and thorough social experience to offer him.

I cited Sandburg's power of realization as proof that he possessed a large reservoir of feeling; I should add, however, that it is a reservoir which produces not a steady flow but geyser-like spouts. It varies enormously in temperature; at times it is full of impurities, and at times it refuses to function. Whatever one says, therefore, about Sandburg's emotion must be extensively qualified. At his best he has tremendous passionate energy, but this energy is intermittent. Only once, I think, throughout "Smoke and Steel," is it sustained for a considerable space —though many perhaps would add "Slabs of the Sunburnt West," and a few might include "Prairie." Otherwise, it shows itself in the intensity which pervades all of some short lyrics, and in the intensity with which here and there throughout his work an image or a figure has been realized. Not infrequently, as in "And So Today," it is obvious that the author is strongly moved, yet the emotion is somehow not communicated to his language, has not arrived at poetic expression. Too commonly Sandburg's feeling, even at its most vehement, tends to be diffusive rather than concentrated: the impulse escapes

too readily into words; not being subjected to the restraint
of a severe taste, it does not have to force its way out, and
it does not develop high pressure. That is why he so
seldom develops and maintains a white inner heat capable
of transforming his ore of experience into the tempered
steel of poetry.

When the inner compulsion is working, he is a consum-
mate artist; when it is not, he is helpless—and apparently
he cannot tell the difference. The results in his writing
are manifold. Since emotion expresses itself primarily
in rhythm, we should expect to find, and we do find, that
Sandburg's rhythm is uncertain. Long stretches of his
work have none at all, or at best the lifeless movement of
dull prose. On the other hand, when he is conceiving his
subject strongly, his rhythm and his tone quality are
admirable, and also remarkably varied in their expressive
quality. On occasion, he can be as noisily cacophonous
as the elevated trains in the Loop, or he can make such
use of verbal jazz as in the obvious, but properly obvious,
lines:

> *Drum on your drums, batter on your banjoes,*
> *sob on the long cool winding saxaphones.*
> *Go to it, O jazzmen.*

> *Sling your knuckles on the bottoms of the happy*
> *tin pans, let your trombones ooze, and go husha-*
> *husha-hush with the slippery sand-paper.*

Not infrequently he imparts to his lines a singing music
which should win over the most conservative believer in
the dictum that poetry is song; witness the falling cadence
of the much-quoted line:

*Pocahontas' body, lovely as a poplar, sweet as a
red haw in November or a pawpaw in May, did
she wonder? does she remember? . . . in the
dust, in the cool tombs?*

And as good an illustration as one could wish of musical
rhythm used expressively is "Monotone":

> *The monotone of the rain is beautiful,*
> *And the sudden rise and slow relapse*
> *Of the long multitudinous rain.*
>
> *The sun on the hills is beautiful,*
> *Or, a captured sunset sea-flung,*
> *Bannered with fire and gold.*
>
> *A face I know is beautiful—*
> *With fire and gold of sky and sea,*
> *And the peace of long warm rain.*

"Monotone" is also sufficient evidence that Sandburg
has a sense of form, when his impulse is concentrated
enough to crystallize his feeling into poetry. It is a form
based upon balance, parallelism, and repetition, both of
ideas and of melodic equivalents. As a rule it is most
evident in shorter lyrics, although the famous "Chicago"
derives its force even more from its perfection of form
than from its vigor of diction; it has been built, it has
structure, architectonics. Likewise "Smoke and Steel"
and "Slabs of the Sunburnt West" form fully integral
and intricately organized units of large dimensions; but in
general the longer chants like "Prairie" are laxer in form,
tending to become sequences of associated lyrics linked

by repetitions and refrains. In such instances an indeterminateness of pattern may be defensible; but no one is likely to maintain that the bulk of Sandburg's work profits from the formlessness which overtakes him when the inner tension is slack. At such moments he indulges freely in prose notations, jottings any good reporter might make, such as "Ice Handler," which begins:

> *I know an ice handler who wears a flannel shirt*
> *with pearl buttons the size of a dollar,*
> *And he lugs a hundred-pound hunk into a saloon*
> *icebox, helps himself to cold ham and rye bread,*
> *Tells the bartender it's hotter than yesterday and will*
> *be hotter yet tomorrow, by Jesus,*
> *And is on his way with his head in the air and a*
> *hard pair of fists.*

The portrait as a whole is not without merit, but it never approaches a poetic intensity. Such pieces, it may be, lend breadth and inclusiveness to Sandburg's record, but one cannot help wishing that they had been fired to the fusing point.

More frequent in Sandburg's product than passion is a milder, tender mood of reverie, wistful and crepuscular; not sentimentality, for it is not false, but rather a soft glow of sentiment bordering on the vague and the luxurious. This mood is usually tinged with a pleasant sadness, and is called forth by twilight, autumn, moonlight, mist, as in "Bringers":

> *Cover me over*
> *In dusk and dust and dreams.*

173

SPOKESMEN

Hear me and cover me,
Bringers of dusk and dust and dreams.

The evocations of this elegiac mood are often charming;
some of Sandburg's most exquisite verses belong to the
group, which, as the majority of readers always prefer
gentle sentiment to hard passion, have greatly increased
his popularity. Nor do I know why one should disparage
these pieces, unless it is that because they are relaxing
they come by and by to cloy a little.

Now and then Sandburg's wistfulness runs into downright melancholy. Like every lover of life, like Horace
and Villon and Keats, he is conscious of the evanescence
of all that he loves.

I cried over beautiful things knowing no beautiful
thing lasts.

The transiency of life, of beauty, of the individual, runs
as an undertone through Sandburg's work, and leaves in
the background a shadowy darkness. Nothing exercises
a stronger fascination, whether attractive or repulsive,
over his imagination than death.

Death is a nurse mother with big arms: 'Twon't
hurt you at all; it's your time now; you just need
a long sleep, child; what have you had anyhow
better than sleep?

Most residents of Chicago must feel from time to time
that a long rest would be not unpleasant; but wherever
Sandburg lived, I think he would feel the same; any one,
I suspect, who, like him, gives so much energy to the out-

side world, who lives so fully, must know such reactions, when not to live at all seems most to be wished for. It is the ebb which follows the flow in the tides of desire.

Another sign of Sandburg's emotional instability is his occasional falling into downright sentimentality. He cannot discriminate between authentic and spurious feeling, or, more accurately, between an emotion proper to poetic expression and one which is essentially unpoetic. "Mamie" in *Chicago Poems,* which I refrain from quoting, is an example of Sandburg at his worst; he is not trying to see or to describe Mamie as she really is, but is engaged in exploiting and reveling in his own pity. A feeling called forth by a preconceived idea has come between him and his subject and has obscured the latter behind a veil; the feeling, that is, has been opposed to realization, and such feeling is sentimentality. Perhaps it should not be called sham, but it is anti-poetic because it precludes, instead of heightening, experience of reality. Always it leads to trite, tawdry phrasing, to rhetorical bombast, and to affected insincerity of form.

Such sentimentality often incapacitates Sandburg when he writes of the rich and the poor, for the reason that he then sees, not life itself, but life obscured by the conventional ideas of the socialist. Amy Lowell objected to his propaganda, and I think rightly—not merely because it is propaganda, for a sense of social injustice may and often does express itself in poetry, but because in Sandburg the propaganda, if present at all, comes first and the poetry second. Not only do his theories sometimes prevent him from seeing actuality, but he uses poetry as a means to a practical end. His aim for the moment is less to render a vivid apprehension than to persuade the reader that something ought to be done about economic

inequality. Even to one in full sympathy with Sandburg's indignation such verses as those which begin "The
Right to Grief" may prove irritating:

> *Take your fill of intimate remorse, perfumed sorrow,*
> *Over the dead child of a millionaire,*
> *And the pity of Death refusing any check on the bank*
> *Which the millionaire might order his secretary to*
> *   scratch off*
> *And get cashed. . . .*

> *I shall cry over the dead child of a stockyards*
> *   hunky—*

and so on. Sandburg's irony is for the most part of this
sort, cheap and obvious.

As Louis Untermeyer says, Sandburg is "a feeler
rather than a thinker." He reaches few conclusions of
any sort, and they are arrived at by way of the emotions. The nearest approach he makes to thinking is in
pondering and wondering. He loses himself in musing;
his is a contemplative type of mind. He is too absorbed
in brooding to reason; consequently his mind is as un-
clarified as his art. The notion that a poet has no need
of thinking is true to the extent that good poetry exists
in which the intellectual element is negligible; but that
is not to say that poetry does not gain enormously from
intellectual expertness and interest. Sandburg's work
could hardly suffer from his being less wholly non-
ratiocinative. It is natural to associate the poverty of the
intellectual element in Sandburg and in his work with
its absence from his environment—an absence vouched
for, tacitly or explicitly, by Dreiser, Anderson, Sinclair

Lewis, and Sandburg himself, among others. It is natural also to connect Sandburg's indifference to reason with his uncritical quality and with the confusion and the unevenness of his work. A world conspicuously lacking in clarity and arrangement seems well fitted to produce just such uncertainty in aim, in style, in feeling, and in art as we find in Sandburg.

He himself inveighs against what he calls "the curse of explanation," as if the effort to arrive at rational understanding were evil. Consequently, he offers us no such formulation of his experience as do Henry Adams and Robinson, or even Dreiser and Anderson. Yet Sandburg has come, as every one must, to a point of view. So far as can be detected, he has arrived intuitively at a kind of naturalism. However his attitude may differ from theirs, he holds much the same view of life as Adams and Dreiser. He too sees man as merely one among many natural objects, subject to the same forces and influences and to no others. For him, the life of a man has no more and no less ultimate significance than the life of a pawpaw or a chipmunk. Here is his summary of the matter:

> *In the loam we sleep,*
> *In the cool moist loam. . . .*
>
> *We stand, then,*
> *To a whiff of life,*
> *Lifted to the silver of the sun*
> *Over and out of the loam*
> *A day.*

He has his full share of the tragic sense of life, modern style—not merely that life is ephemeral, but that its brevity consists so largely of unavailing effort and suffering.   He is acutely conscious of man's helplessness, yet he manages to avoid the pessimistic conclusion.

For, attached to life as he is, he cannot feel that it is altogether futile.   If we are the playthings of immeasurable, incomprehensible forces, at any rate none of these forces is stronger than the love of life itself; so, though it may be irrational, let us satisfy this instinct as fully as we can.

> *Take any streetful of people buying clothes and*
> *groceries, cheering a hero or throwing confetti*
> *and blowing tin horns . . . tell me if the lovers*
> *are losers . . . tell me if any get more than the*
> *lovers . . . in the dust . . . in the cool tombs.*

If Sandburg has any notion of a *summun bonum,* it is that experience has value for its own sake, that in itself it is a not unworthy end.   If all we know, is a whiff of life, then let us make the most of it.   This idea, which in itself is far from novel, is given a fresh nuance by Sandburg in his idolatry of work and force.   Since the only reason we can detect for living is to live, the best form of living is the most intense, and that is doing, making, creating.   Hence Sandburg's affection for all exhibitions of energy, especially in new forms—airplanes, submarines, radio—because they are harnessings of more and more force.   Hence his insistence on the present and the future, his impatience with the hampering past:

> *I speak of new cities and new people.*
> *I tell you the past is a bucket of ashes.*
> *I tell you yesterday is a wind gone down.*

Where Adams' worship of power was practical in that he
wished to control it, Sandburg's is poetic, for he wishes
to share in it and to experience it—although I fear that
his idolatry also has something of the savage's uncritical
reverence. His passion for work, which runs like a blast
through "Smoke and Steel," is succinctly expressed in
"Prayers of Steel":

> *Lay me on an anvil, O God.*
> *Beat me and hammer me into a crowbar.*
> *Let me pry loose old walls.*
> *Let me lift and loosen old foundations.*

Like Dreiser's, Sandburg's view of life is closely related to his environment; the difference is chiefly that
Sandburg has escaped the desire for exploitation and self-
advancement, which hardly appears in his version of the
world at all. Perhaps this fact is due to his having concerned himself and associated much with the proletariat,
who are less obsessed by the craze for making good than
are the *petite bourgeoisie,* but it is probably more a matter
of personal temperament. Sandburg's picture is of a
world in which the practical temper has been active, but it
is preëminently a poet's picture, and therefore one in
which the practical impulse does not directly appear. It
appears indirectly in the ugliness and chaos of his world,
in its lack of common purpose, and in its irrationality
and unintelligibility. Sandburg assumes, so far as one
can tell, that these qualities are inevitable, that human
life has been and must be a catch-as-catch-can struggle;
his socialism, so far as his poetry shows, is confined to a
wish to even up the chances of the fighters, in order that
artificial injustice may not be added to inherent natural
injustice.

As befits a resident of a meaningless world, Sandburg deduces little from his experience because little is deducible, as Henry Adams likewise discovered. Sandburg is a thorough agnostic—more thorough than Adams, for Sandburg does not even lay down the dogma that existence cannot have any meaning. He is sure of nothing, save that he doubts, and wonders. His strongest conviction is of his own and everybody's invincible ignorance.

> *"I ask why I go on five crutches,*
> *tongues, ears, nostrils—all cripples—*
> *eyes and nose—both cripples—*
> *I ask why these five cripples*
> *limp and squint and gag with me. . . .*

> *"And away and away on some other green moon*
> *is a sea-kept child who lacks a nose I got*
> *and fingers like mine and all I have.*
> *And yet the sea-kept child knows more than*
> *I do and sings secrets alien to me as light*
> *to a nosing mole underground.*
> *I understand this child as a yellow-belly*
> *catfish in China understands peach pickers*
> *at sunrise in September in a Michigan orchard."*

Here is his cosmogony:

> *Eighteen old giants throw a red gold shadow ball; they pass it along; hands go up and stop it; they bat up flies and practice; they begin the game, they knock it for home runs and two-baggers; the pitcher puts it across in an out- and an in-shoot drop; the Devil is the Umpire; God is the Umpire; the game is called on account of darkness.*

The rest is silence; when we don't know, how can we say? In a world so strange as this of ours, anything may be true. Sandburg is fully conscious of its mystery, of the mystery pertaining to common things, visible in their curious relations and correspondences and hints of meaning. It is this consciousness that gives him a bent toward symbolism, that makes him, like a transcendentalist, see the material as replete with implications and overtones. His habit of mind has grown increasingly symbolic. An obvious instance is "Flying Fish":

Child of water, child of air, fin thing and wing thing . . . I have lived in many half worlds myself . . . and so I know you.

Much has been made of Sandburg's mysticism, but I doubt whether, in the strict sense of the word, he is a mystic at all. That he is not an orthodox mystic is of course clear; there is no sign in him of that "flight of the Alone to the Alone" which since Plotinus has been the ordinary course of the mystic. Nor do I think that Sandburg is truly a mystic of the cosmic or pantheistic sort, like Walt Whitman. A mystic is never a sceptic. The outstanding mark of mystical experience, of every type, is that it is absolutely authoritative, that it carries a complete certainty of conviction and a feeling of security, very different from Sandburg's puzzled questioning. He approaches mysticism most closely in "Slabs of the Sunburnt West," a meditation on nature, man, and God filled with profound emotion, with wonder, and with awe. But the experience leaves a conviction, not of certainty, but of nescience. Instead of an intuitive apprehension of unquestionable, ultimate reality, Sandburg feels rather his own inadequacy, helplessness, and isolation. That he approaches mysticism I grant, even that in him there is a mystical element in his sense of mystery and in his power of identifying himself with the outside world. I should say that he has attained the contemplative stage on the mystic way, and that he may have had moments of illumination, but that he has never approached the higher degrees of union. His seems to be a deeply religious nature which has never found a religion.

The best term that I can find for Sandburg is that of psalmist—not in form only, although his predilection for the form of the Psalms may be significant, but in deeper ways. His feeling for the sky, the ocean, the winds, for all the more grandiose aspects of nature, for vastness in time and space, is like that of the Psalms. He is given to wondering how the foundations of the hills were laid and how the sea was poured forth. "Slabs of the Sunburnt West" in its theme and mood and even its conclusions as to human impotence affords strange parallels to passages in the Book of Job. Sandburg's poetry is in truth a veritable Psalm of Life—for he is essentially an accepting, yea-saying psalmist.

In contemporary verse, Sandburg's work stands out for its breadth, volume, and body. Many of our poets are far more perfect, have rid themselves more successfully of alloy; but not one of them has Sandburg's massive bulk. No doubt his work suffers both in material and in form from the peculiarities of his environment, but at least he is not at all undernourished; he has derived ample sustenance from his surroundings. If discipline in taste is the more important for the individual's achievement and reputation, yet the nourishment provided the artist's imagination is the more important for national literature—and that is where Sandburg excels, and for the historian of national literature is most significant. He proves that it is possible for a man endowed with the poetic temper to lead the life of realization to good purpose among us. Furthermore, Sandburg has extraordinary social value in that only Whitman has done more in the arduous labor of opening up the country and subjecting it to artistic treatment. He has made the way easier not only for all other artists, but also for all who are inclined to follow the life of realization.

BIBLIOGRAPHY

SANDBURG, CARL. *Chicago Poems.* New York, 1916, Henry Holt and Company.

—— *Cornhuskers.* New York, 1918, Henry Holt and Company.

—— *Smoke and Steel.* New York, 1920, Harcourt, Brace & Company.

—— *Slabs of the Sunburnt West.* New York, 1922, Harcourt, Brace & Company.

—— *Rootabaga Stories.* New York, 1922, Harcourt, Brace & Company.

—— *Rootabaga Pigeons.* New York, 1923, Harcourt, Brace & Company.

—— *Abraham Lincoln, the Prairie Years.* 2 vols. New York, 1926, Harcourt, Brace & Company.

—— *Selected Poems.* New York, 1926, Harcourt, Brace & Company.

—— Editor, *The American Songbag.* New York, 1927, Harcourt, Brace & Company.

IX

VACHEL LINDSAY

N the introduction to his *Collected Poems,* Vachel Lindsay tells an anecdote of his childhood as significant as it is delightful, of how he took part in a kind of masque written by his mother and staged in the Campbellite church of Springfield, Illinois. It was a "colloquy," called "Olympus," in which all the Greek deities appeared.

My uncle, Johnson Lindsay, was Neptune, since he had a wonderful, long, beautiful red beard, and was exceedingly tall and handsome besides; a Neptune of Neptunes, when draped in seaweed. The Sunday School superintendent impersonated Bacchus. How they let him get into the pulpit with all those grapes on him I do not know. But he laughed hard, and Peter Paul Rubens would have been proud of him. I was too young to know what the church elders said about him. My mother was a riot in those days. How she did it in the midst of that rigor I do not know. . . .

My Sunday School teacher was chosen by my mother to be Venus in this colloquy. Venus was as voluminously robed and as magnificently crowned as is the Statue of Liberty. . . .

I was six or seven years old at this particular time, and I was Cupid. . . . My mother took off most of my clothes. She put a pink slip on me, and sewed dove's wings to the back of it. I was given silver pasteboard arrows, and a silver pasteboard bow, and a silver quiver on my shoulder, under the wings. I climbed into that pulpit hand in hand with the beautiful Venus, my Sunday School teacher.

Beside that episode should be set a statement Lindsay once made to a Canadian audience, after he had been described as having come from "humble and poverty-stricken antecedents." He said: "I am not only sophisticated, but all my ancestors were sophisticated."

It looks like a far cry from that colloquy to the higher vaudeville which Lindsay began to practice about 1914, and which was a blending of the Greek choric ode with Keith and Proctor. This higher vaudeville included not only his writing but also his recitation, and both were designed to bring poetry back to its proper place as an art of the people and as an art of the ear. These poems were popular in subject, treatment, and style, and as Lindsay chanted them, with the audience joining in and growling like lions or singing refrains, they seemed at the time as if they might succeed in reinstating poetry as one of the folk-arts. At any rate, there could be no doubt as to its place as one of the lively arts. It was, in the best sense of the word, vulgar. But all that is past, for Lindsay has repudiated his higher vaudeville—a term which I daresay he bitterly regrets having invented—in favor of a return to the more evangelical and less authentic and robust art of his childhood.

This regression was the greater pity because all his work that up to the present has proved itself enduring came out of the higher vaudeville. Essentially he is known as the author of some half-dozen poems: "The Chinese Nightingale," "The Congo," "General William Booth Enters into Heaven," "The Santa Fé Trail," "Abraham Lincoln Walks at Midnight," "Bryan, Bryan, Bryan, Bryan." To these six might be added perhaps a dozen others of much the same calibre and type. The rest of his *Collected Poems* are best forgotten—are necessarily forgotten by his admirers. Of all living American poets, his reputation rests upon the smallest achievement—smallest in bulk, that is. Yet the volume of the *Collected Poems* runs to four hundred and sixty-four pages. The collection was a mistake: Lindsay's reputation would be more secure were he known only through the selections of the anthologists.

Concerning the great bulk of the *Collected Poems* little need be said. The best of it is like "The Chinese Nightingale," but slighter; it consists of fancy designs cut out in tissue paper, some of which, such as the little moon poems, are charming. Another portion of it might be described as "The Ghosts of the Buffaloes" gone to seed —dealing, that is, with similar material, but jumbled and unformed. Yet another part is hortatory and didactic. Almost all of it suffers from one great defect: it is mechanical. Its feeling is forced, and its style is banal. The writer's excitement has an artificial look and his words are flat and trite. Its whimsy is determined, its jollity metallic, and its preachment solemnly oracular. The time has not yet come, however, for Lindsay's obituary to be written; if he seems just now to be at a moment of slack water after a time of ebb, it would be rash to say that another tide will not set in. Already in his latest books, *The Candle in the Cabin* and *Going-to-the-Stars,* there is perceptible, I think, light though these verses may be, both a fresher feeling than he has shown for some years and a new and promising point of view. He is apparently engaged in an effort which, if it succeeds, will make his work at least as interesting as it has ever been, for he is working toward a kind of poetry which would be, even more truly than the higher vaudeville, a genuine folk-art.

All Lindsay's erstwhile admirers must wish him well in this undertaking, for unless he can carry it through, his career will be the most tragic in contemporary letters; unless he can add to his achievement in the future, no other writer will have done so little with so much ability. His is not the usual story of the promising youngster, clever and shallow, whose precocious flash is soon burnt out for lack of fuel, for Lindsay had, and no doubt has, real power. His achievement has not yet been commensurate with his possibilities. What has prevented him from realizing those possibilities, from effectuating himself? What malign blight fell upon him and for a time wasted his robust vigor? Heywood Broun answers as follows:

Fundamentally, Mr. Lindsay is a remarkable poet; altogether he never comes to as much as he should. Probably he never had much of a chance. He grew up in the Babbitt country. He was, when young, a Babbitt himself, and to this day he has not ceased trying to transmute the activities of Babbittry into the stuff of dreams and fantasy.

But that Broun is in error the slightest glance at Lindsay's biography is enough to show.

His activities have been many and varied, but none of them have been tainted with Babbittry—if Babbittry means the ordinary doings of the average successful business man. It is true that Lindsay has indulged in uplift, and that in particular he has delivered lectures for the Y.M.C.A. and the Anti-Saloon League—but those were not among the recreations of Zenith's realtor. And Lindsay's other activities have been above reproach. Besides his writing of poetry and his reciting tours, there

were his years as an art student, and his excursions into
such labors as the following:

Once I spent three months pushing a truck in the whole-
sale toy department of Marshall Fields, Chicago. Once I
worked three months for a gas-tubing factory in New York
City. Once I spent two weeks digging for the Springfield,
Illinois, Department of Public Property, where they were
installing a new boiler at the Water Works. Once I spent
three days south of Springfield cutting corn for a silo, with
as rare a gang of dollar-a-day thugs as ever remained unhung.

There were also his three famous tramps as a beggar,
which he says were deliberate acts of defiance.

Each time I broke loose, and went on the road, in the
spring, after a winter of art lecturing, it was definitely an
act of protest against the United States commercial standard,
a protest against the type of life set forth for all time in two
books of Sinclair Lewis: *Babbitt* and *Main Street*.

After I had been twice on the road, and proved my independence in a fashion, there were days in my home town
when the Babbitts were about ready to send me to jail or
burn me at the stake, for some sort of witchcraft, dimly
apprehended. . . .

I was told by the Babbitts on every hand that I must quit
being an artist, or beg. So I said, for the third time, "I
will beg."

The anti-Babbitt side of Lindsay comes out most
clearly in his travel books, *A Handy Guide for Beggars*
and *Adventures While Preaching the Gospel of Beauty*.
Even in them, to be sure, there are false as well as true
strains of humor, and forced as well as genuine love of
humanity: the author himself is sometimes guilty of "the

fine manly handclasp, the glitter of teeth, the pat on the back," which he notes in one professional social server. But for the most part they are entirely delightful and amusing accounts of his wanderings, recorded with appreciation of landscape and human appearances and with a surprising flair for human character. When writing the books, if not when making the trips, he forgot his obsessions and purposes and contented himself with relating his experiences, as if he had tramped, not to defy Babbitts nor to preach gospels, but for the fun of it.

Lindsay is a difficult mixture, an amphibious creature, the duck-billed platypus of contemporary writing, neither fish, flesh, nor fowl. The simplest way of putting it is to say that he is still but half emancipated from his environment. I feel sure that nature intended him for a poet, that the poetic temper is innate in him. In his books of travel and in his twenty or so memorable poems, he shows himself a man who cares intensely for living and for experience, and a man moreover with a singular knack for getting into the heart of the populace. This Lindsay is a simple, childlike, even a primitive being, a kindly savage—perhaps because he has never had a chance to grow up. For this is the unacknowledged, though fundamental, Lindsay, who has been suppressed in the interest of all sorts of conscious aims and purposes. He is permitted to appear only through the half-dramatic disguise of negroes, Indians, children, and plebeians.

We have Lindsay's word for it that he has found his environment hostile. Against one phase of this environment he reacted strongly from the first: he never submitted to the worship of success, to the practical *ethos*. He was never even tempted to be a Babbitt. On the contrary, in answer to the unfriendliness about him, he did what many poetically inclined Americans have done; he tried to escape into realms of fantasy, and half succeeded. Hence the flimsy romanticism in his poetry. But the practical temper was not the only enemy in his surroundings—and the others he unfortunately embraced. The timid refinement and gentility, the sentimental strain, purified and emasculated, the evangelical puritanism, no less than practicality, were inimical to him as a poet, but were, one gathers, presented to him in the guise of art. That "colloquy," that Sunday school saturnalia which adapted antique paganism to the tastes of Midwestern Protestanism, is emblematic of Lindsay's conflict. All his life he has been, if not Bacchus, at least a faun trying to masquerade as a Sunday school superintendent— luckily, with imperfect success. Lindsay, like Dreiser, is an example of how the young may be so thoroughly trained in false modes of thought and feeling as never to be able to escape. The result, as usual, is instability, immaturity, and lack of integrity.

The preceding conjectures receive some corroboration from the emotional qualities of Lindsay's verse. Seldom is his writing vibrant with feeling; his emotion rarely communicates itself to the rhythm of the line. Even his best work, with all its vitality and animation, has little depth or intensity. Yet, though he fails to get it into his poetry, he himself is by no means devoid of strong feeling. Few readers will deny what he says of himself in these lines:

> *Why do I faint with love*
> *Till the prairies dip and reel?*
> *My heart is a kicking horse*
> *Shod with Kentucky steel.*

His failure in communication is somewhat explained by his treatment of sex. In the whole volume of his collected work, there is not one love poem, although there are many which profess to be love poems. Until lately Lindsay has always spoken of love as if he were an elderly gentleman addressing a child of six: his tone has been one of playful and chivalric compliment, much too remote to be taken seriously. It is nothing if not pure, like —to borrow one of his own figures—moonlight on lilies. The whole point of "The Chinese Nightingale" is that in all life only youth and love in springtime are memorable. Yet the feeling of the lovers is never conveyed; we are merely told that they "had thoughts of desire which were noble and grave," whatever that may mean. So throughout all his work but the most recent, love is only a pretty toy for the fancy to play with and decorate. The most encouraging aspect of *The Candle in the Cabin* is that at last in it Lindsay seems to have accepted love and desire as what they actually are.

The earlier attitude, which was a defensive one, was symptomatic: Lindsay has been terribly afraid of desire, in whatever form it has presented itself. This fear he has expressed most fully in "The Firemen's Ball," in which he represents the world as perishing in the fire of passion while true love dies, and in connection with which he quotes the words of Buddha: "A disciple . . . divests himself of passion. By absence of passion he is made free." Elsewhere he makes Buddha say:

I bring you my fair Law of Peace
And from your withering passion full release.

One hopes and has reason for hoping, that in the future

Lindsay will accept passion as a creative, rather than denounce it as a destructive, force.

In so far as he has feared desire, Lindsay has shrunk from reality. I suspect that he condemned his own poetic wish for realization. Venus—Love—Life itself—has been to him either a terror or a Sunday-school teacher. He has had two dominant conscious attitudes toward experience: it has been something to flee from into dream and reverie, or it has been something that teaches lessons. Correspondingly, for him his poetry has had two functions: it has been either a refuge from actuality or a vehicle for edification. The latter I shall return to shortly; as for the former, he has practiced his own doctrine of escape all too well, though not always.

> *Dream, boy, dream,*
> *If you anywise can.*
> *To dream is the work*
> *Of beast or man.*

That is why Lindsay has moved about in a world rather less than half realized.

Because his conscious attitude has been hostile to realization, because he has not valued experience for its own sake, his poetry has suffered in form and in content. Its frequent foggy dimness is due to the fact that his emotion, instead of being used to fire his imagination and concentrate it to a sharp focus, instead of being channeled in "passionate apprehension," has been dissipated and diffused in clouds of fancy. He has been as indifferent to exactness of expression as to distinctness of experience. Therefore his work has tended to be not only fumbling in utterance but meager in substance. The objection is not that Lindsay is not a realist, for none of the greatest poets have been realists. It is that his fancifulness is thin and feeble, because his imagination has not been fed and nourished by complete realization of reality. The poet may transport us to regions as remote as he pleases; he may transmute his material into the strangest and most bizarre forms—but he must have the material to transmute. Not the maddest alchemist tried to make gold out of nothing; and the poet's base metal is experience. Lindsay has collected little of it, comparatively speaking, and has done little with it, because he has underrated its value.

Of the poetic qualities I have been attributing to Lindsay's work, no more striking illustration could be asked than "The Chinese Nightingale," which is Lindsay's own favorite and which has always enjoyed wide popularity, but which I cannot call better than the best of his failures. It is a very pretty piece, full of pleasant sentiment and pretty fancies and pretty melodies, but comparatively deficient in vigor. It ought to have not only the delicate fancifulness but the delicate precision and sharpness of the old Chinese paintings. No doubt as he indicates in the line, "Who shall end my dream's confusion?" he did not intend the poem to have verisimilitude, but he can scarcely have meant it to be blurred and ineffective. Yet the central and crucial passage contains lines of meaningless padding; and a vagueness of conception and an inaccuracy in the choice of words are shown in such verses as these:

And heard the curled waves of the harbor moan—

Hear the howl of the silver seas—

193

Partly because of the writing and partly because of the unrestrained profusion of undefined images, the poem is dim and vague, lost in its "rainbow mist." Furthermore, its fancy and sentiment, though agreeable, do not rise to the level of poetic intensity; it is confectionery rather than creation.

Moreover, Lindsay has regarded poetry as an instrument not only for escaping but also for saving the world. His verse, he says, has been "a weapon in a strenuous battlefield"; it has been part of his "crusade." He has been a propagandist and a preacher; indeed, moral fervor has been the primary motive of his life. There have been other poets with moral enthusiasm, who have been none the worse poets on that account; the love of righteousness can express itself in poetry as well as other emotions. But at least at the time of writing the poet must be intent upon expressing his feeling, not upon accomplishing some ulterior end; his mood for the moment must be poetic, not practical—and moral ardor is peculiarly liable to lead to unpoetic writing, to didacticism. Lindsay's zeal for virtue has at times made him adopt a pulpit manner of exhortation. Furthermore, although one may insist, contrary to current prejudice, that morality is not necessarily fatal to art, one must confess that it all depends on the morality. A conception of goodness which emphasizes veracity and devotion and which aims at yielding life more abundantly strengthens the artist in his endeavors as much as a negative conception hinders him. But that Lindsay's enthusiasm has led him away from experience rather than to a completer life we have already seen. Mid-American evangelicalism has never been turned into song because it is opposed to the very vital breath of the poet.

It is easier to see that Lindsay has a "message" than to say what the contents of that message may be. His mental processes are entirely non-rational. He would be the first to claim the title of seer, prophet, visionary, dreamer, rather than of thinker. Americans—perhaps Emerson is responsible—have always rather scorned the process of reasoning, for which they have felt no aptitude. The absence of the logical element from Lindsay's mind has produced strange results. It has enabled him to cherish an equal admiration for Confucius, Buddha, Napoleon, St. Paul, Mohammed, St. Francis, Darwin, and Roosevelt. No wonder he feels that all nations and all churches are on the point of becoming one: if all men's minds worked like his, such a union might easily take place. But, for good and evil, the minds of other men persist in making distinctions and discriminations of which he knows nothing. What he may do in the future —whether or not he will arrive, or indeed has already arrived, at an ordered and coherent point of view—one cannot say; all that can be inferred from the *Collected Poems* and the prose manifestoes is that apparently Lindsay's gospel is confused, unintelligible, and self-contradictory because it is the manifestation of an inner chaos. His ideas are not integrated because he himself lacks integrity. Each of his mutually opposed impulses at once embodies itself in his thought, and he is apparently unconscious of their inconsistency. That is why one cannot make true statements concerning him: whatever one says is bound to be disproved by a passage somewhere in his books. The best one can hope for is to trace out and place side by side in all their antagonism some of his major tendencies. His undiscriminateness is an outcome of his thoroughly uncritical habit of mind, which prevents him from having tried standards or a scale of values by which to judge either his work or his notions. He has shown himself unable to distinguish true from false in thought or feeling, or real from unreal.

The slightness of his sense of reality betrays itself in his thought as in his verse. His gospel is a compound of moral enthusiasm and fantasy. He has been much given to wish-thinking. Whatever has presented itself to him as desirable has straightway become actual; his only concession has been to project it into the remote future. His visions of the United States hereafter are quite unrelated to any existing facts of American life. He has been as much the slave of his fancy as any child. Indeed, the extreme infantility which has been conspicuous in much of his writing continued to grow on him so long as he got more and more out of touch with reality and lived more and more exclusively in his dream-world. In the old days he had comprehensible ideas; at times he was a hedonist, as in "The Chinese Nightingale," celebrating the joys of youth and love; at times he went so far as to be an antinomian, now in the "mad, bad, glad" manner of Swinburne, and now in the manner of Blake, as in the lines:

> *God loves the golden leopard*
> *Though he may spoil her lair.*
> *God smites, yet loves the lion.*
> *God makes the panther fair:*

and in his reflection on the career of Alexander:

> *God make us splendid, though by grievous wrong.*
> *God make us fierce and strong.*

196

Another predilection was for Buddhism; at yet another time the title he was most eager to claim for himself was that of Franciscan. Not all beggars, however, are followers of St. Francis, even when they are beggars for conscience' sake. St. Francis, like his Exemplar, tried to show men the way to a more abundant life; he laid all his stress on the first and great commandment, confident that if it were obeyed other matters would take care of themselves, whereas American Protestanism since the seventeenth century has shown no sign of acquaintance with the first commandment—I do not mean the first of the Decalogue. St. Francis' ideal was always personal and individual, not social; he had no taint of utopianism. The Franciscan spirit is at the opposite pole from the negative puritanism and the external, taboo morality of such organizations as the Y.M.C.A. and the Anti-Saloon League, as witness its flowering in art and poetry. Lindsay's work would have profited if he had been a more complete Franciscan.

It is true that Lindsay called his original evangel "the gospel of beauty," and that he has devoted his moral earnestness to defending the cause of loveliness as he has seen it. The trouble is that he has seen it as something remote or at best as something imported from the fairyland of dreams into actuality. He has not seen it as rooted in an intense awareness of what is, however ugly in itself. He has seen it, not as something that grows or is shaped out of life, but as an exotic that flourishes only in the airy regions of conceit. In some of his earlier and better work, to be sure, his practice was quite the reverse; and in his summary of his earlier creed, which he called "The New Localism," there was a hint of some

197

recognition of the value of experience: Young Americans, he says,

. . . should, if led by the spirit, wander over the whole nation in search of the secret of democratic beauty with their hearts at the same time filled to overflowing with the righteousness of God. Then they should come back to their own hearth and neighborhood and gather a little circle of their own sort of workers about them and strive to make the neighborhood and home more beautiful and democratic and holy with their special art. . . . They should labor in their little circle expecting neither reward nor honors. . . . In their darkest hours they should be made strong by the vision of a completely beautiful neighborhood and the passion for a completely democratic art. . . .

Religion, equality, and beauty! By these America shall come into a glory that shall justify the yearnings of the sages for her perfection.

If Lindsay had devoted himself more to the beginning and less to the end of that statement, he would have done better. But as a matter of fact he has rarely mentioned the individual because he has been obsessed by his vision of a beloved community.

Yet Lindsay cannot justly be called a utopian: his prophecy is not of a Spotless Town inhabited by impeccable wax figures. He says wise words on the subject:

Citizens of America, wise or foolish, when they look into the coming days, have the submarine mood of Verne, the press-the-button complacency of Bellamy, the wireless telegraph enthusiasm of Wells. . . . They order machinery piled to the skies. They see the redeemed United States running deftly in its jeweled sockets, ticking like a watch. . . .

VACHEL LINDSAY

We shall have a tin heaven and a tin earth, if the scientists
are allowed exclusive command of our highest hours.

Lindsay's own reading of the future is embodied chiefly
in *The Golden Book of Springfield;* it is not dull, and
it is not perfect. Beyond that I can scarcely describe it.
It is an apocalypse, a delirium from a Sangamon County
Patmos. It is a kind of jazz version of a medieval walled
town, with incessant pageants and pilgrimages and pro-
cessions and festivals and rituals and what-not. Apparently it is his conception of "the whole of the United
States as a permanent World Fair," which he regards as a
desirable consummation. It has something to do with
the Map of the Universe which is prefixed to his *Collected
Poems,* and which, he says, "is a mere kindergarten map,
and makes no pretensions to profundity," yet which "has
dominated all his verses" and which, according to his
own statement, he intends to devote his life to expounding
on his transcontinental tours. It is related to that "Mystic
Springfield," in which, as he says, he has spent most of
his life.

For many reasons, then, Lindsay has shown a strong
tendency to underrate the importance and the worth of
actuality; he has never recognized the value of the poetic
temper and never espoused the life of realization—which,
I feel sure, is as much as to say that he has denied himself his birthright. For I have no doubt that he is a born
poet. Indoctrinated as he was in the genteel tradition,
puritanic and sentimental, with its sterilized refinement,
and taught by both friend and foe that art was a shadowy
affair having little to do with the substantial business of
men, the wonder is that his native bent has proved strong
enough to produce what it has, in spite of himself and

199

his environment. It is all but a miracle that the little cupid in the pulpit, with his dove's wings and tinsel arrows, could ever grow up to say with truth:

> *I am the Kallyope . . .*
> *Music of the mob am I,*
> *Circus day's tremendous cry . . .*
> *I am but the pioneer*
> *Voice of the Democracy;*
> *I am the gutter dream. . . .*

"The Kallyope Yell" is by no means Lindsay's best; and even his best are not great poems, for they lack too many of the elements which may lend greatness to poetry—high passion, finished art, a sense of drama and an understanding of human character, the wisdom of patient meditation, depth of inner experience. Yet at one time he was, more genuinely than any other, "the pioneer voice of the Democracy." His imagination penetrated what common experience we have as a nation and discovered the lowest common denominator, and embodied the results in forms expressive of the common spirit—really expressive, and therefore poetic.

Lindsay first became famous because of his novelty. For half a century American verse had been retired, personal, exclusive, delicate, and mournful. Lindsay was the opposite; instead of writing to express his *Weltschmerz*, he was not even solemn, much less melancholy. He had verve and go and high spirits; he was not afraid to be amusing. Furthermore, not only did he differ from his immediate predecessors, but in his "higher vaudeville" he had invented something new in the whole history of poetry—not in form, but in union of form, subject, and spirit. In a day when most verse was the record of infinitesimal impressions and insignificant emotions, his poems were big in conception and unflagging in the fire and vigor of their working out. They combined vivacity with strength. Fortunately, the spirit of the higher vaudeville, though repudiated by its creator, has proved contagious, and the work which Lindsay began is being carried on by others—the clearest of signs that his discovery was one of vital importance.

What first struck every one in Lindsay's poems was his rhythm. Nowadays he grows so violent when called a jazz poet that I hasten to add that, though I see no reason why he should not write jazz, it is a fact that he seldom does so. His most characteristic meter, the pæonic, is no novelty in English verse.

And a thigh-bone beating on a tin-pan gong. . . .

With a bright-brown breast and a bronze-brown wing. . . .

Big-voiced lasses made their banjoes bang. . . .

While smoke-black freights on the double-track railroad. . . .

The basic rhythm which underlies the special accent imparted by Lindsay may be as old as the English language; at any rate, it was a favorite with Swinburne and Kipling decades before jazz was heard of. It lacks the peculiar syncopation and cross-accent of jazz. The only poem of Lindsay's which approaches the jazz rhythm is "Daniel":

SPOKESMEN

Daniel was the chief hired man of the land.
He stirred up the jazz in the palace band.

So we will not accuse him of being a jazz poet, but merely insist that he used to be the master of a peculiarly spirited and infectious rhythm—and one, as he treated it, peculiarly American. At first one is tempted to say that this rhythm is not musical at all—that is, that it is no more musical than the effect one can get by beating two sticks or stones together, that it is rhythm pure and simple, with no melody, no timbre. However, while it is true that the drums and traps are the most prominent instruments in Lindsay's orchestra, it is amazing, in the first place, what variety of effects he can get from them, from the shrill clash of the cymbals to the boom of the bass drum; and in the second place, if we listen attentively, we hear from time to time the sounds of flutes and violins. These predominate throughout "The Chinese Nightingale," and are not absent from even so noisy a piece as "The Santa Fé Trail."

This is the order of the music of the morning:—
First, from the far East comes but a crooning.
The crooning turns to a sunrise singing. . . .

And all of the tunes, till the night comes down
On hay-stack, and ant-hill, and wind-bitten town.
Then far in the west, as in the beginning,
Dim in the distance, sweet in retreating,
Hark to the faint-horn, quaint-horn, saint-horn. . . .

Indeed, one of Lindsay's chief merits is his use of variety in rhythm and tone-quality. He is a master both

of gradual transition and of sharp contrast. His odes
have lyric structure and arrangement; they are planned
with definite effects and climaxes in mind. Furthermore,
they have intellectual structure also. They are by no
means mere riots of sound. See, for instance, how carefully "The Congo" is made, with its three sections, each
divided into two parts, with the refrain in each making
the transition from the American negro to the African.
And "The Santa Fé Trail" evinces the same strong sense
of form, the same ability to make the musical pattern and
the intellectual plan define and enhance each other. No
small part of the effectiveness of these pieces is derived
from this classic quality, which may or may not have
been suggested by the strophe, antistrophe, and epode of
the Greek choric odes.

Because Lindsay feels that his treatment of rhythm
and his use of music have received too much attention, he
goes to the other extreme and disparages their importance,
as in the introduction to the *Collected Poems:* "I petition
that my verse be judged not as a series of experiments in
sound, but for lifetime and even hereditary thoughts and
memories of painting." Nor is it merely the contrari-
ness of human nature which makes him wish to be taken
as a sort of imagist, for his imagery is more noteworthy
than his sound. His writing is full of pictures: "The
Congo" is a series of passages like this:

Just then from the doorway, as fat as shotes,
Came the cake-walk princes in their long red coats,
Canes with a brilliant lacquer shine,
And tall silk hats that were red as wine.

Seldom, to be sure, are his pictures so precise as that;
they usually are a little vague and slightly confused.

Lindsay's imagination does not commonly work in exact, clear-cut images, and his rendering of them into words often leaves something to be desired in accuracy and distinctness.

Yet, in spite of these occasional imperfections and in spite of the fact that he perversely underrates the importance of his rhythms, he is right at least to the extent that his peculiar excellence lies in something which is closely related to his use of imagery. It is what I can call only his myth-making faculty. These myths, it is true, consist of scenes; however, it is not their merit as pictures or as word-painting that matters; theirs is quite another and a not specifically æsthetic appeal. They partake of the nature of visions: the figure of Lincoln walking through the streets of Springfield in the darkness; the tremendous rush of the Indian gods and the ghost-herds of buffaloes through the night sky over the prairie; Johnny Appleseed sowing his trees beside the trails through the wilderness; the hurrahing streets of Springfield when Bryan spoke in 1896; all the United States whirling westward in automobiles over Kansas; the entry of Booth's tattered army into Heaven. Such phantasms have an epic scope, legendary, fabulous, racial.

All Lindsay's best work has this folk-quality. No one equals him in ability to discern symbols of national significance underlying the national life. He has been able to tap a new source of great power. His achievement is akin to Irving's in "Rip Van Winkle" and "The Legend of Sleepy Hollow"; and Lindsay's instinct is the truer of the two, for he does not import his material into the national consciousness, but perceives what is already there. Always at his best he has this intimate relationship with the American scene; like other American writers, he profits by staying close to the soil, for the reason presumably that American life grows thinner and thinner as one ascends the economic scale. Probably he belittles his best work because his successes depend upon his sinking to a primitive or barbaric level—to the level of the negro, of the Salvation Army, of the child in "Bryan, Bryan" and in "John L. Sullivan," of the mob in "The Kallyope Yell," and of the mythopœic savage in "The Ghosts of the Buffaloes" and "In Praise of Johnny Appleseed." He is afraid that he himself will seem naïve, that his auditors will not recognize that these poems are semi-dramatic. He does not wish to be thought an inspired member of the proletariat, as of course he is not—unfortunately. It is his weakness as a folk-artist that he is, as he says, "sophisticated"; it is his strength that at times he is able to free himself amazingly from his contamination and enter into the deepest chambers of the American spirit.

In his visionary and symbolic turn, as long as it was controlled by his artisan's instinct and by a relation to actuality, lay his signal strength; but out of that strength came forth a weakness which for a while led him away into more and more remote and insignificant realms of fancy. At the present moment he seems to be getting his feet back on the earth, and he may recover his architectonic skill and his ability as a craftsman. But he is still given now and then to a feeble reëchoing of his first strong strains, and if one can be sure of anything it is that he cannot return to what he used to be but must develop a new style, perhaps without the high spirits of his youth but not necessarily without equal merits of another sort. In his most recent verses there is a new treatment of love, as I have said, and there is also a new feeling for nature, particularly for the high mountains and the wilds. There is likewise a growing sympathy with the Indian out of which much may come.

Lindsay has said more than once that he is developing a system of "United States hieroglyphics," and while his remarks on this subject are not intelligible to me, I suppose that he refers to the fundamental symbols or patterns which underlie American life. Few undertakings are of greater moment, and no one is better equipped for it by nature than Lindsay. But for success in it there are two or three requisites: one is that these "hieroglyphics" must be discerned in the actual experience of the American people and not in a no man's land of fancy, and another is that before they are worth anything they will have to be shaped and made explicit and embodied in carefully elaborated forms of art. If Lindsay could fulfill this achievement, he would have more than any one else to tell concerning American life. As it is, he has already told much in his best work, and even more, indirectly and unconsciously, in his other work.

BIBLIOGRAPHY

LINDSAY, VACHEL. *General William Booth Enters Into Heaven.* New York, 1913, The Macmillan Company.
—— *Adventures While Preaching the Gospel of Beauty.* New York, 1913, The Macmillan Company.
—— *The Congo.* New York, 1915, The Macmillan Company.
—— *The Art of the Moving Picture.* New York, 1915. Revised edition, New York, 1922, The Macmillan Company.
—— *A Handy Guide for Beggars.* New York, 1916, The Macmillan Company.

VACHEL LINDSAY

LINDSAY, VACHEL. *The Chinese Nightingale.* New York, 1917, The Macmillan Company.

—— *The Golden Book of Springfield.* New York, 1920, The Macmillan Company.

—— *The Golden Whales of California.* New York, 1920, The Macmillan Company.

—— *Collected Poems.* New York, 1923. Revised edition, New York, 1925, The Macmillan Company.

—— *Going-to-the-Sun.* New York, 1923, D. Appleton and Company.

—— *Going-to-the-Stars.* New York, 1926, D. Appleton and Company.

—— *The Candle in the Cabin.* New York, 1926, D. Appleton and Company.

X

SINCLAIR LEWIS

INCLAIR LEWIS has said of himself: "He has only one illusion: that he is not a journalist and 'photographic realist' but a stylist whose chief concerns in writing are warmth and lucidity." Such illusions are not uncommon: the scientist who prides himself on his violin-playing, the statesman who would like to be known as a poet—most men would rather think of themselves as excelling in another activity than that in which they are eminent. Lewis's wish need not prevent us from adopting the general view of him, namely, that though he is a "photographic realist" and also, at times, something of a novelist or creative artist, yet after all he is primarily a satirist—unless indeed he is even more interesting as a product than as a critic of American society. Surely no one else serves so well as he to illustrate the relation between literature and a practical world: in such a world he has himself lived all his life, and such a world he portrays and holds up to ridicule and obloquy.

No small part of his effectiveness is due to the amazing skill with which he reproduces his world. His knack for mimicry is unsurpassed. He is a master of that species of art to which belong glass flowers, imitation fruit, Mme. Tussaud's waxworks, and barnyard symphonies, which aims at deceiving the spectator into thinking that the work in question is not an artificial product but the real thing.

Of this art Zeuxis, who painted grapes so truly that birds came and pecked at them, is the most eminent practitioner; but Lewis's standard is often little short of the Zeuxine. Dyer's Drug Store, with its "greasy marble soda-fountain with an electric lamp of red and green and curdled-yellow mosaic," Babbitt's Dutch Colonial house in Floral Heights, with its bathroom in which "the towel rack was a rod of clear glass set in nickel," and its bedroom in which were "the bureau with its great clear mirror, Mrs. Babbitt's dressing-table with toilet articles of almost solid silver, the plain twin beds, between them a small table holding a standard electric bedside lamp, a glass of water, and a standard bedside book with colored illustrations"—thus thoroughly are the houses and stores and office buildings in Gopher Prairie and in Zenith represented for us down to the last minute particular. The inhabitants also are portrayed in corresponding fashion, as to their looks, their habits, their talk, their thoughts. Nothing could be more lifelike than Lewis's counterfeit world in all its accurate and unbearable detail. His novels are triumphant feats of memory and observation.

Not of course that they are not also much else besides; for one thing, his mimicry is all charged with hostile criticism and all edged with a satirical intent which little or nothing escapes. His is a world ruled by the desire of each individual for his own self-aggrandizement, and it shows the effects of such a rule plainly in its appearance. Viewed externally, Gopher Prairie is most conspicuous for its hit-or-miss ugliness, its lack of attraction for the eye or any other organ of sense. It looks as if its inhabitants were more or less permanently camping out, not as if they had built themselves a lasting habitation. It is dreary, haphazard, uncared for—only one degree better

than the boom towns of the last century, thrown together
by pioneers just to "do" for a while, and betraying essentially much the same spirit. Yet Gopher Prairie has
passed the stage of pioneering; it is established and prosperous, but the people do not know what to do with their
prosperity, as witness the interiors of their houses, with
their shiny golden-oak furniture and their hideous carpets.
Not a room in any of the dwellings nor a structure in the
village—still less the village as a whole—was made with
the design of its being well fitted to human life. All of it
cries aloud an indifference to humane living. It is an
accurate index to the attitude of the people.

Zenith, on the other hand, has attained a real beauty
in its grouped towering skyscrapers, yet wholly by luck
and accident, not purpose. And this beauty is only in the
large; a closer inspection, though it shows comfort and
luxury and even a kind of æsthetic striving, reveals this
effort at beauty as spurious: from the Old English dining
room of the Athletic Club to the sepia photographs on
the living-room walls in Floral Heights, the taste for art
is affected and unreal. The material showiness of Zenith
is no improvement over the ugliness of Gopher Prairie, for
it is conventional only, and the inhabitants find their
truest pleasure in the accumulation of ingenious mechanical contrivances and conveniences. Zenith has arrived at
the perfection of a mechanical luxury in which the only
flaw is that it is altogether inhuman.

Life dehumanized by indifference or enmity to all human values—that is the keynote of both Gopher Prairie
and Zenith. And nowhere does this animosity show itself
more plainly than in hostility to truth and art. The creed
of both towns is the philosophy of boosting, a hollow
optimism and false cheeriness which leads directly to

hypocrisy, as in making believe that business knavery is social service. Toward ideas likely to break this bubble of pretense the people are bitterly opposed; toward new ideas they are lazily contemptuous; toward other ideas they are apathetic. In both places, to be sure, there is a conventional gesture at the pursuit of culture: in Gopher Prairie the Thanatopsis Club listens to papers on the English Poets, and in Zenith a symphony orchestra is advocated as a means of civic advertisement. Yet intellectually both are cities of the dead, and in both the dead are resolved that no one shall live.

In *Main Street* and in *Babbitt*, the life of the mind is noticeable only because of the void left unfilled; in *Arrowsmith*, however, Lewis has devoted all of a long book to the tribulations of a seeker for truth in the United States, and his handling of the theme is masterly. The hero is a physician who becomes a bacteriologist. Before he finally takes refuge in the wilds of Vermont where he can pursue his researches undisturbed, he encounters all the difficulties which the United States puts in the way of a doctor and an investigator who would like to be honest; he struggles with the commercialism of the medical school, the quackery which thrives in the country, the politics and fraud of a Department of Public Health in a small city, the more refined commercialism of a metropolitan clinic, and the social and financial temptations of a great institute for research. He is offered every possible inducement to prostitute himself to an easy success—manifest, worldly success. Nor is he indifferent to the pressures which are brought to bear on him; on the contrary, being a scientist by instinct rather than by reasoned conviction, he wins out only in spite of himself. He would like to succeed, he has been contaminated by the success-worship with which he is surrounded, but he is unable to cope with an ineluctable honesty and stubborn drive in himself. In the end, he succumbs to his own integrity. When one reflects that of all thinkers the scientist is among us much the most favored, and that among scientists none is more encouraged than the medical man, one realizes that Lewis has wisely taken for his theme the form of intellectual life in which it appears at its best. Martin's troubles would have been still more serious had he been a chemist, economist, historian, philosopher, or artist.

The intellectual life, however, is not the worst sufferer in the society Lewis deals with. The other humane activities fare no better; and of them all probably none is so debased as religion. In Gopher Prairie religion takes the form of repressive puritanism and prurient espionage. In Zenith it is only one form of boosting, with a go-getter in the pulpit and the best of hustlers in the Sunday school. Nothing in Lewis's work reads so like outrageous burlesque as his account of Babbitt's campaign to increase attendance at the Sunday school; yet no student of Mencken's *Americana* will dare to say that Lewis has not been scrupulously truthful. There is nothing unusual in "the good time the Sacred Trinity class of girls had at their wieniewurst party," nor in the publicity given "the value of the Prayer-life in attaining financial success." If Lewis goes so far as to fall into low farce, it is only in pursuit of absolute verisimilitude.

No doubt every detail of *Elmer Gantry* is faithfully accurate, and one ought to be grateful to Lewis for so detailed a clinical report on the morbid symptoms which attack religion in a land where the religious spirit is dead. Nothing is omitted, no possible fraud or quackery or hypocrisy or iniquity—nothing is missing but religion. And that perhaps is why one is less grateful than one ought to be. In the other books, there is always in some form or other some norm for comparison, some principle of protest—as there is in Carol Kennicott's aspirations, in Babbitt's sense of defeat, and most conspicuously in Arrowsmith's stubborn loyalty to science. The absence of relief—even comic relief—in *Elmer Gantry* may account for the fact that the book is so difficult to read and therefore, unfortunately, so much less effective as satire than its predecessors. It is too bad, for never has Lewis had so good a subject or such wealth of material. But perhaps I do *Elmer Gantry* an injustice; possibly the very qualities which make it inferior to *Arrowsmith* and the rest adapt it all the better to the audience at which it is aimed. However that may be, it can be studied with profit as a sociological survey—even if it cannot be read with pleasure as a work of literature—for as a report on the status of what passes as religion in most of the nation it has the virtue of completeness.

Furthermore, since Lewis's folk are not alive in senses, mind, or spirit, they could scarcely be expected to have a social life. They carry on, of course, a group existence, for solitude is terrifying to them. Yet when they have gathered together, they have nothing to say to one another. They tell stories, they talk about business and the weather and housekeeping and automobiles, they gossip endlessly and often maliciously. Their curiosity as to each other's doings, which is equalled only by their indifference to each other as persons, is not a friendly and welcoming curiosity. They do not really care to get acquainted with one another; they have, and are capable of having, no true personal relations. Sometimes they seek distraction in noise and artificial gaiety. Constantly they simulate goodfellowship and practise a forced and humorless jocularity, raucous and mechanical. Their sociability is ghastly as any lifeless imitation of a living thing must be ghastly. It is a dance of galvanized dead. Lewis's world is a social desert, and for the best of reasons, that it is a human desert. It is a social void because each of its members is personally a human emptiness.

The central vacuum at the core of these people' is the secret which explains their manifestations. Having no substance in themselves, they are incapable of being genuine. They are not individual persons; they have never developed personality. A search for the real Babbitt reveals simply that there is no "real" Babbitt. There are several Babbitts who have never been integrated. And so with the others: in their inner vacancy, they necessarily have no integrity, and therefore they are insecure and uncertain. Having no guide, no standard, in themselves, they are driven to adopting the standards and the ideas of the herd. Their only existence is in the pack— naturally they fight for their tribal taboos with the ferocity of savages. It is impossible that they should be anything but standardized and uniform, since the wellsprings of individuality have gone dry in them; and it is inevitable that their uneasiness should make them defend themselves by assuming a blatant self-satisfaction and a bloodthirsty intolerance. Being unsure, they are self-conscious and snobbish and cruel. Their ignorance leads to bigotry and to scornful and uncomfortable ridicule of what they do not understand—which is everything unlike themselves. The women are devoted to a conception derived from without, an inherited convention, of what constitutes gentility, refinement, "niceness." The men, after their own fashion, are equally fanatical in behalf of their own notions of respectability and propriety in behavior. To both men and women, life is a hollow shell of deportment, and of course they hate any one who threatens to crack the shell.

If in the land which Lewis depicts "life at its most passionate is but a low-grade infection," the explanation is not far to seek. This society from the beginning has been developed under the dominance of one motive: the self-advancement of its separate members. The men are ruled mainly by the desire to get rich, the women by the desire to rise socially, but the two are ultimately the same. Both, in order to get up in the world, have denied themselves all other interests and experiences. They have starved themselves, until in the midst of the utmost material profusion they are dying of inanition. An unspoiled peasantry is rich in life in comparison with them, for they do not even live and grow like good vegetables, having cut themselves off from the source of nourishment. The instincts which cannot be entirely killed, such as sex, take on queer distorted forms among them. They are famine-sufferers who alienate sympathy by their own pride in their misshapenness and by their fierce determination that every one else shall be as deformed as themselves. Were it not for their complacency and contemptuousness, they would be pathetic—and at times, in spite of everything, they are pathetic. For these folk, who enjoy ample opportunity to do whatever they like and who do not know what to do with themselves, suffer from an obscure but acute dissatisfaction. After all, the impulse to live cannot be altogether extinguished; it can only be frustrated. The victim, though self-sacrificed, realizes that he has missed something. Mrs. Babbitt turns for succor to vaporous forms of New Thought; Zilla Riesling finds an outlet in a degraded and vindictive religiosity.

But the spiritual malady which afflicts Zenith is most fully analyzed in the person of Babbitt himself. He feels vague longings which cannot be satisfied by the mechanical toys which are his "substitutes for joy and passion and wisdom," his "symbols of truth and beauty"; there is in him a wish for something beyond even electric cigar-lighters. When illness gives him an opportunity to stop and reflect, he is conscious that something is wrong:

He lay on the sleeping-porch and watched the winter sun slide along the taut curtains, turning their ruddy khaki to pale blood red. The shadow of the draw-rope was dense black, in an enticing ripple on the canvas. He found pleasure in the curve of it, sighed as the fading light blurred it. He was conscious of life, and a little sad. With no Vergil Gunches before whom to set his face in resolute optimism, he beheld, and half admitted that he beheld, his way of life as incredibly mechanical. Mechanical business—a brisk selling of badly built houses. Mechanical religion—a dry, hard church, shut off from the real life of the streets, inhumanly respectable as a top-hat. Mechanical golf and dinner-parties and bridge and conversation. Save with Paul Riesling, mechanical friendships—back-slapping and jocular, never daring to essay the test of quietness. . . .

It was coming to him that perhaps all life as he knew it and vigorously practiced it was futile; that heaven as portrayed by the Reverend Dr. John Jennison Drew was neither very probable nor very interesting; that he hadn't much pleasure out of making money; that it was of doubtful worth to rear children merely that they might rear children who would rear children. What was it all about? What did he want?

Babbitt seeks relief in philandering and in drink, but finds hardly even a momentary distraction. He attempts a timid excursion into liberal thought—liberal for Zenith —but is frightened and cajoled back into orthodoxy. His only real happiness he finds in a few days' vacation with Paul Riesling in the Maine woods.

The discontent which is common among the pillars of Zenith's civilization flares at times into open rebellion among the less compliant members of the community. Paul Riesling, who should have been a violinist and who instead went into the tar-roofing business, is in complete revolt and is finally reduced to committing murder. Chump Frink, the syndicated poet, gets drunk and lets out the secret of his thwarted aspirations. Gopher Prairie likewise has many malcontents: Guy Pollock, the lawyer, the one civilized man in the town, a victim to what he calls "the village virus"; Raymie Wutherspoon, the shoe clerk, with his futile yearnings toward sweetness and light; Erik Valborg, the tailor's assistant, with a spark, but only a spark, of the true fire. Not the least tragic aspect of both city and country is the effect they have on such as these, denying them possibility of healthy growth, condemning them to ineffectuality if not to freakishness. The rebels are as badly off as the conformists; for in a society in which the bread of life is nowhere to be found, the few isolated seekers for it are in a hopeless situation, foredoomed to being stunted and distorted both by lack of nourishment and by the hostility of their environment.

In short, in *Main Street, Babbitt, Arrowsmith,* and *Elmer Gantry,* Sinclair Lewis has rendered in minute detail a vast panorama of an almost ideal practical society. To be sure, in my account of his work I have exaggerated the effect by omitting the shades and qualifications which are frequent in his books; nor does he himself analyze or explain the phenomena he depicts. Furthermore, Lewis himself, in spite of his fullness, has perforce selected and emphasized certain aspects of American life, so that his work cannot be taken as a complete portrait of the United States. His achievement is to have rendered more effectively than any one else several of the most conspicuous phases of our civilization. I hardly think that any one will deny that the United States recognized itself in Lewis's portrait, which therefore, though unflattering, may be accepted as on the whole a good likeness. We are all certain to find our neighbors in the picture, and likely, somewhere or other, if we try, to find ourselves. Nor is the author himself absent. No special discernment is needed to detect a self-delineation in Lewis's novels, for after all the world he deals with is no more the world of Carol Kennicott, George F. Babbitt, Martin Arrowsmith, and Elmer Gantry than it is the world of Sinclair Lewis. He belongs to it as completely as do any of his creatures. He too was bred and born in the briar patch, and he has not escaped unscratched.

As a novelist Lewis has several peculiarities and limitations all of which point to a poverty of invention or imagination. One of his these, his fondness and aptitude for mimicry, has already been discussed. Closely allied to this trait is his extreme dependence on his own experience and on his power of observation. Another indication of the same weakness is the care with which he gets up his subjects, as he got up aviation for *The Trail of the Hawk*, or medicine and bacteriology for *Arrowsmith*. Furthermore, it is significant that his interest is in social types and classes rather than in individuals as human beings.

With few exceptions, his treatment of his characters is external only; he confines himself largely to the socially representative surface, rarely exercising much insight or sympathy. He is above all a collector of specimens. May the explanation of this clinging to actuality and to externals not be that his imagination has failed to find adequate nutriment in his experience, especially in his social experience?

However that may be, of one thing there can be no doubt: that he has hated his environment, with a cordial and malignant hatred. That detestation has made him a satirist, and has barbed his satire and tipped it with venom. But his satire is no plainer a sign of his hatred than is his observation: he is as watchful as a wild animal on the lookout for its foes, or as a Red Indian in the enemy's country. His eye is always alert and keen for inconsistencies or weaknesses in his prey—and how quickly he pounces! Years of malicious scrutiny have gone to the making of his last four volumes. Such observation is but one sign of a defensive attitude. Undoubtedly, his hostility is only a reply to the hostility which he has had himself to encounter from his environment, such as every artist has to encounter in a practical society. But for the artist to adopt an answering unfriendliness is disastrous, because it prevents him from receiving and welcoming experience. From such a defensive shield, experience, which ought to be soaked up, rattles off like hail from a tin roof. I should judge that Lewis had been irritated rather than absorbed by his experience. His observation seems at the other extreme from realization; it seems vigilant and wary, whereas realization demands self-surrender and self-forgetfulness, and is possible only in friendly surroundings. If it be true that his imaginative power is somewhat lean and scanty, the fact would be in part accounted for by the enmity between him and his surroundings.

But to have evoked this enmity is not the only unfortunate effect which his environment has had on Lewis. Although he has changed not at all in essentials, some of his characteristics are disclosed more plainly in his early than in his later novels. *Our Mr. Wrenn, The Trail of the Hawk, The Job,* and *Free Air* assist materially toward an understanding of the author of *Main Street* and *Elmer Gantry.* In the former, for example, he betrays his defensive attitude in the extraordinary precautions he takes lest his readers misjudge him. He makes greater use of irony as a defensive weapon than any other writer I know of; he early made the discovery that if only he were ironical and showed that he knew better, he could be as romantic and sentimental and playful as he pleased. He writes as if always conscious of a hostile audience. He takes needless pains to make clear that he is more sophisticated than his characters, as if there were danger of our identifying him with them. He makes fun of their ingenuous enthusiasms, even when these enthusiasms have the best of causes. The result of it all is that he often seems unduly afraid of giving himself away.

In this respect he resembles his characters; nothing in them is more striking than their morbid self-consciousness. Only Will Kennicott and Leora are free from it. The others, especially those in the early books, are always wondering what people will think, always suspecting that they are the objects of observation and comment—and in Lewis's novels they are generally right. They are constantly posing and pretending, for the benefit even of waiters and elevator-boys. They do not dare to be natural;

they are self-distrustful, uncertain, and insecure. They are self-analytical and self-contemptuous for their lack of sincerity; yet they continue to pose to themselves, adopting one attitude after another. That is to say, they conceive the object of life to be to pass themselves off as something they are not. This idea the author himself seems to share; he seems to think that the solution of all problems and difficulties is to find the one right pose, the one correct attitude.

Just as his people have no inner standards of their own, because they are not integral personalities, because they have not, in fact, developed any real personality at all, so Lewis himself shifts his point of view so often that finally we come to wonder whether he has any. One of the great advantages of *Arrowsmith* over its forerunners and its successor is that in it there seemed to emerge an almost established point of view. Otherwise, one would be inclined to call Lewis a man of multiple personality—save that all these personalities have a look of being assumed for effect. All the Lewises are disdainful of one another. When he has been romantic, he throws in a jibe at sentiment lest we think him sentimental; when he has been cynical, he grows tender lest he be thought hard; when he has been severe with a member of the Babbittry, he emphasizes the virtues of the common people and the absurdities of highbrows and social leaders. All his manifold attitudes, however, may be resolved into four: most conspicuously, he is the satirist who has flayed American society; least obviously, he is the artist whom one feels sure nature intended him to be; in addition, and above all in the early novels, he is a romanticist, and he is a philistine—these two bitterly abusive of each other. That is, besides his other reactions, he has tried to escape from his environment, and he has tried, with more success, to conform to it.

His romanticism is of two kinds. In the first place, there is in him much of the conventional romanticist and even of the sentimentalist. He has said of himself that he is "known publicly as a scolding corn-belt realist, but actually (as betrayed by the samite-yclad, Tennyson-and-water verse which he wrote when he was in college) a yearner over what in private he probably calls 'quaint ivied cottages.'" This is the Lewis who flees from reality to fantasy, who sympathizes with Carol in her dislike of Gopher Prairie and in her longing for "a reed hut on fantastic piles above the mud of a jungle river," and who invents for Babbitt a dream of a fairy child playmate, "more romantic than scarlet pagodas by a silver sea." Then there is the second sort of romanticist, who has taken a tip from Arnold Bennett and gone in for the romance of the commonplace, who records the Swede farm-girl Bea's glamorous impressions of Main Street, who dilates on the excitement, adventure, and beauty of life in Zenith and who has no use for "Lloyd Mallam, the poet, owner of the Hafiz Book Shop," who wrote "a rondeau to show how diverting was life amid the feuds of medieval Florence, but how dull it was in so obvious a place as Zenith." To establishing the strangeness and beauty of humdrum life Lewis devoted his first four books; he undertakes to prove in *Our Mr. Wrenn* that a clerk's life in a Harlem flat is more romantic than travel in foreign lands, and in *The Job* that a stenographer is more romantic than Clytemnestra. This process is really no less an escape from reality than is the old-fashioned romance, for it consists, not in bringing out the essential quality and verity of ordinary life, but in casting a glamour over it and falsifying and sentimentalizing and prettifying it. Although romanticist the second is always highly contemptuous of romanticist the first, there is no essential difference between them.

Closely akin to the romanticist of the second sort is the Lewis who speaks as a man of the soil, one of the common herd, a Rotarian; he points out the essential goodness of small towns and their inhabitants and of boosters; he is homey and folksy, and strongly opposed to people whom he suspects of thinking that they are superior. This side of Lewis, plain enough in all his writing, is especially pronounced in the novels which preceded *Main Street;* in the first of them, the account of Wrenn's marketing the Dixieland Inkwell, a glorification of the romance of business, is sheer Babbittry, and the account of Mrs. Arty's boarding-house, a glorification of folks who are just folks, is sheer Main-Streetism. In *Free Air,* an extravaganza on the theme of "Out Where the West Begins," the heroine learns during her trans-continental journey that "what had seemed rudeness in garage men and hotel clerks was often a resentful reflection of her own Eastern attitude that she was necessarily superior to a race she had been trained to call 'common people.'" According to Lewis the superiority is all the other way: people who have enjoyed the hereditary advantages of wealth, social position, and education are ridiculous and contemptible—unless, like Claire, they have the good luck to be regenerated by the Great West. His whole tendency in his first four stories is to bring a warm glow of self-satisfaction to the heart of the great American majority, to strengthen and entrench the folk of Zenith and of Gopher Prairie in their complacency and also in their intolerance of every one unlike themselves.

In short, he has not escaped contamination, but has partially conformed to his environment. One of the Lewises is a philistine.

Wonder has often been expressed at Lewis's popularity —that attacks such as his on American life and the American gods should meet a reception so enthusiastic. Yet I think his vogue is easily understood. For one thing, no doubt all the Zeniths enjoyed *Main Street* and all the Gopher Prairies *Babbitt,* and all who live on farms or in big cities liked both books. Moreover, Lewis caters to all tastes because he shares all points of view. For instance, I happened to see the play *Main Street* acted by a provincial stock company, and was amazed to find how readily the animus of the book had been shifted: a slight change had turned it into a traditional hick comedy—the rustics humorous but lovable and even admirable—and directed all the satire against Carol, Erik Valborg, and the other highbrows. Probably many readers took the novel so in the first place. In any case, whatever one's likes and dislikes, whether boosters, malcontents, romantics, radicals, social leaders, villagers, bohemians, or conventional people, one can find aid and comfort in the work of Sinclair Lewis.

Furthermore, Lewis's style must have contributed enormously to his success. It is of just the sort to please the people of whom he writes. His technique of raillery he has learned from Sam Clark and Vergil Gunch; he merely turns their type of wit and humor back upon themselves. All his satire is a long *tu quoque.* His crusade against the shortcomings of the clergy is conducted in the same spirit as Elmer Gantry's crusade against vice. His irony and sarcasm are of the cheap and showy variety popular on Main Street and in the Zenith Athletic Club:

Babbitt's preparations for leaving the office to its feeble self during the hour and a half of his lunch-period were somewhat less elaborate than the plans for a general European war. . . .

. . . the lithograph of a smirking young woman with cherry cheeks who proclaimed in the exalted poetry of advertising, "My tootsies never got hep to what pedal perfection was till I got a pair of clever classy Cleopatra Shoes."

Surely the point of these jibes would be plain even to Uncle Whittier or the Widow Bogart. Moreover, Lewis must think that his imitations or quotations of the speeches, advertisements, and conversation in *Babbitt* are amusing—that it is funny, that is, that the speakers should think themselves funny—and not merely dreary and faintly obscene. One comes finally to suspect, from his asperity, that not long ago the writer himself enjoyed such mispronunciations as *animiles, intellekschool, bacheldore, Heavings.* The reviewer who said that in *Elmer Gantry* Lewis had sent the preachers a comic valentine hit off Lewis's style to perfection. Lewis seems to aim at much the same stage of mental development as the movies, which is said to be the average age of fourteen. His manner is founded on the best uses of salesmanship, publicity, and advertising. It is heavily playful and vivacious, highly and crudely colored, brisk and snappy. He avails himself of all the stock tricks of a reporter to give a fillip to jaded attention. His people do not run, they "gallop"; instead of speaking, they "warble" or "gurgle" or "carol"; commonplace folk are "vanilla-flavored"; interior decorators are "daffodilic young men," "achingly well-dressed"; dancing becomes "the refined

titilations of communal embracing." No wonder Lewis
has sold satire to the nation—he has made it attractive
with a coat of brilliant if inexpensive varnish. The excellence of his rare intervals of real writing is lost in the
general glare.

For, though no one unaided could have guessed that
Lewis thought himself "a stylist whose chief concerns in
writing are warmth and lucidity," there are such intervals,
and they serve to remind us from time to time of Lewis
the artist, by no means insensible to beauty or devoid of
the tragic sense of life. The account of Carl Ericson's
boyhood in *The Trail of the Hawk* is full of poetry, and
there are bits in the story of his *Wanderjahre* that make
one wish Lewis had seen fit to develop the picaresque
possibilities more fully. In *The Job,* the death of Una
Golden's mother is powerfully felt and strongly written.
And, although Carol Kennicott is mainly a medium and an
object of satire, she is also a created character, as is Babbitt likewise. But Will Kennicott, who is little analyzed
or dissected, is the best evidence before *Arrowsmith* that
Lewis has the ability to create people. *Arrowsmith* itself,
however, is the final proof of his creative power. Leora,
Martin's first wife, is by general consent Lewis's masterpiece in the creation of character. Not only is she lik-
able, but she is indubitably real; though she is portrayed
casually and without effort, few other characters in American fiction equal her in absolute final reality. And Martin
suffers only in comparison with Leora; although far more
difficult than either Carol or Babbitt, he is more under-
standingly and more successfully portrayed. Yet even
Leora interests Lewis less than his national portrait gallery of typical frauds and fakirs. He prefers to stay
safely on the surface of social appearances. He shows

little of Sherwood Anderson's hunger to delve into the lives of men and women.

The very mention of Anderson brings into sharp relief Lewis's limitations—his superficiality, his meretricious writing, his lack of passion and of thoughtfulness. If it were objected that the comparison has no point, Lewis being a satirist, I should reply that it is possible for a satirist to manifest penetration, strong feeling, and intellectual power, seeing that other satirists have obviously possessed these qualities. Yet I feel sure that Lewis has many unrealized capabilites. Underneath all the masks he puts on to rebuff or to placate the world, there seems to lurk a boyish artist, immature and shy and eager, full of fancy and sentiment, who has never grown up and ripened—denied his proper development, probably, by the necessity of manufacturing those protective masks. He is uncomfortable in the presence of other people, and feels at ease only with nature, on which he lavishes exquisite praise. The world would have none of him; so he will have none of the world. His world was a poor one at best, but he has denied himself even what little it might have offered. That is why he is still a boy, with a boy's insecurity and self-doubt hidden behind a forced rudeness and boldness.

In *Arrowsmith,* his seventh novel, Lewis showed signs of beginning to develop a point of view, an inner standard of measurement. But that it is too late now for him to abandon his assumed attitudes and adopt the position proper to the artist, with the self-reliance which can come only from a sense of there being a pivot or point of rest in himself, *Elmer Gantry* is sufficient evidence. To the present, at any rate, Lewis is significant mainly as a social rather than as a literary phenomenon. And though this

fact heightens his immediate importance, it detracts ultimately even from his social importance. While many of
his contemporaries, who have succeeded in maintaining
their integrity unimpaired, impart to their readers an intenser realization of the world they live in, the net result
of Lewis's work is not a truer apprehension or a deeper
insight, but an increase in mutual dissatisfaction: he has
made Americans more outspoken and more hostile critics
of one another. But perhaps after all it is better so:
Lewis's romanticism and philistinism and vulgarity of
style make him powerful because they make him popular.
The attack on American practicality needs its shock troops
—could we afford to give up so effective a critic for a
better writer? Perhaps it is worth spoiling an artist to
have him take so salutary a revenge. Lewis is the most
successful critic of American society because he is himself
the best proof that his charges are just.

BIBLIOGRAPHY

LEWIS, SINCLAIR. *Our Mr. Wrenn*. New York, 1914,
Harcourt, Brace & Company.
——— *The Trail of the Hawk*. New York, 1915, Harcourt,
Brace & Company.
——— *The Job*. New York, 1917, Harcourt, Brace & Com-
pany.
——— *The Innocents*. New York, 1917, Harcourt, Brace
& Company.
——— *Free Air*. New York, 1919, Harcourt, Brace &
Company.
——— *Main Street*. New York, 1920, Harcourt, Brace &
Company.
——— *Babbitt*. New York, 1922, Harcourt, Brace & Com-
pany.

SINCLAIR LEWIS

LEWIS, SINCLAIR. *Arrowsmith*. New York, 1925. Harcourt, Brace & Company.

——— *Mantrap*. New York, 1926, Harcourt, Brace & Company.

——— *Elmer Gantry*. New York, 1927, Harcourt, Brace & Company.

SHERMAN, STUART P. *The Significance of Sinclair Lewis*. New York, 1922, Harcourt, Brace & Company.

XI

EUGENE O'NEILL

NO other American writing to-day has so many ardent well-wishers as Eugene O'Neill. In part this is because he is the father of the American drama, and was long our one dramatist; in part, perhaps, because something in his work peculiarly comes home to us. One need only recur to the time when *The Witching Hour* and *The Great Divide* were the great American dramas to realize afresh the debt of gratitude we owe O'Neill. But our feeling toward him is only in part gratitude; it is mixed with a sense, not only that he is possessed of extraordinary powers, but that somehow he has not yet quite succeeded in making the most of those powers. For that reason— because we are aware of a kind of greatness in the man which has never yet achieved full expression, and because what he has to say is of importance to us—we approach each new play of his in a prayerful attitude, offering supplications that this time he may have been enabled to produce work which will fulfill our hopes of him. We have watched his progress from days of his first one-act plays with their promising strength, through the realism of *Beyond the Horizon, Diff'rent,* and *Anna Christie,* and the failure of *The Straw, The First Man,* and *Welded,* and the experiments and expressionism of *The Emperor Jones, The Hairy Ape, All God's Chillun,* and *Desire*

under the Elms, to the mystery of *The Fountain* and *The Great God Brown.* And while *The Great God Brown* is by all odds his finest work, and finer work in many respects than the other plays would have led one to expect of O'Neill, it still leaves one with the tantalizing feeling that the dramatist is capable of doing still better, that his definitive masterpiece is just around the corner.

Of our ten writers, O'Neill has the most tenuous relation to American life. Even less than Robinson's is his work intentionally or obviously American. Only in *Marco Millions* is he an avowed critic of American society, and can scarcely even there be called a portrayer of it. His themes are not peculiarly American, and he never stresses the social background. No one would be likely to think of calling his plays tragedies of American life as one naturally speaks of such plays as *The Show-Off* or *The First Year* as comedies of American life. In *The First Man* there is a touch of social satire, and the New England setting counts for something in *Diff'rent* and in *Desire under the Elms;* but only in his one satire is O'Neill preoccupied with the social aspect of the United States. All that can be said is that, since he is an American, he lays his plays in this country with as little self-consciousness as a Frenchman or a Russian lays his in France or Russia. In other words, save for one play, O'Neill's only significance for our inquiry is that, in so far as the phrase has any meaning at all, he is a product of the United States. He therefore raises in a particularly acute and difficult form the question whether, except in so far as a writer chooses to confess and confide in us what he thinks of his environment, we can trace any connection between his work and his surroundings. We have to try to guess, from the qualities of the world he has created, how he has been affected by the actual world, to draw from the imaginative experience he offers us some conclusions as to the qualities of the experience he has himself been afforded.

The most striking aspect of the world of all save the latest of O'Neill's plays—for *The Great God Brown, The Fountain,* and *Marco Millions* are so different from the others that they must be reserved for separate discussion —is that it is a tragic world in which the tragedy is singularly bleak and unrelieved. The older writers of tragedy give us some compensation, slight though it be; their protagonists go down to defeat, of course, but they go down in a blaze of glory. There is a kind of recompense for their defeat if only in our sense of their greatness; and more often than not their outward defeat is somewhat atoned for by their winning a spiritual victory. And although that is not the modern point of view, yet there are moderns who do not leave us altogether without alleviation. In Hardy, for instance, although life is wanton and cruel and futile, there is something redeeming in humanity; however bad according to human notions the universe may be, at least in some men and women there is a saving beauty and nobility. Or in Dreiser, if there is little to be said even for humanity, one finds at any rate a huge gusto for experience.

O'Neill, however, like many other contemporaries, denies us even these poor mitigations. Not only, like most moderns, does he see man as a subordinate part of nature, the sport of incomprehensible and meaningless natural forces within and without himself, a passive and helpless victim who can only suffer and vainly struggle in the grip of powers which he cannot understand, let alone cope with; not only, that is, is O'Neill a naturalist and a determinist: he is also a pessimist, who sees everything as predetermined for the worst. In all tragedy we expect the protagonist to lose his battle outwardly, and in modern tragedy we expect him to succumb to nature; but O'Neill goes farther. He shows us man as undergoing an inner defeat. For the defeat his protagonists suffer is spiritual; they end in a spiritual frustration, a spiritual failure. His is an extreme development of what we have found to be the special theme of contemporary American tragedy. His favorite topic is the degradation and disintegration of character. His heroes lose both the world and also their own souls. Irony is fundamental in O'Neill's view, for the disparity between human wishes and the brute facts is inevitable, and it is a bitter irony. Indeed, since not only all man's hopes but the very self of man is doomed to betrayal, and since all aspiration and all effort are futile, ironic is not so good a word for such a world as sardonic. Not that all O'Neill's plays are utter gloom, for at least he is not a misanthrope. But the most that can be said is that he treats his poor creatures with pity, not with contempt. The dramatist at any rate is sympathetic, though life is inane and inscrutable, derisively and ingeniously malignant.

The agencies of destruction in O'Neill's world are varied and complex. Usually both external and internal forces are pitted against the individual, and usually he is a willing and unconscious accomplice in his own undoing. That he has bad luck is commonly the least of his troubles, although O'Neill, in a few of his earliest pieces, made considerable use of chance and circumstance. In the later plays it is not an intangible evil fate that pursues man. Sometimes he is broken by the might of nature, as when the Emperor Jones reverts to savagery and is finally crushed by the sheer weight of the tropic night. *Thirst,* published in O'Neill's first volume, 1914, deals in the sensationalism of mere physical horror, and while the author has long since outgrown such crudity, he has never forgotten the part played by the primal facts of existence. They are the foundation of all he writes. Sometimes society takes the rôle of hostile victor; it destroys the Hairy Ape when he refuses to be only a slave to a machine, it all but destroys Anna Christie, and it furnishes the matrix for the tragedy of *All God's Chillun.* As for conflicts between individuals, although such conflicts occur frequently in O'Neill's work, which without them would lack an essential of drama, they never furnish the main theme. They are incidental; and for that matter even the forces of nature and society are secondary. For always the interest is focused on the mental process of the victim, and ordinarily the destructive force itself is an inner one: the mind goes to pieces because of its own inner conflict.

Gold, though not one of O'Neill's successes, is in many respects characteristic. It opens with emphasis on the elemental fact of maddening thirst; its real theme is avarice. The latter aided by the former, masters and corrupts an upright, God-fearing sea-captain; he falls into delusion, connives at murder, and deteriorates until he goes insane and ruins his family and dies. In *Diff'rent,* the debasing impulse is sex—that is, sex denied: Emma Crosby, after thinking her sailor lover "diff'rent" from other men, finds that he is made of common clay and rejects him; thirty years later nature has her revenge, and Emma's long-suppressed instincts express themselves in an unseemly infatuation for an unmitigated young cad. The end is suicide. Similarly, in *All God's Chillun* the

disruptive agency is race-prejudice, conflicting with love
and leading to homicidal mania and presumably death.
In *Desire under the Elms* avarice is at war with sex.
But perhaps *Beyond the Horizon* is the most typical
example of O'Neill's tragedy. Fundamentally the catastrophe is caused by the trickery and illusions of sex.
Because Ruth chooses the wrong brother, there is a three-
fold failure: Robert, the romantic dreamer, sinks under
the burdens of a farmer's life; Ruth, who in prosperity
might have made an excellent and contented wife, is reduced by poverty first to bitterness and then to apathy;
and Andrew, who should have stayed on the farm he
loved, takes to the sea and becomes infected with the virus
of making good and getting rich. All three end in a
spiritual defeat, unnecessary and yet inevitable, due partly
to circumstance, somewhat more to external nature, most
of all to sex. All things work together for the ruin of
men, with a sort of mocking grimness.

O'Neill's dramatic world, then, has obvious limits: not
only is it tragic, but it is confined to the tragedy of
frustration. Such limitation is an unavoidable consequence of the author's view of life; however, his world is
still further restricted in ways which are not unavoidable.
He chooses for the most part to deal with the disinherited.
Almost without exception he portrays only the more unfortunate among farmers and laborers. Peasants, sailors,
stokers, prostitutes, negroes—these are his types, as his
locale is the sea, the unproductive farm, and the slum.
His settings and his characters have little diversity; the
imaginative experience he offers us is not varied or wide
in scope. Furthermore, it suffers from a still more serious
restriction. The point about O'Neill's folk is less that
they have been denied the good things of the world

than that they have been denied life itself. In a few of them the lack is innate; they must have been feeble organisms to begin with. But in most of them the difficulty is not congenital weakness so much as malnutrition. They are thwarted, starved, stunted, and twisted like trees that have tried to grow in a bad soil and a bitter climate. Even at the opening of the play, before the process of deterioration has begun, they are unfavorable specimens of humanity. The characters of *Desire under the Elms* are extreme instances—sucked dry, perverted and obscene, denuded of every humane impulse, balked of any healthy growth, left with only hatred, greed, and lust, they are worm-eaten fruit which rots while still green because it never has a chance to ripen.

If O'Neill's world has an effect of narrowness and scantness, this effect is in part due to the materials with which he works, for a dramatic world of human abundance cannot be created out of dehumanized human beings. There is, however, another reason why his world lacks body and fullness. His particular mode of characterization does not leave an impression of solidity, and in general his concern is not to project a fully imagined and created world, an independent, self-sufficient, opaque, three-dimensional affair in which solid, fully existing men and women move about. Seldom does he give us that complete realization, complete illusion of actuality, which distinguishes the first act of *Anna Christie* and the early one-act masterpiece, *The Moon of the Caribbees*. Than the latter, indeed, we could ask no better illustration of the quality absent from his later work. This little piece has no plot; it is just a scene of drunkenness and lust in the tropic night under the full moon with negroes chanting in the distance. It is sordid, not at all prettified, yet

intensely poetic, with the poetry of a thing completely
realized, completely imagined, and vividly rendered.
And as with his scenes in general, so it is likewise with
his individual men and women. From the beginning he
has never given us subtly complex characterization.
Always he has dealt in characters of one syllable, his
delineation has been notably simple, stressing one or two
traits only, expressing the simplest of emotions, requiring
the actor's presence to fill in the outline; but at its best
this delineation has been bold and clear, like a strong
sketch. In her review of *Beyond the Horizon,* Miss Lola
Ridge commented that the characters were not fully projected, not independent; they exist as sketches rather than
in the round.

In the preceding, I have meant not to find fault but
merely to attempt a description of O'Neill's world and
especially of his characterization. His method, I think,
entails a certain loss; but it may well be that the gain is
the greater. In any case, his type of mind works in a
special way, and it has its appropriate merits as well as its
limitations. There is a striking parallel between O'Neill
and Sherwood Anderson. As with the latter, O'Neill's
is not the imagination that bodies forth so much as the
insight that penetrates. Neither of the two concerns himself much with surfaces and accidents and details; both,
in their indifference to appearances and their eagerness to
go below to the primary motives, neglect the concrete
minutiæ which lend verisimilitude to a portrait. Because
O'Neill's whole interest is centered on the essential springs
of action, his people are likely to appear elementary—I
think the truer word is elemental. They are manifestations of such primal forces as hate and fear and cupidity
and sexual desire. They are stripped of all save the one

or two vital energies of the moment, and if they seem at times unduly simple and rudimentary or even abstract, this bareness may be more than compensated for by a gain in strength. There is no dissipation; everything contributes to heightening the pressure, and this concentration raises the intensity to its highest pitch. If one must have both abstractness and intensity or neither, no one I suppose would hesitate in choosing. I suspect, however, that the best dramatists succeed in achieving intensity without sacrificing the concrete individualities of their characters.

Anderson's intensity I ventured to call lyric; O'Neill's, needless to say, is dramatic. It appears, that is, in various forms of conflict. At times this conflict is internal, as when the Emperor Jones struggles with his fear, or as when her racial animosity and her love for her colored husband battle within Ella Downey. But almost always the contest is objectified in the relations of people. The interplay and interaction of character goes on continuously in his work; there is constant collision or coöperation of desire and impulse, of attraction and repulsion, leading from crisis to crisis. To follow the pattern of reciprocal action and reaction through any of his better plays, through *Beyond the Horizon* watching the effect of Ruth on Robert, of their love on Andrew, of Andrew on Ruth, and so on, or through *Desire under the Elms* tracing the complicated relations of Abbie and Eben and the older Cabot, is to realize that O'Neill's world is never inert or static but always dynamic. There is unbroken development and movement forward; his people are never as they were five minutes before, and at the final curtain they have altered as completely as a series of human eruptions and tempests and conflagrations can alter them.

One of his dramas might be described as the automatic
working-out of a complicated system of forces which at
the start are in a state of unstable equilibrium. Possibly
that description sounds unduly mechanical; yet it is
significant that one is tempted in discussing O'Neill to
use physical rather than human terms, to speak of forces
rather than of human individuals. His people as people
seldom represent a highly or fully developed grade of
mankind, but they are the channels through which mighty
and universal forces effectuate themselves—all of which
is merely to say that although O'Neill's may not be a
world of human abundance, it is none the less powerfully
and unremittingly dramatic.

Again and again in reading books by Americans one is
amazed to find how much can be done with how little.
To enumerate the elements which have gone to the making
of other dramatists' work and which are absent from
O'Neill's is to wonder what he can have left. If denied
the play of wit and ideas and of philosophic reflection,
if bereft of the appeal of sensuous beauty, if compelled to
deal with characters who have never known the life of
the senses, of art, of religion, of the intellect, above all
if deprived of the social complex with all its traditions and
nuances, most dramatists I fancy would be hard put to it.
Yet O'Neill does without all these things, even including
the social fabric. True, his characters have personal
relations with one another, but as individuals rather than
as members of a social organism. And society has a rôle
in some of his plays, but an impersonal rôle, as in *The
Hairy Ape* it appears in the symbolic form of the puppets
on Fifth Avenue and of the steel cage in the prison, or as
in *All God's Chillun* it appears in the almost equally
symbolic form of throngs of whites and negroes. The

extremely simple village life in *Diff'rent* is the nearest O'Neill has come (except for *The First Man*) to handling a social group. We never feel that his people are threads in a social mesh, but rather that they are detached and semi-isolated. And that they lack all the elements of interest derived from a rich social experience, even of the sort which may be enjoyed by peasants, goes without saying, as they lack the elements of interest derived from other humane activities. They have known work and action of such elemental sorts as sailing and farming, and they have their elemental passions. Perhaps from dealing with life reduced to its basic terms O'Neill gains a kind of impressiveness, but he also foregoes most of the elements which contribute to enriching the appeal of dramatic as of other literature.

To read O'Neill, then, or to witness his plays is to live temporarily in an intense but a simplified and even impoverished world, a world narrow in range and meager in substance. Scanty to begin with, this world has been further stripped and denuded by its creator's preoccupation with primal forces only. And not only is it so to speak an emaciated skeleton world, but also one which by subordinating man and making him the helpless victim of larger forces, and by depicting him as always undergoing a spiritual defeat, is thoroughly hostile to human life. In fact, in spite of the violent forms in which life manifests itself, the ruling principle of this world is death, not life. It crushes and kills. Existence is a process of dehumanization. To read O'Neill may be a salutary and bracing experience, for he is a corrective, a bitter herb, a perpetual northeast wind, and he brings us squarely face to face with one aspect of life which, though we may think it partial, we recognize as true; but we soon begin to long for a more nourishing imaginative diet—we cannot live long at a time in a world so fatal to life as his. Such are the qualities of the experience he offers us, of the world he has imagined: what do they have to tell concerning the man who has produced them?

In the first place, although I have spoken of O'Neill as simplifying his characters and stripping them of non-essentials, I have no doubt that to speak thus is to falsify; for nothing seems more likely than that his is the type of mind which begins with an abstract theme and works toward the concrete embodiment, that he first conceives his plays in the form of abstract propositions. If true, this would account for much—for the fact that, as *The Straw* and *The First Man* bear witness, without a strong and simple theme he is lost. His action, when too fully embodied in individuals—that is, when treated with a thoroughgoing realism—does not come clean, but gets fouled and muddled, as it does in *Anna Christie*. His people alone are not of enough interest to carry the play; in fact, in and of themselves, apart from what happens to them, they would cause us little concern or curiosity. Again, it would account for the fact that his growing tendency has been away from the concrete toward the abstract and the schematic. Even in *The Hairy Ape,* Yank remains more of a symbol than a person. Indeed, it looks as if O'Neill felt more at home with symbols than with people. One reason why he was the first American playwright to join the anti-realistic reaction called expressionism may be that the newer technique offered him a line of less resistance than the old, in that it freed him from the necessity of trying to transform his forces into concrete individuals, and gave him a chance to solve many of his problems, as in *All God's Chillun,* by means of devices which are facilely mechanical. His plays have tended more and more to work themselves out like the equations of physics.

His preference for abstraction may be debatable, but there will be none to deny the second trait deduced from his world—namely, that he feels it intensely, that he himself takes it hard. Therein consists his evident claim to greatness. O'Neill has a strength of feeling granted to few; it is comparable to Dreiser's, and is the source of the excellences which raise him above the level of merely talented writers. It charges his work with emotion, so that somehow his readers and auditors know that he is no detached observer of his own creation; somehow we come to share his feeling and like him are profoundly moved by his spectacle. His pity and his sympathy touch and penetrate every one on his stage, until finally they seem to brood over the audience as well, and indeed over all human beings. Here surely, in his all-embracing pity and sympathy, in his deep fellow-feeling with luckless humanity, in his acute sense of life's inherent tragedy, lies the wellspring of his penetrating insight into humanity, of his understanding of men and women. The pressure of his commiseration makes him feel his way into people, and the breadth of his compassion enables him to include the world—not, of course, that he is able to portray all the world dramatically, but that his interpretation of life is universally applicable. That interpretation we may disagree with, but we shall hardly deny that it goes deep and that it has been born out of travail. I hesitate to call O'Neill a thinker, for in his plays there is little sign of logical processes; but by means of intuition guided by his feeling he has arrived at understanding. If he has reasoned little about life, he has contemplated it long and hard.

It is this greatness in O'Neill that makes us such ardent well-wishers and followers of his career; we long for this greatness to receive completely adequate expression. If only he could write always up to his highest level and successfully carry out his designs, if only his performance were equal to his conception!—for even his failures are conceived in passion. But always somewhere there is the flaw, the break. Now and then that very emotion which is ordinarily his strength betrays him. Once in a while his sympathy with the underdog leads him to portray his outcasts not as they are but as he would like comfortable people to think they are. In *The Web,* published in 1914, he surrendered to the sentimental convention of the noble prostitute and the noble criminal; O'Neill seems to assume that because a man is a thief or a woman a harlot, it follows that he or she is morally superior. This sentimentality is seen at its worst in the confusion which obscures Anna Christie, who entered a brothel in order to escape being a nurse-maid, yet who hates men and her trade violently, and who by a few days at sea is "washed clean" and "not like that any more"—although she was never, it seems, "like that" or anything but "clean" in her inclinations. Somewhat the same confusion hangs about the figure of Ella Downey in *All God's Chillun.* It looks as if in O'Neill, though it shows itself only in moments of aberration, there were a soft streak which he has to guard against and watch, lest his feelings dim and confound the clarity of his imagination.

Such confusion is one sign that O'Neill sometimes loses command of his feeling; another sign is his frequent, indeed usual, failure to carry us through with him to the end. Ludwig Lewisohn has said that he "conceives his actions powerfully and philosophically," but that "the moment he begins to write, he abandons the leadership of his conception." The latter statement, though too extreme, points to a truth—that the mastery with which O'Neill begins does not last out the piece, that his feeling gets out of hand. In his wish to drive it home, to rub our noses in the human misery which outrages him, he goes so far that we revolt and in our reaction withdraw our belief, as at the end of *Diff'rent*. O'Neill seems to underestimate the savage clinging to life of the human organism. Suicide and madness are ticklish matters which he takes far too casually; for them to seem credible to us, we must be worked up as strongly as the *dramatis personæ*, the feelings of the characters must be fully communicated to us. In most of O'Neill's plays—all indeed except *The Hairy Ape* and *The Emperor Jones*—there comes a moment when an emotional pitch is reached beyond which the writer does not carry us. Then all sorts of disasters happen. His people no longer work out their own destiny; they seem as obviously managed as marionettes. In *Desire under the Elms,* the best example of such disintegration, the chief characters shift and break up before our eyes. They who have been hard and bitter grow soft, sentimental, and relatively commonplace. They say and do things utterly unlike themselves. The play dissolves into hysterics, and we become incredulous and indifferent.

Such collapses bespeak a lack of control over the imagination; they also bespeak a limitation in the power of writing, of handling words. It is easy to say that at the end of his plays O'Neill flees for refuge to theatrical claptrap, but as a matter of fact hardly any story is too preposterous to be successfully treated if the dramatist can write well enough to carry us with him and force our belief. This, of course, is a matter chiefly of the dialogue, and O'Neill's dialogue, though for the most part quite adequate, is rarely more than adequate. That is to say, it does not often have that felicity of expression which startles one by its aptness and inevitability and which is the unmistakable mark of creative genius. Only at times in O'Neill's best work, as in the speeches of the Emperor Jones and of Yank, do we get utterances which bear the absolute stamp of the speaker's personality. It is noteworthy that O'Neill's successes are in dialect and in the vernacular, and that his success is greatest with the most inarticulate characters, in whom an incomplete and impeded utterance is expected. And his power of expression is apparently unable to rise above a certain range of intensity; above that limit, his words strike us as false, but I suspect that they are more accurately described as inadequate. The strange thing is that we feel these shortcomings not as fixed and inevitable limits of capacity, but as bonds which O'Neill may break at any moment. That is why, with the announcement of each new play, we hope again that at last he may be able to bring it off, that this time his execution will be worthy of his conception.

And finally there came almost the longed-for play, for over half the sentences I have been writing ought to be qualified with the phrase, "except for *The Great God Brown,*" a piece of work so astounding, so uncanny, so unlike everything else of O'Neill's, that it requires separate consideration. I confess at once that I do not understand it; I believe, moreover, that the author himself does not wholly understand it—if he did, he would have solved the riddle of existence, he would know what God and Man are. Intuitively, he has dived into the lowest and most secret caverns of man's soul and has dredged up wonders from depths so profound that neither he nor we know what to make of these strange sea-children in the common light of day. He has penetrated far into the heart of the mystery, only to find the mystery grown more mysterious. He has written a symbolic dramatization of human psychology, a philosophic poem that is also tensely dramatic. His characters are both symbols and persons: Dion Anthony, who is half Dionysus-Mephistopheles and half St. Anthony, is a would-be artist, and is likewise life and love, disdain and denial; William Brown is first a man from whom the electric touch of life has been withheld, and later, after he comes to life, a human being tortured and ruined by the vital force; Margaret is girl, wife, and mother, and perhaps Madonna; Cybel is Cybele, goddess of mother earth and divine harlot.

Some of O'Neill's traits are still obvious in *The Great God Brown*—his tendency to symbolize, for instance, and his preference for the elemental and abstract have been given free rein. His passion and his insight are the same, but raised to a higher degree than one would have thought possible for him. But the differences are more striking. First of all, he has been able to control and to sustain his effort throughout; here not only is there no going to pieces, but there is even no such unevenness as in *The Emperor Jones* and *The Hairy Ape*. But most astonishing is his ability to write, his power of expression especially on the highest emotional levels. The play is full of passages of breath-taking poetry. By frankly abandoning all effort at realism, he seems to have freed himself for soaring flights unlike anything in his previous work. The poet in him whom one had begun to fear was tongue-tied has found his proper utterance at last. The tragedy is no longer unrelieved, for it is not stark but clothed in the beauty of poetry.

The Great God Brown is all but a tragedy of futility and defeat. None of the characters finds the world propitious to human welfare, and Brown in particular finds the gift of life destructive and ruinous. But in this connection, although it is all in some sense or other Brown's play, Dion, "born with ghosts in his eyes and brave enough to go looking into his own dark," is the most interesting of the four. Perhaps, since Dion is explicitly the artist, it is not unreasonable to associate him especially with the dramatist. Dion is impotent because he is a split personality, one half, the saint, a "sniveling, cringing, life-denying devil of mockery and scorn." His own account of what caused him to be split and therefore uncreative is as follows:

Listen! One day when I was four years old, a boy sneaked up behind me when I was drawing a picture in the sand he couldn't draw and hit me on the head with a stick and kicked out my picture and laughed when I cried. It wasn't what he'd done that made me cry, but him! I had loved and trusted him and suddenly the good God was disproved in his person and the evil and injustice of Man was born! Everyone called me cry-baby, so I became silent for life and designed a mask of the Bad Boy Pan in which to live and rebel against that other boy's God and protect myself from His cruelty.

The malignity of others made the artist develop a mask for self-protection; yet by doing so he divided himself into two warring parts which separately or together are incapable of creation. The fable, as it concerns American artists, need scarcely be moralized.

Dion, so far as appears, ends in utter frustration. But not Brown; and the play closes on a note of mystic rapture in Brown's last words:

"Blessed are they that weep, for they shall laugh!" Only he that has wept can laugh! The laughter of Heaven sows earth with a rain of tears, and out of Earth's transfigured birth-pain the laughter of Man returns to bless and play again in innumerable dancing gales of flame upon the knees of God!

And Cybel adds:

Always spring comes again bearing life! Always again! Always, always forever again!—Spring again!—life again! —summer and fall and death and peace again!—(*with agonized sorrow*)—but always, always, love and conception and birth and pain again—spring bearing the intolerable chalice of life again!—(*then with agonized exultance*)— bearing the glorious, blazing crown of life again!

Most significant is the fact that O'Neill has devoted the whole of *The Fountain* to the development of this theme, which is conspicuous also in *Marco Millions.* Ponce de León exclaims:

Age—Youth—They are the same rhythm of eternal life! . . . I see! Fountain Everlasting, time without end! Soaring flame of the spirit transfiguring Death! All is within! All things dissolve, flow on eternally! O aspiring fire of life, sweep the dark soul of man! Let us burn in thy unity! . . . O God, Fountain of Eternity, Thou art the All

248

in One, the One in All—the Eternal Becoming which is Beauty! . . . I have found my Fountain! O Fountain of Eternity, take back this drop, my soul!

Here indeed is a change from the desolation of his earlier work, with its pictures of human beings blighted and broken by the mere process of existence. They still are broken, but as a vase of perfume is broken; they are shattered, not slowly drained of life. If this fundamental alteration in his view of life corresponds to something in O'Neill's experience, if he has found a principle of life as well as of death in the world, if he has discovered a fountain for himself, what may he not do in the future? He leaves his admirers still looking hopefully forward. *The Great God Brown* has shown that he possesses powers we did not know of; it makes us more sanguine, but it is not itself the play which embodies all that he is capable of.

Still less is either *The Fountain* or *Marco Millions* the desired play. The former is often poetic, but is of interest chiefly for its relation in its central idea to *The Great God Brown*—an interest which attaches likewise to *Marco Millions*. But the latter is also of some importance as O'Neill's one incursion into satire. Although the scenes are laid in Venice and Asia, no one can fail to compare the hero with the famous realtor of Zenith. O'Neill has taken his turn at Babbitt-baiting. Unfortunately, not the heartiest agreement with O'Neill's point of view can make one feel that his effort has been a success; such matters had better be left to Sinclair Lewis. Yet the play has its significance because it contains the most clear-cut opposition of the poetic to the practical temper to be found in contemporary literature. No judgment could be more thoroughgoing than Kublai's on Marco:

He has not even a mortal soul, he has only an acquisitive instinct. We have given him every opportunity to learn. He has memorized everything and learned nothing. He has looked at everything and seen nothing. He has lusted for everything and loved nothing. He is only a shrewd and crafty greed. I shall send him home to his native wallow.

Kublai's own philosophy—and O'Neill's—is in his prayer:

In silence—for one concentrated moment—be proud of life! Know in your heart that the living of life can be noble! Know that the dying of death can be noble! Be exalted by life! Be inspired by death! Be humbly proud! Be proudly grateful! Be immortal because life is immortal. Contain the harmony of womb and grave within you! Possess life as a lover—then sleep requited in the arms of death!

If we try, finally, to trace a connection between O'Neill's work and his environment, we find a suggestive parallel between his earlier picture of the world and his own difficulties as a writer. Concerning most of his characters he has emphasized two things: one, that they are starved for lack of the food of life; the other, that they are unable to control their lives. But these are the very qualities which O'Neill's writing has also shown: he has often been unable to rule his inspiration, and his characterization has been somewhat lean, as if his imagination had not been well fed. That is, to judge by his work, he is in these two respects like his own creatures. But this is simply to say that his work has been conditioned by his own experience. Toward the creation of his imagined world his temperament and his environment have collaborated, and the problem is to resolve the product into its original elements. Such a task is less difficult with writers who are avowed critics and portrayers of American society. O'Neill affords no such aid. One can only ask how far his work conforms to what one normally expects to find in the literature of a practical society, and compare it with the work of his contemporaries, to see if they afford illuminating parallels.

If a practical society has a twofold effect on a writer's mind, warping it and starving it, O'Neill may possibly show some traces of having been affected by his surroundings. "Warping" is scarcely a word applicable to him; yet his lack of control indicates an uncertainty or instability which is often found in artists who have been bred in a hostile society. If O'Neill lacks the sureness which comes from solid and self-confident integration and unity, if like his characters—above all, like Dion—he is at odds with himself, it may be for the reason that he has been at odds with his world. However, the signs of starvation can be spoken of much more positively. O'Neill's tragedy has sounded till lately like the cry of a man to whom the cup of life has been denied. Since he sees the world as unfriendly to human life, he has presumably found his own world so. Certainly his work has the "gaunt emaciation" which is anticipated in the literature of a practical society. If his dramatic world is narrow and meager, his characterization incomplete, if his imagination is not hale and robust, it is because that imagination, feeding upon a devitalized life, a life inimical to human values, has suffered from undernourishment. He has instinctively come to portray human existence as a tragedy of spiritual frustration because that aspect of existence has been most conspicuous in his surroundings, and he has felt it so keenly because he has felt it threatening himself. He has been thwarted of what, in view of his great capabilities, should have been his full achievement.

Moreover, as we have found, the majority of our best writers agree that spiritual frustration is the common condition of American life. From E. A. Robinson to Sinclair Lewis, they are unanimous in their indictment. Nor are many of them hesitant in pointing out the baneful effect of this life on the creative spirit, especially of the artist. With their corroboration, then, we may make bold to conclude that O'Neill's difficulties result in part from his environment, and also that the tragedy of O'Neill is the tragedy of America. But while most of his contemporaries have succeeded in their search for vital sustenance by bringing the poetic temper to bear upon the world about them, O'Neill has turned to the world within, and apparently has found what he sought. Neither alone will suffice, for to great literature as to good living both the outer and the inner world must contribute equally; O'Neill, however, has at last tapped one of the two great sources of life. If America cannot draw upon both sources, it will not be the fault of her writers.

BIBLIOGRAPHY

O'NEILL, EUGENE. *Thirst, and Other One-Act Plays.* Boston, 1914, The Gorham Press.
—— *Before Breakfast.* New York, 1916, Frank Shay.
—— *The Moon of the Caribbees, and Six Other Plays of the Sea.* New York, 1919, Boni & Liveright.
—— *Beyond the Horizon.* New York, 1920, Boni & Liveright.

EUGENE O'NEILL

O'NEILL, EUGENE. *Gold.* New York, 1920, Boni & Liveright.

—— *The Emperor Jones; Diff'rent; The Straw.* New York, 1921, Boni & Liveright.

—— *The Hairy Ape; Anna Christie; The First Man.* New York, 1922, Boni & Liveright.

—— *All God's Chillun Got Wings,* and *Welded.* New York, 1924, Boni & Liveright.

—— *Collected Plays* (4 volumes). New York, 1925, Boni & Liveright.

Volume   I: *Beyond the Horizon; The Straw; Before Breakfast.*

Volume II: *Anna Christie; All God's Chillun Got Wings; Diff'rent.*

Volume III: *The Emperor Jones; Gold; The First Man; The Dreamy Kid.*

Volume IV: *Desire under the Elms; The Hairy Ape; Welded.*

—— *Desire under the Elms.* New York, 1925, Boni & Liveright.

—— *The Great God Brown; The Fountain; The Moon of the Caribbees; and Other Plays.* New York, 1926, Boni & Liveright.

—— *Marco Millions.* New York, 1927, Boni & Liveright.

—— *Lazarus Laughed.* New York, 1927, Boni & Liveright.

—— *Strange Interlude.* New York, 1928, Boni & Liveright.

CLARK, BARRETT H. *Eugene O'Neill.* New York, 1926, Robert M. McBride & Company.

XII

THE AMERICAN SITUATION

UR undertaking was to discover if possible what contemporary literature has to tell concerning American life, and our first question must be to what extent our writers portray the United States as a practical society. Are most of their characters governed by the practical ideal? The answer must be in the negative. The pursuit of success, as success is popularly understood, figures conspicuously in some of the novels and in the autobiographies of Dreiser and of Anderson, and in the books of Sinclair Lewis. Otherwise, it is little emphasized. When dealt with, it is represented as bringing little or no satisfaction. That is all; certainly it is not the common theme of current writing —good writing, that is. No doubt this fact goes to show —what we already know—that Americans are not exclusively practical, that not every minute in the lives of all of them is devoted to making good; but beyond that I think it shows little. Assuredly the fact that success-worship is not the general topic of our best literature does not prove that the practical purpose is not on the whole more prevalent among Americans than any other purpose. For one thing, it is not a subject which, unless glorified as in the popular magazines or satirized as by Lewis and some others, is likely to appeal to writers. It is too non-human, it brings too little of human nature into play, is too deficient in dramatic or emotional interest, to furnish the stuff for good novels or plays or poetry. Therefore it is wisely subordinated or eliminated. Furthermore, it is pertinent to ask what motive, if not the practical, is represented as dominating American life?

Not the poetic temper, at any rate: it figures less conspicuously than the practical. There are few characters in any of the books who show signs of a disinterested love of thought or knowledge or beauty or any other kind of experience. There are faint traces, perhaps, of something of the sort in Dreiser's "Genius" and in some of Frost's Yankees, and rather plainer traces in Lewis's Carol Kennicott; there is Robinson's "gleam" in his long poems, and there are men in some of Anderson's stories who are in pursuit of a mystic experience; but Martin Arrowsmith and Miss Cather's protagonists alone exhibit the poetic temper in a robust form. And many of these folk cannot find fulfillment for their impulses, and all of them are in conflict with their environment: not one of the communities portrayed but is unfriendly to the life of realization. Tilbury Town, Winesburg, Gopher Prairie, Zenith, Chicago, and Nebraska—from Maine to Colorado it is the same story, and we may be sure that the South and the Far West escape only because they have not been treated to critical observation. According to our writers the United States has physical beauty only in nature, and perhaps by accident in such manifestations of industrial achievement as locomotives, steel mills, and skyscrapers. The conscious, intentional production of beauty is unheard of, presumably because it is not valued. Nor do these authors tell of a community in which there is a play of thought or emotion, or a healthy religion, or, with the possible exception of Dreiser's financial circles, a delight in work or conflict or action.

Inevitably in such a country as they depict there can be no social life, for there is not even the social fabric which must be the basis of social life. There is no social organism, because what should be its members are detached and unrelated, like a heap of pebbles. What is portrayed for us is a social chaos which is singularly standardized and uniform, of which the outstanding social qualities are dullness and intolerance, a prying and repressive and negative moralism, and an appearance of hypocrisy which arises from a manifest incongruity between action and professed belief, between cherished sentimental illusions and peccant behavior. I confess that this account is only a summary of a general impression left by contemporary writing, and that to be accurate it would need extensive qualification; but I should say that though it may be impossible to indict a nation, our present writers have come nearer to succeeding in the attempt than any other group I know of in any country.

Van Wyck Brooks has written, "Considered with reference to its higher manifestations, life itself has been thus far, in modern America, a failure," and the only alteration which an inspection of current literature enforces is the omission of the qualifying phrase: judging by the volumes under discussion, one can say quite blankly that life in modern America is a failure. That is, to repeat once more two phrases of Van Wyck Brooks', the nation, if its literature may be believed, "sends up to heaven the stench of atrophied personality," and "the individual as a spiritual unit invariably suffers defeat." As I have said before, the most striking trait of American life is that it is so frequently a tragedy of frustration—tragic because it involves a futile waste of human material, of desires and aspirations which are thwarted for the reason that in an inane and meaningless chaos no medium is provided for their fulfillment—"the living force within could not find expression," again to quote Anderson's words.

This then is a country which supplies neither the experience upon which personality feeds nor the necessary channels through which creative impulses may effectuate themselves. If our writers do not specifically justify us in saying offhand that the practical temper is dominant in the United States, and justify us much less in thinking the poetic temper dominant, neither do they justify us in regarding any other purpose or ideal as dominant. In fact, to make a deduction from the books under consideration, one would say that one great defect of American life is that it is governed by no purpose or ideal; its aimlessness is one of its most conspicuous features. Yet here we find a world depicted which has all the symptoms or consequences or secondary features of a practical society: the easiest solution seems to me to be that though the practical point of view is and has been by no means universal in the United States, it has been on the whole rather more influential than any other in the development of American life. I think contemporary writers tend to warrant that conclusion.

Furthermore, the view of life most prevalent in our literature—namely, the naturalistic view—looks like the natural if not inevitable product of a practical society. Briefly, in so far as one can condense ideas so divergent as those of our ten authors, I should describe that view as a belief that man has the same status and destiny as any other natural object, subject to the same forces and to no others, that he is usually the victim of these forces, that human life is a pathetic spectacle, futile and mean-

ingless. But is not this a mere generalization and applica-
tion to the universe of the social conditions I have just
been describing? Conceivably, of course, it might be
maintained that the naturalistic theory came first, derived from natural science or foreign literature; but the
evidence, except in the case of Henry Adams, is conclusive
to the contrary. Dreiser in this matter is no doubt
typical: in his autobiography he makes plain that his
reading served only to clarify and confirm views which
he had already formed from his own experience and
observation. And not only are these views traceable to
American conditions, but one can go farther, I think,
and say that the mother of American naturalism, with
all its peculiarities, is practicality—science and foreign
literature having acted at most only as midwife.

Practicality or success-worship sets up for the individual a non-human ideal, a quantitative scale of
acquisition, of getting more and more not of money only
but also of power and position, a goal not of being but
of having. It is indifferent to humane values, and even
hostile to them, because it forgets and must forcibly keep
out of mind all non-self-seeking impulses and any
standard of a human better or worse. It necessarily
implies economic individualism in an extreme form—
every man for himself, with the usual corollary—which
in turn inevitably produces social chaos, since it precludes
any communal purpose. But such a community, providing no nourishment for human growth and no means
of expressing disinterested desires, assures that its members as human entities will be failures. It also assures
that they will be uniform and standardized, in lack of
development, as embryos are more uniform than adults;
with little capacity for resistance, they will conform the

more readily to the pressure of the practical mold, and the result will be, perhaps inequality of possessions, but certainly not the diversity in character which can be produced only by fullness of growth.

In the second place, success-worship and economic individualism, living as they do by the law of the jungle, of the survival of the fittest, impose upon their followers a cult of blind force and strength, a power-worship. This cult, when adopted by a community, brings it about that progress is measured in quantitative terms of wealth or size or height or speed or horse power. And in both the individual and the community the result is the enslavement of human beings to non-human forces. The man, for instance, whose chief aim is to get gold, has made himself the servant of gold; he must do as gold bids and go where gold calls him, whether to the Sierra Nevadas or to the Klondike. And the society whose aim is the production of more power, of more and bigger things, must sell its members—and has no objection to selling even its children—into bondage to coal, steam, steel, electricity, and the like. Thus power-worship leads to determinism, to a slavery none the less real because self-imposed of men to inanimate forces.

A practical society presents two paradoxes, that of chaos and standardization, and that of economic individualism and determinism: but all come alike from the original success-worship of the individual. And finally, if the practice of such a society is reduced to theory and formulated, and then generalized and applied to the universe, the result will be a philosophy which holds that man's life is determined by natural forces, that the universe is chaotic and purposeless, and that man is foredoomed to failure as an individual—which of course is the American naturalistic philosophy in its utmost form. American literature is naturalistic because American life is naturalistic; and both are so because practicality has always been more influential than any other point of view in the United States.

As to why things should be as they are portrayed in the picture of American life which we have derived from our ten writers, few of them offer much explanation, nor can merely laying the blame on practicality, even if accepted, be regarded as satisfactory. Henry Adams and Dreiser content themselves with saying that such has always been and must always be human existence, the universe being what it is. Robinson and some others seem to regard Americans as perversely not individualistic and self-reliant enough, assigning no cause for this sheeplikeness. Sherwood Anderson attributes the trouble partly to the passion for getting on and up in the world, but chiefly to the industrial system with its factories and machinery. Puritanism has often been represented as the great American curse. In my opinion, the likeliest explanation is that social conditions and almost everything else American go back ultimately to the great American fact —namely, that Europeans came here and found an undeveloped and almost empty continent of vast natural resources. A large majority of them were drawn hither in the first place by economic motives; they arrived with the practical point of view, and great numbers of them at once became pioneers.

And a pioneer, whether he liked it or not, was promptly forced to be practical. His own life and the lives of his family often depended on his watching the main chance. He had as little opportunity for reflection or appreciation as a soldier in battle, and the man whose enjoyment of the adventure and excitement of the situation was not consumed in anxiety must have been rare. Behind us now lie three hundred years of pioneering, ten generations of pioneers, and they have bequeathed a habit of mind which is not easily shaken off, even when it has become unnecessary. And they have left an even more serious legacy—a society built up for the most part as it were inadvertently, a society which "just growed," while its makers were absorbed only in their own advancement, a society created less *for* than *by* each individual's looking out for his own interests, and neither for nor by any process of humane living—a society therefore impervious to any wish for realization.

But even more important than the pioneer's practicality, I am sure, is the psychological effect of pioneering —and here, so far as I have been able to discover, we enter an unexplored tract of ignorance. Van Wyck Brooks has discussed the problem, but has not, I think, for all his acumen, solved it. What is the mental result when men go from a relatively high civilization to live in the wilderness? I have no answer, except that the result cannot be an altogether happy one. Even when the two levels are much the same, the experiment is rarely successful; transplantation seems not to be good for the human mental organism. Then to revert to a savage way of life, to abandon all other interests in a primeval struggle for existence—it may develop certain basic moral qualities of courage, fortitude, and the like, but I suspect that it often involves an equivalent debasement. And the experience, bad enough for the men, must have been much worse for the women. As for the children born in log huts in the forests or in sod huts on the plains, their situation presented still other difficulties. The

261

problem is all the more unsolvable because history presents no earlier but only contemporaneous or later analogies. The Goths and Vandals entering the Roman Empire and passing from a lower to a higher culture are altogether different. It has been suggested to me that a study of the war neuroses of soldiers in the trenches might throw some light on pioneer life and thus on American history —and I daresay it might. But until the matter is competently studied, one can only speculate. Whoever will solve the riddle will provide a new understanding of American life and thought and art.

If pioneering and the frontier are the great facts concerning the United States, there are also others of scarcely less consequence, some of which have been mentioned. One is the puritan tradition, in all its metamorphoses, and with the added note that the Mississippi Valley was settled not only by New Englanders but first by the southern Scotch-Irish who were no less Calvinists than the Yankees. Puritanism, which at certain times and places was not altogether without virtue, has received of late somewhat more than its due of blame; yet it has not proved itself favorable to fullness of life, and it must bear a good part of the responsibility for the American situation.

More, however, belongs to industrialism. After the Civil War when modern invention in machinery and transportation abetted the pioneering impulse to exploit the western half of the continent, the country threw itself into an orgy of practicality; the temptation of unparalleled opportunity was more than human nature could be expected to bear, and Mark Twain's "Gilded Age" was the result. Furthermore, there is no doubt good reason for Anderson's hostility—and Carlyle's and Ruskin's and Morris's before him—to machinery and factories. Probably likewise to the list of malign influences should be added economic competition, and perhaps even the capitalistic system, unless it can be shown that they do not necessarily foster undue success-worship, which up to the present they have undoubtedly promoted. In any case, the United States alone among nations has had to stand the combined and simultaneous attack of the three most dehumanizing of agencies—pioneering, puritanism, and industrialism—and that the country has suffered from the onslaught is no cause for astonishment.

With American life thus devitalized, and with no strong desire in Americans to cultivate or criticize their own experience, the development of American culture was in addition rendered apparently superfluous by the ease with which the results of alien culture could be imported. Hence has arisen the curious lack of relation, noted by all observers, between American life and American theories and concepts. Emerson commented on this split in his own way when he said, "Our people have their intellectual culture from one country and their duties from another." Santayana has analyzed the condition with great acuteness; speaking of "the conscious minds of cultivated Americans," he says:

In them the head as yet did not belong to the trunk. . . . Their culture was half a pious survival, half an intentional acquirement; it was not the inevitable flowering of a fresh experience. . . . To be on speaking terms with these fine things was a part of social respectability, like having family silver. High thoughts must be at hand, like those candlesticks, probably candleless, sometimes displayed as a seemly ornament in a room blazing with electric light. . . . Hence a curious alternation and irrelevance, as between weekdays and Sabbaths, between American ways and American opinions.

Van Wyck Brooks, who has treated the matter better than any one else, has summarized it perfectly:

In the American mind, Nietzsche and A. C. Benson—the lion and the lamb—lie down quite peacefully together, chewing the cud of culture.

European thought and art have helped us not to interpret our own experience, but to avoid it; what evanescent impulses Americans have had toward reflection have been too easily satisfied, and we have been able to escape the arduous task of wrestling with our own experience by a flight to the accumulated riches of an older civilization. That I take to be the reason why American life has always run thickest at the bottom, among the least educated, and thinnest at the top, among those whose apparent advantages have been greatest, and why the best American literature has always been most deeply embedded in the American soil, and has often been written by men least influenced by the European tradition.

Foreign guides have been useless or worse in leading us to interpret our own experience, and we have had few native guides of consequence. To those we have had, we have paid little attention, preferring to go it blindly. On the result we have small excuse to congratulate ourselves: with all our booming prosperity,

There are too many sleepers in your land,
And in too many places,
Defeat, indifference, and forsworn command
Are like a mask upon too many faces.

The word which contemporary literature has to say concerning American life is briefly this, that the United States, inevitably perhaps, but none the less disastrously, in devoting itself to acquisition, aggrandizement, and exploitation, has denied life itself, and has failed therefore to find either happiness for the individual or national welfare. It is high time that, having completed our task of exploitation, we set ourselves to the no less laborious task of realization—high time we undertook to develop human as well as material values, lest in the end we find ourselves failures in all that matters. And this enterprise I see signs for hoping that we have entered upon, that the practical temper is waning and the poetic temper waxing among us.

For one thing, to turn from the picture which our writers present of the United States and to ask whether their work and they themselves look like the products of a wholly practical society is to see at once that they do not. To be sure, some scars can be detected, some traces are discernible of the starving and warping which such a society inflicts upon its artists. A few of them only—Sandburg, Miss Cather, perhaps Frost—show signs of having had a rich sensuous experience, of having acquired a large store of imagery; and these few have drawn largely from nature. Most of them afford little gratification and exhibit little sense of the beauty of color and sound and form. Their emotional development is perhaps better, but a union of vigor and volume of feeling with control and discipline is rare among them. They tend rather either to intensity, sometimes a little shrill, or to unchecked riot. Of them all, Robinson, Anderson, Sandburg, and in his latest work O'Neill manifest some sort of religious impulse or seeking for religious experience, and their seeking has seldom if ever found an adequate object or mode of expression. The intellectual aspect of their work is weakest of all; for thinking, for the rational process as distinguished from contemplating, brooding, and pondering, they have, excepting Henry Adams, no knack and no liking.

In the matter of social experience, they have fared somewhat better only. Here it is hard to separate the subjects with which they deal from their manner of dealing with them; but if one tries, one will decide, I think, that the limitations of their human world, its comparative meagerness and monotony and poverty in human relationships, are not imposed solely by the material in which they work. I question, that is, whether if they chose to try they could create an imagined world abounding in fully grown personality and in human drama. Furthermore, I wonder whether their clinging to actuality, their imagining worlds so very similar to the worlds they have themselves known, is not indicative of a slight infertility of imagination. Most of their work has a touch of that gauntness or emaciation, a deficiency in variety, body, mass, which springs from underfeeding of the imagination—from having lived, that is, in a world which affords inadequate experience.

These writers have been injured less by warping than by starvation. Dreiser, Sandburg, and Lindsay suffer acutely from want of discipline and standards, having taken on and conveyed to their writing the chaotic quality of their surroundings, and in these men and above all in Lewis, and possibly in O'Neill, are marks of that instability or immaturity or uncertainty which arises when the environment opposes the artist's temper. Adams, Dreiser, Lindsay, and Lewis have conformed in various

ways to their surroundings and more or less accepted the
prevailing point of view, but only Lindsay and Lewis
have failed to free themselves from the false thought and
feeling of either sentimentality or empty optimism or
negative puritanism or the flimsy romanticism of escape.
And finally none of these ten has been prevented from
trying to do his best; they have not prostituted themselves to purveying the literary confections agreeable to
practical people.

If the foregoing account sounds like a fairly complete
condemnation, it is misleading. In it I have tried to
collect and summarize all the traces I could detect of these
writers' having been adversely affected by practicality,
and I have kept in mind as a basis for comparison the
qualities of the literature produced in countries and epochs
peculiarly favorable to art. I do not consider the characteristics I have been enumerating as the most striking
traits of our modern Americans, but quite the reverse—
as often all but obliterated vestiges of injury. On the
contrary, the outstanding features of the best American
writing in the last fifteen years have been a profound
sense of the tragedy and pathos of humanity, authentic
passion and especially passion for truth, insight, sympathy, and poignancy. And the expression has frequently
been excellent; Robinson, Frost, Anderson, Willa Cather,
O'Neill, and sometimes others have succeeded in per-
fecting literary forms all the better because highly personal and idiomatic, and because developed *ab ovo* and
under difficulty. A considerable body of their work can
be trusted to possess permanent literary value, and not
merely historical or social interest.

They suffice to disprove Van Wyck Brooks' remark
that "the blighted career, the arrested career, the diverted

career, are, with us, the rule," and also his other remark, which before I quoted in part:

Considered with reference to its higher manifestations, life itself has been thus far in modern America a failure. Of this the failure of our literature is merely emblematic.

However, our literature, though the maddest patriot would hardly compare it with the major literatures in their good periods, is not a failure, but more than respectable. Even if we hope for better to come, we have no cause for present discontent. But in that case, as to at least one of its higher manifestations American life is not a failure. Would it be going too far to paraphrase Brooks and say that the success of our literature is emblematic of the success of our national life? No doubt; yet it may be asserted that our writers disprove not only Brooks but themselves as well: if their picture of the United States told the whole truth, their books could never have come out of this country. Here is an apparent contradiction, one solution of which may be that, since the ten I have discussed were born on the average about 1878, the world they portray is probably for the most part the world they knew in their youth— the United States from 1885, say, to 1900. They tell far more about the end of the nineteenth century than about conditions of the last fifteen years.

Possibly the nation has partially managed to free itself from the Age of Exploitation, as its writers have managed to extricate themselves from the predicament into which they were born. For to varying degrees they have emancipated themselves and succeeded in adopting the poetic temper and in following the life of realization.

Their work is precisely what Santayana said was lacking: "the inevitable flowering of a fresh experience." They have been engaged in literary pioneering, in getting acquainted with their world. That no doubt is why they are so dependent on external actuality, why they keep so close to the ground. They have been doing the spadework essential to the growth of American literature. For the present I take to be only a halfway stage. The first need was to make possible a vital and fecund contact with America, a consciousness of America which must precede any attempt to deal with American experience. They have done well to devote themselves to the apprehension and realization of their environment. If it be true that for a great literature (as for good living) there is needed a rich experience both outer and inner, digested and assimilated, thought about, shaped, and transmuted, yet the first step must be the cultivation of the outer experience, the making of the right relation between the individual and his world. Until this step had been taken, the other steps would have been premature: without the requisite fund of experience, reflection works idly in a void, and imagination is insubstantial. Therefore our writers are right to confine themselves to laying a foundation for American culture on a full and sharp experience of American life.

By so doing, they make the task easier for other writers and for artists of other sorts, and for other people too. For once experience has been recorded in any medium, it enables others not only to share that experience, but also to gather fresh experience of their own. It gives them new eyes and ears. To read *My Antonia* or *Winesburg, Ohio,* or *Cornhuskers* is to have one's perceptions of the Great Plains, the prairies, farmers, and villagers quickened and made more penetrating. That is why it is vitally important that the nation should be rendered in art. Fortunately, the poetic temper is catching. Readers of novels and poems become infected with it, and apply it to their own lives. Thus a body of national experience is accumulated, which is the raw material of a healthy national life. Signs are not lacking that the leaven has been working in the United States for some time past.

For one thing, the nation has produced and supported these writers. I do not forget that, as Sir Leslie Stephen said, "produced" used in such a connection means "failed to extinguish." Nor do I mean that Frost and Sandburg and Anderson and Miss Cather have enjoyed such enthusiastic welcomes as Harold Bell Wright, Edgar Rice Burroughs, and Edgar Guest. But they have somehow managed to continue, and they have at least not been impelled to do bad work. They have received recognition fairly widespread and popular. Sinclair Lewis rivals even Zane Grey in the magnitude of his clientele. All this can mean only one thing, that enormous reservoirs of discontent have collected in the United States, and that at last they have been tapped. Astonishing numbers of people, it seems, are dissatisfied with their lives and their surroundings. Perhaps they cannot tell why and do not know what they want, but at any rate they have taken the first great step: they want a change. This is much; but even more auspicious is the fact that Americans for the first time in their history are seeking honest self-knowledge instead of self-glorification. The nation is self-conscious, with an eager curiosity as to all that concerns itself past or present, with a genuine desire to get acquainted with itself. It is willing to be told bitter truth, so long as it is told something about itself.

If any one is sceptical as to the awakening in the United States, I invite him to revert in his mind to the year 1910 or thereabouts, and ask himself whether the United States is not more alive now than then. Compare, say, the periodicals of the present with those of 1910; most of our best were unborn, and those that did exist were uniformly dull. Try to imagine *The American Mercury* in 1910! Or base the comparison upon anything connected with the theater—best of all upon the plays written by Americans. If one turns to poetry or architecture or, I daresay, music or painting or sculpture, there is the same story. Even if one is not enamoured of such things as little theaters and poetry magazines, one must admit that their prevalence means something. All over the United States there is a stirring and a striving—after no one knows what. But the new life has already by its achievements established a claim to respect. It has produced buildings and books and plays and pictures which entitle it to admiration.

Yet I do not wish to represent the United States as a butterfly spreading its bright wings in the sunlight. If no longer the grub it was, it has scarcely more than begun to crack the chrysalis. Many no doubt will think that of late the shell has grown harder and more restrictive than ever. They will point to innumerable acts and agencies for the suppression of freedom in speech and action. They will insist with truth that obscurantists and puritans and patriots are more zealous and more harsh and impudent than ever. It is possible to reply that all this ferocity on the part of the majority is a reaction against the restiveness of the minority, and is a part of the awakening. But it is true that the American situation, whatever currents may be moving under

the surface, has as yet undergone no sweeping transformation. The signs of life I mentioned are too
sporadic to quicken the whole monstrous bulk. Nor do I
see hope of a complete change in the near future; the
obstacles are too many and too great.

All the old forces except pioneering are still operative,
and even if no longer all-powerful, still prevailing. We
are daily reminded of the absolute rule which taboo
morality exercises over us. The problem of machinery
versus men does not approach solution. To make good
is still the general aim of American youth, and this
ambition with its attendant practicality and competition
and cut-throat individualism is still fostered by capitalism
through all its subsidiary agents. Furthermore, there is
the incalculable inertia of more than one hundred million
people whose lives have run into the mold of a society
fashioned for and by practicality. And even if the
hundred million could be converted and inoculated with
the desire to live, their desire would be thwarted by the
lack of means of expression. The outlook is not
triumphant, nor is the guerilla warfare of the rebels likely
to lead to an immediate victory.

Innumerable saviours are at hand, of course: the
socialists with their socialism and the syndicalists with
their syndicalism and the intellectuals with their individualism. The last at least avoid one mistake: they do
not promote a utopia, a frictionless communal machine
in which men and women are to be smooth-working cogs.
At least they begin with the unit. But to keep saying,
"Be yourselves" to people whose trouble is that they have
no selves and that their environment gives them slight
chance to develop selves, is of doubtful utility. The best
because the only thing is to trust with the gravest mis-

givings to the slow processes of time, noping that the alteration which our contemporary literature and other arts show as already beginning will continue until the national point of view shall be shifted from the practical to the poetic temper. When that millennium dawns, the United States will be ready to make a start, ready to attack its real problem of devising a less naturalistic life which will lead not to frustration but to human fulfillment. In the meantime, as Marcus Aurelius found it possible to live well even in a palace, so an increasing number of people are finding it possible not only to live but to do creative work of high merit even in the United States.

GENERAL BIBLIOGRAPHY

BOYNTON, PERCY HOLMES. *Some Contemporary Americans.* Chicago, 1924, The University of Chicago Press.

——— *More Contemporary Americans.* Chicago, 1927, The University of Chicago Press.

BROOKS, VAN WYCK. *America's Coming-of-Age.* New York, 1915, The Viking Press.

——— *Letters and Leadership.* New York, 1918, The Viking Press.

——— *The Ordeal of Mark Twain.* New York, 1920, E. P. Dutton and Company.

——— *The Pilgrimage of Henry James.* New York, 1925, E. P. Dutton and Company.

——— *Emerson and Others.* New York, 1927, E. P. Dutton and Company.

BROWN, ROLLO WALTER. *The Creative Spirit: an Inquiry into American Life.* New York, 1925, Harper & Brothers.

273

SPOKESMEN

CLARK, BARRETT H. *A Study of the Modern Drama* (Revised Edition). New York, 1928, D. Appleton and Company.

EASTMAN, MAX. *The Enjoyment of Poetry.* New York, 1913, Charles Scribner's Sons.

GOLDBERG, ISAAC. *The Drama of Transition.* New York, 1922, D. Appleton and Company.

LEWISOHN, LUDWIG. *Up Stream.* New York, 1922, Boni & Liveright.

LOWELL, AMY. *Tendencies in Modern American Poetry.* New York, 1917, The Macmillan Company.

MANLY, JOHN MATHEWS, and RICKERT, EDITH. *Contemporary American Literature: Bibliographies and Study Outlines.* New York, 1922, Harcourt, Brace & Company.

MENCKEN, H. L. *A Book of Prefaces.* New York, 1917, Alfred A. Knopf.

—— *Prejudices* (six series). New York, 1919-1927, Alfred A. Knopf.

MICHAUD, RÉGIS. *Le Roman américain d'aujourd'hui.* Paris, 1926, Boivin et Cie.

MUMFORD, LEWIS. *Sticks and Stones: a Study of American Architecture and Civilization.* New York, 1924, Boni & Liveright.

—— *The Golden Day: a Study in American Experience and Culture.* New York, 1926, Boni & Liveright.

SANTAYANA, GEORGE. *Character and Opinion in the United States.* New York, 1920, Charles Scribner's Sons.

STEARNS, HAROLD E., editor. *Civilization in the United States; an Inquiry by Thirty Americans.* New York, 1922, Harcourt, Brace & Company.

UNTERMEYER, LOUIS. *American Poetry since 1900.* New York, 1923, Henry Holt and Company.

VAN DOREN, CARL. *Contemporary American Novelists.* New York, 1922, The Macmillan Company.

—— *Many Minds.* New York, 1924, Alfred A. Knopf.

INDEX

275

INDEX

(1)